NEOCYBERNETICS AND NARRATIVE

Cary Wolfe, Series Editor

(continued on page 213)

NEOCYBERNETICS AND NARRATIVE

BRUCE CLARKE

posthumanities 29

University of Minnesota Press

Minneapolis

London

Portions of the Introduction were published as "From Information to Cognition: The Systems Counterculture, Heinz von Foerster's Pedagogy, and Second-Order Cybernetics," *Constructivist Foundations* 7, no. 3 (2012): 196–207, http://www.uni-vie.ac.at/constructivism/journal/7/3/196.clarke.

Portions of chapter 1 were published as "Gaming the Trace: Systems Theory for Comparative Literature," in *Comparatist* 37 (2013): 186–99; copyright 2013 by the Southern Comparative Literature Association; reprinted by permission of the University of North Carolina Press.

Portions of chapter 1 were published as "Friedrich Kittler's Technosublime: *Gramaphone, Film, Typewriter,*" *Electronic Book Review* 10 (1999), http://www.altx.com/ebr/reviews/rev10/r10cla.htm.

Portions of chapter 2 were published as "Systems Theory," in *Routledge Companion to Literature and Science,* ed. Bruce Clarke with Manuela Rossini, 214–25 (New York: Routledge, 2010).

Portions of chapter 2 were published as "Communication" and as "Information" in *Critical Terms for Media Studies,* ed. W. J. T. Mitchell and Mark B. N. Hansen, 157–71 (Chicago: University of Chicago Press, 2010); copyright 2010 by the University of Chicago; all rights reserved.

Portions of chapter 5 were published as "Embodied Mediation: *Avatar* and Its Systems," *Zeitschrift für Medien- und Kulturforschung* 3, no. 1 (2012): 25–42.

Published by the University of Minnesota Press
111 Third Avenue South, Suite 290
Minneapolis, MN 55401–2520
http://www.upress.umn.edu

Library of Congress Cataloging-in-Publication Data
Clarke, Bruce.
    Neocybernetics and Narration / Bruce Clarke.
        (Posthumanities ; 29)
    Includes bibliographical references and index.
    ISBN 978-0-8166-9102-9 (pb : acid-free paper)
    ISBN 978-0-8166-9100-5 (hc : acid-free paper)
    1. Narration (Rhetoric).   2. Cybernetics in literature.   3. System theory
in literature.   I. Title.
    PN212.C55 2014
    808—dc23

                                                                2013049861

Printed in the United States of America on acid-free paper

The University of Minnesota is an equal-opportunity educator and employer.

20 19 18 17 16 15 14   10 9 8 7 6 5 4 3 2 1

CONTENTS

INTRODUCTION

Mysteries of Cognition

> Living systems are cognitive systems, and living, as a process, is a process of cognition.
> **—HUMBERTO MATURANA,** "NEUROPHYSIOLOGY OF COGNITION"

> But what is "Spirit" if not a metaphorical circumlocution for the mystery of communication?
> **—NIKLAS LUHMANN,** *ART AS A SOCIAL SYSTEM*

OF THE MANY SYSTEMS discourses taken up in the theory discourse of the posthumanities, the most refined and capacious line of thought is the second-order systems theory formulated by biologists Humberto Maturana and Francisco Varela, incubated by cyberneticist Heinz von Foerster, and then extensively cultivated by sociologist Niklas Luhmann. Grounded as well in the work of social scientist Gregory Bateson and mathematician George Spencer-Brown, this second-order or neocybernetic line of systems discourse has borne the widest and most promising dissemination beyond the home disciplines of cybernetics, and the most searching theoretical development beyond science proper and into the discursive disciplines. For the kind of work done in the posthumanities, Luhmann's social systems theory in particular represents the second-order line's most thorough unfolding to date.

To sharpen second-order systems theory's scholarly profile and enhance its intellectual cred, *Neocybernetics and Narrative* reviews the state and status of these neocybernetic formations, fills in some important historical moments in their development, and models their forms of attention to literary, cinematic, and critical works. This study samples and applies primary concepts of second-order systems theory—in particular, recursive forms and self-referential systems—in their own right. It also interrogates two key discourses in systems theory's immediate environment: media theory and narrative theory. It puts into play the treatments of second-order systems theory in my *Posthuman Metamorphosis* and those that Mark Hansen and I collected in *Emergence and Embodiment*. In hopes of moving the critical arguments forward, I draw out issues left latent in those previous works.

Key among those latent issues is the matter of cognition, in particular, as that concept is redefined in neocybernetic theory. Drawing from the nexus of sources listed previously, I work with an understanding of cognition first developed at the turn of the 1970s by von Foerster and Maturana (Figure 1). In an interview published in 2007, Maturana underscores cognition as the central concern of his own research carried out while on fellowships at von Foerster's Biological Computer Laboratory (BCL). Asked what he may have contributed to von Foerster's thinking, Maturana contends that

> my way of facing the questions about cognition in the domain of biology made a difference: introducing the observer as an active participant in the generation of understanding and in the process of explaining the observer. That was my concern: explaining the observer, not merely claiming, the observer is there, but explaining it.[1]

"Introducing the observer as an active participant . . . in the process of explaining the observer" is a classic second-order statement. Its recursive arc perfectly captures what "second-order" means—the redoubling or rendering circular of an input or an outcome, the reentry of a product into the process of its own ongoing production. In "Interview on von Foerster," Maturana goes on to recollect a watershed moment at the BCL, when his interactions with von Foerster assist a conceptual transition away from an earlier control- and information-theoretical cybernetics:

> When I came back in 1968 . . . I put my emphasis on circularity, on the observer participating, on the distinction by an observer. . . . [von Foerster] was still speaking in those days about information and information in the environment. I remember that during one of my first lectures in Illinois I said: "Information does not exist, it is a useless notion in biology . . . . It is a useful notion for design for understanding systems that are very well specified, you may describe relations in these terms but living systems do not operate in those terms." (45)

Seemingly responding to Maturana's challenge, in 1970, von Foerster seizes and refines the case against "information in the environment"— that is, against a positivist approach to information as a preconstituted, empirical datum simply awaiting a passive reception to be registered as a fact of nature. Stating the contrary position with maximum compression, von Foerster now declares: "The environment contains no information. The environment is as it is."[2] It is a simple if radical point, marking the reformation of cognition within a self-referential cybernetics, the priority now accorded to systemic cognition as responsible for its own informatic constructions. An environment contains everything that is not the system that cognizes it, but whatever "information" an observer comes to have about it refers to that observer in the first instance. It begins as the product of a cognitive operation, which may then be available for attribution to the environment of the system. That product is necessarily a selection of internal states, carried out by and within that system, and achieving a determinate meaning for itself by leaving aside other possibilities. If this reversal of cognitive attitude from passive registration to active selection and subsequent construction is somewhat less of a radical gesture in the present moment, nonetheless, it remains a widely disputed repudiation of objectivistic truisms in favor of what we would now call a form of epistemological constructivism.

The discourse of cognition in second-order cybernetics also undercuts the usual delimited sense of cognition as conscious awareness or psychic experience: this opening up of the concept to nonconscious and nonhuman forms of sentience is its particular entrée into posthumanism. Given Maturana's disciplinary location, the neocybernetic concept of cognition makes particular reference to biological systems, starting with "the cell, the smallest autopoietic structure known today . . . the minimal unit that is capable of incessant self-organizing metabolism."[3] For instance, we now know that evolutionary processes of biological variation occur not merely at the genomic level but primarily at the level of the entire living cell as an integrated system. Such processes involve not only the active mixing and mingling of genetic elements but also the sentience possessed by any given cell to select its own states according to the environmental contingencies of the moment. As molecular biologist James Shapiro writes in *Evolution: A View from the 21st Century*: "Without an elaborate sensory apparatus to pick up signals about chemicals in the environment (nutrients, poisons, signals emitted by other cells)

Figure 1. Ken Wilson, Humberto Maturana, and Heinz von Foerster at the Biological Computer Laboratory, University of Illinois at Urbana-Champaign, spring 1974. Courtesy of Ken Wilson.

or to keep track of intracellular events (DNA replication, organelle growth, oxidative damage), a cell's opportunity to proliferate or contribute to whole-organism development would be severely restricted. Life requires cognition at all levels" (7).

This is a major epistemological position for a contemporary biologist to take, and with this remark, Shapiro places himself on the same page with the line of biological autopoietic theory developed by Maturana and Varela. Of course, Shapiro possesses a generation of new knowledge about cellular processes, but it is striking that he has assessed the evidence so as to arrive within the overall milieu of Maturana's earlier bioepistemological positions. Shapiro's molecular biology fills in the evolutionary processes of self-change that are grounded in the self-maintenance of cellular autopoietic operation. In defining the living cell as an autopoietic or "self-producing" system—a system whose product is itself—Maturana and Varela stress that the self-produced and self-maintained boundedness of the cell is both a product of and the necessary occasion for its metabolic workings and their operational autonomy.

In his collaborations with Varela, Maturana continues to call this living capacity of the cellular system to enclose its own operations and thus to self-regulate its commerce with its environment "cognition."

Second-order systems theory marks the point at which cybernetic discourse grasps the constitutive nature of this operational closure across natural systems—bodies, minds, and societies—and applies its principles to itself. In an interview given in 1976, Varela drives this point home:

> When you have a closed interaction of chemical productions, you can have a cell, and not before that. When you have a closed interaction of descriptions, you can have self-consciousness, and not before. When you have a closed interaction of species, you have an ecological system, and not before. That is, the closure, the self-referential-ness, seem to be the hinges upon which the emergent properties of a system turn.[4]

The observer or cognitive system—even in or precisely due to *its* operational closure—is immersed but not merged in an environment variously perfused with structural openings and points of closure, other nodes of systemic withdrawal, and other observers. It is necessarily implicated in its own selections of possible knowledge. Acknowledging these inevitable contingencies, second-order systems theory selects for itself the burden of recovering self-reference from its long exile from Western thought and making its epistemological repercussions explicit.

In a 1973 paper, "On Constructing a Reality," referencing Maturana's 1970 paper "Neurophysiology of Cognition" in relation to visual and perceptual blind spots, von Foerster provides a template for this process of recovery. Working within Maturana's bioepistemological domain, he proposes "to interpret cognitive processes as never-ending recursive processes of computation."[5] That is, such processes are not to be treated as neural registrations of sensory transmissions, but rather as closed-operational translations ("computations") internally producing cognitive qualities from sensory reports of external quantities—for instance, a note of a certain pitch and timbre from the overlaid frequencies of a set of aural oscillations. This argument leads von Foerster to "the postulate of cognitive homeostasis: The nervous system is organized (or organizes itself) so that it computes a stable reality. This postulate stipulates 'autonomy,' that is 'self-regulation,' for every living organism" (225). Or, the "stability" of the environment as observed by any particular bounded biopsychic consortium of systems (or "person") is an autonomous production referring in the first instance to that consortium's capacity for coordinated self-regulation, and only then, to an environment that, in any event, "is as it is."

In a crucial development, second-order systems theory eventually lifts off from the living domains of biological and neurological systems when Luhmann perfects a *metabiotic*—psychic and social—extension of the concept of autopoiesis. This allows for a multiple account of cognition based on the "interpenetration" of these two "meaning systems."[6] Through social systems theory, one approaches not just the cognitive states of individual minds but also the social-systemic cognitions constituted by autonomous processes of communication, for which no individual mind can be solely accountable. In this manner Luhmann's discourse deposits media theory squarely within the common interstice—in the environment of the systemic interpenetration—between psychic and social systems. This complex articulation enables social systems theory to gather grammatology, structural linguistics, and narratology together and supplement them all with a strong account of how observing systems operate on mediatic and semiotic structures.

Thus, while the biological sources of neocybernetic cognitive discourse are straightforwardly scientific, they have long been thoroughly supplemented by extrascientific—sociological, philosophical, and other theoretical—elaborations. Accordingly, my treatment of cognition does not presume to call itself "cognitive science" or to be supposed a dedicated application of what currently goes by that name. And despite the ample enthusiasm for and accomplishments of "cognitive approaches to narrative," neither is that the path I am taking here.[7] There are many rooms in the mansion of contemporary cognitive science, and most of the schools there are practicing varieties of cognitivism that are far afield from my neocybernetic approach. I recall a comment by the eclectic humanities theorist W. J. T. Mitchell after attending the Society for Literature and Science Conference in 1998 at the University of Florida, a meeting coordinated with the opening on that campus of the McKnight Brain Institute. After several days of intensive exposure to big cognitive science, Mitchell offered a remark summing up my own feeling exactly: "The brain isn't all it's cracked up to be."[8]

The closest I get to a version of contemporary cognitive science would be a partial resonance with enactive cognitive science, a school of thought developing from Varela's turn, as named in the subtitle of Evan Thompson's article: "Life and Mind: From Autopoiesis to Neurophenomenology." This work is very much a variant form of neocybernetics.[9] However, to my mind, in its stress on systemic continuity rather than operational distinction between life and mind, enactive cognitive science so far has sidestepped the full potential of the neocybernetic amplification of cognition. And enactive or not, contemporary cognitive science tends to hew to a phenomenological frame narrowing the objects of its attention to psychic matters. Its approaches to communication— the technical materialities or the mediated sociality of communication as a systemic process over and above, and operationally discontinuous with, life and mind—are thus less than satisfactory, at least for my work here.[10] The metabiotic turn in Luhmann's systems theory factors in psychic operation but closes its boundaries and so places it in more rigorous relation to other kinds of cognition. His theory is indispensable precisely because its virtual extensions of autopoietic form and operation have cleared the decks for a comprehensive and differential discourse of cognition embracing but transcending both its biological roots and the particular varieties of experience of human minds, while detailing the ahuman operationality of communication, human and otherwise.[11]

Scientize it as one may, cognition per se remains as mysterious as life is in any of its forms, as any moment of the consciousness of one human mind must remain for any other human mind or, again, as the social communication of a bacterial colony or a pod of dolphins must remain for their human observers.[12] Formal descriptions of such cognitive objects underscore the limits to knowledge and control imposed by the recursively closed operations of self-constitution evident in self-referential systems, if not also by the "withdrawal" of objects altogether.[13] And given this understanding of the closure of cognition as the necessary condition for the possibility of an autopoietic system's producing itself as well as constructing an internal model of its environment, some common elements of the popular discourses of information and informatic cybernetics abroad in current cyberculture come under critique. *Neocybernetics and Narrative* focuses its skepticism in particular on those elements of info- and cyberdiscourse that cluster around the terms *noise* and *flow*. Such discourses model cognition on open vectors of informatic input, schemas proper to technological devices, Maturana's "designed" or "well specified" systems, but not to bodies, minds, or other complex systemic consortia distributing cognitions contributed from autopoietic sources. More sophisticated theories of transmission, noise, and networks in the work of Friedrich Kittler, Michel Serres, and Bruno Latour also call for a scrupulous neocybernetic cognitive accounting, which I have ventured to provide.

Let us clear away a semantic issue: the term "structure" is often used interchangeably with the term "system." For instance, following Saussure, one speaks of language in its paradigmatic dimension, *langue,* as the "linguistic system." This reasonable locution developed well before current systems theory arrived, but now that it is here, one can say that a linguistic "system" does not operate in and of itself, that is, it is not self-operating or autopoietic. Instead, it is a massive, complex, collectively evolving *structure* that provides a template for systems using linguistic codes as elements of *their* operations. As a structure, *langue* evolves over time because it is operated on by meaning systems whose evolution—that is, whose incremental self-differentiation from moment to moment—is an ongoing product of their forms of operation. More broadly, because structures of any description do not operate themselves, they cannot observe themselves. Rather, as Luhmann notes, "the descriptive marking of structures is completely relative to a system's operations."[14] In particular, narrative structures do nothing until they are operated on by observing systems—readers and viewers interpenetrated by psychic *and* social dynamics.

Media theory and narrative theory both produce superb insights in their own spheres. Now that media theory has arrived, one can see that narrative theory becomes a particular species of its genus. Narrative theory may be called on whenever the transmission being mediated takes a narrative form. Nonetheless, the objects of both media and narrative theories are essentially *structures*—media or textual objects under transmission and reception, and/or the (nonautopoietic) technological or scriptive systems that perform the coding and decoding, the transmitting and receiving. Narrative theory is an explicit development of linguistic structuralism, while media theory works out of an amplification of information theory. Although modern narrative theory responds directly to the rise of information theory—since the narrative signal can be fit directly into its communicational diagram—narratology's sources are older and elsewhere. But media theory in particular, as well as much of poststructuralism in general, is deeply if sometimes covertly beholden to information theory.[15] One thing this means is that neither media nor narrative theory is a discourse of cognitive systems, nor is either rooted in a discourse of cognitive systems.

Neither systems for coding and transmission (such as digital media) nor coded structures (such as narrative texts) are capable of cognizing on their own—that is, of making internal or self-referential sense of either themselves or their objects. So, if one stays within these domains, one must either leave the autopoietic-cognitive element aside, which is OK, or else smuggle it in, which is not OK—or at least, not productive of an adequate theoretical accounting of its phenomenon. However, one can work toward larger critical ends and/or in better critical faith, I think, if one brings the right level of the appropriate systems theory into the media or narrative mix. This would be the level that has been the discursive object of second-order cybernetics—cognitive systems, as grounded in the autopoiesis of living systems and then elaborated by social systems theory. To complete the cognitive, sense- or meaning-making circuit without any reversion to a subject-centered or intersubjective hermeneutics, one can factor self-referential systems, the worldly realm of autopoietic system-environments, into one's critical networks. The chapters that follow show a number of different ways to do that and, in the process, make the meanings that befall their constructor.

Chapter 1, "Systems, Media, Narrative," opens with a short history and introductory sketch of systems theory culminating in the arrival of the concept of autopoiesis. Kittler's *Gramophone, Film, Typewriter* comes in to juxtapose systems theory to media theory and give the latter a pointed introductory rehearsal. After a corresponding review of concepts basic to narrative theory, I align the three nodes of my discussion—systems, media, and narrative—in terms of their connections and their outer and inner differentiations. The power of narrative structures is approached with a consideration first of the trace—the informatic event of minimal inscription—and next of the cognitive moment latent in the reception of the trace. The term *semiolepsis* captures this combination of grammatological event and observing process, and relates these dynamics to the mytheme of metempsychosis. The tale of the transmission of the soul from one body to another comes forward as an allegory of the narrative reception of the trace. The opening chapter closes by extending the argument about the differentiation of transmission and cognition through an approach to the topic of telepathy. As a notion possessing ostensible mediatic and narrative elements, telepathy may also be submitted to a telling systems-theoretical decoding, which I set up with brief readings of Jacques Derrida's "Telepathy" and Octavia Butler's novel *Mind of My Mind*.

Chapter 2, "Communication and Information," opens with a general discussion of communications theory in relation to media theory, first of all, in order to delineate some basic distinctions between the two. Broadly speaking, communication tends to the social, media to the technological. The social moment of communication is explored through a contrast between Jürgen Habermas on intersubjectivity and consensus and Luhmann on closure and emergence. We turn next to information theory, as that can pivot on the disposition of noise relative to transmitted signal. A general reflection on informatic noise prepares for a substantial reading of some seminal work of Michel Serres at the four-way intersection named in his famous paper with the English title, "The Origin of Language: Biology, Information Theory, and Thermodynamics." Serres puts the concept of noise to work with his signature informatic reading of dialogue, and also with an adaptation of information theory to biological systems theory. I argue that, despite the popularity his approach has enjoyed, it does not actually work with regard to biological systems—which are, in the autopoietic conception, cognitive systems. It is instead, in Serrean parlance, a kind of parasiting of biology by physics, in which a discourse of energy feeds on a discourse of life, instead of the other way around, which would be more ecologically proper. The chapter ends by suggesting that the second-order discourse of self-referential form as coordinated with autopoietic systems theory offers a worldly alternative to the usual genuflections at the altar of noise.

Chapter 3, "Feedback Loops," further develops the second-order discourse of form and the form-theoretical concept of reentry, first through popular examples of loopings—such as the lap game that makes an unsupported circle out of its players, and sonic feedback in rock music. It proceeds to embedded reportage in the mass media, paradoxical play frames, and eventually, matters of narrative recursion in the novelistic technique of Virginia Woolf's *Mrs. Dalloway* and of cinematic metalepsis in Michel Gondry's film *Eternal Sunshine of the Spotless Mind*. The vogue for embedded media during the Iraq War is viewed against the longer backdrop of feedback discourse in cybernetics and the interplay of first- and second-order observation. A brief treatment of reentry and time in Spencer-Brown's *Laws of Form* sets up its adaptation in Luhmann to the temporalization of complexity in social systems. Spencer-Brown's calculus of distinctions also erects a wide and adaptable bridge between literary and cinematic narrative forms: I model this with the readings of Woolf's novelistic and Gondry's cinematic devices. In a final section, with a looping flourish underscored by a glance at reverse narratives and Christopher Nolan's film *Memento,* narrative time is reprised as an allegory of systems time.

Chapter 4, "Observing *Aramis,*" stands alone in being focused largely on a single text, Bruno Latour's brilliant, underappreciated, passingly strange and elusive work, *Aramis, or the Love of Technology.* But the chapter begins by enlisting some assistance from Gilbert Simondon's *On the Mode of Existence of Technical Objects.* Their respective philosophies of technology would appear to make parallel connections: Simondon's general recovery of technical objects covering the particular case in Latour's recovery of the failed public rapid transit system called Aramis. However, the two discourses diverge insofar as for Latour, Aramis remains a project that falls short of producing an object. The greatness of *Aramis* lies not in its sociological analysis, which is fine enough, but in its literary recovery of the Aramis project for the creation of a truly unique technosocial novel. In a quasi-historical, quasi-fictive mediation of the lapsed twenty-year effort to design and perfect a technological system, taking the literary license to create alter egos and to endow inanimate entities with voice and agency, Latour brings a suite of narrative and rhetorical devices to bear on a self-referential interrogation of the philosophical implications of actor-network theory. I submit *Aramis* to what may be its only sustained narratological reading, and at the end, draw out of that exercise a comparison of Latour's actor-network concept to Luhmann's social systems theory.

Chapter 5, "Mediations of Gaia," brings the cognitive issue home to living systems and their environments with some recent theorizing and storytelling in relation to ecological matters. The psychic and social discourses of self-referential systems come back to their biological origins and move out to their Gaian contexts. In its transversal coupling of geobiological cycles and material-energetic flows, ecosystem ecology provides a framework comprehending Gaian science and neocybernetics. Comparing their approaches to the idea of ecology and the discourse of systems in Gregory Bateson's *Steps to an Ecology of Mind* and Félix Guattari's *The Three Ecologies* and *Chaosmosis,* one can mark significant differences in their respective intellectual cultures. Ecosystem ecology directly informs Bateson's discourse of mind, while Varela's brand of systems theory is located in dialogue with Guattari's ethico-aesthetic paradigm. But still, how is one to communicate about Earth if one cannot communicate *with* it? Luhmann takes up this paradox in *Ecological Communication,* and Richard Doyle takes a quite different aim at the same basic quandary in *Darwin's Pharmacy.* His "ecodelia" is a pharmacologically mediated quest for, so to speak, ecological telepathy.

The movie *Avatar* evokes that ecodelic vision with a bioengineered prosthesis capable of projecting a paraplegic jarhead into a Gaian wonder world. On Pandora, the Na'vi have organs—let us say, media links—that plug directly into and so communicate through Eywa's planetary system. Neither this depiction of an organic global network, nor Gaia theory proper, has escaped the notice of Bruno Latour. His comments connecting it to *Avatar* begin my interrogation of the movie's mise-en-scène of the avatar system—its telling, its design specs, and its phantasmagoric realizations of technological metempsychoses. However, it turns out that an actual media technology exterior to that frame feeds another digital "transmission of soul" back into the physiological metamorphoses of the story world. Finally, while in its original theorization, Gaia theory draws on the first-order cybernetics of homeostatic self-regulation, when seen in philosophical hindsight, the intuition of Gaia is already a symptom of a concurrent turn toward self-referential systems. The recognition of Gaia is both conceptually and temporally parallel with the discourse of cognition that emerges within second-order systems theory.

An autopoietic spin on the Gaia concept would deem the higher-order planetary couplings of geological and biological systems precisely *metabiotic* in their own physical and material-organic right. Psychic and social systems are also higher-order natural systems that self-produce their own metabiotic forms only within that Gaian environmental matrix of geobiological systems. While the autopoietic "selves" of psychic and social systems are not materially bounded, they are nonetheless fully systemic—coemergent, coevolving, functionally bounded differential forms of virtual autopoiesis spun off from the literal metabolic looping of living systems. In this way, the concept of autopoiesis as elaborated in second-order systems theory comprehends these multileveled mysteries of cognitive operation. In their structural couplings as well as their operational differentiations, the autopoietic interconnections among natural systems can guide our critical efforts at comprehensive thinking past the pitfalls of holistic totalization and specious unification. We observe instead systemic autonomies, an infinitely differentiated but resonant and always potentially sociable play of forms, manifold nodes and networks of knowing, within which are embedded our own observations and fabrications, our constructions and communications, and our fiascoes and felicities.

1 SYSTEMS, MEDIA, NARRATIVE

From the Trace to the Telepathic Imaginary

Systems

"The narratives of the world are numberless," Roland Barthes begins his famous essay, and continues: "Narrative is first and foremost a prodigious variety of genres, themselves distributed amongst different substances—as though any material were fit to receive man's stories."[1] If we were to substitute "systems" for Barthes's "narratives" and "stories," and "media" for "substances" and "material," we would have a proper statement in each case. The systems of the world are also numberless, and the materialities involved in their constitution and communication are equally open-ended. However, while a system may be any complex totality composed of interdependent elements, the strong sense of the system concept denotes a complex ensemble unified in such a way that a *process* emerges from, and only from, the interdependent interactions of those elements. Systems theories attend to both the elements and the processes of the systems they observe.

An element-process distinction can now be observed between Barthes's statement about narrative and the strong definition of systems. As a complex structure of signs, the literary object, such as a narrative text, is a social element and media object ready to be taken up and processed by an observing system. However, the narrative subject—the observer of the text—can be one of, or comprised of, multiple systems, most immediately the psychic systems (or minds) producing perceptions and intuitions of the text and the social systems (or conversations) within which the text circulates as an element of literary communication. At least one more distinction must be noted right away: in their prodigious variety, systems may be physical or technological, biological or cultural, natural or designed, or some combination of these. Unlike stories, nothing restricts the nature of systems to "man's" dominion.

A major complication of systems theory is the proliferation of *its* genres. A "prodigious variety" of kinds and conceptual models of systems have been treated under the heading of systems theory. We have narrowed this profusion down to a pair of interrelated developments. At mid-twentieth century, at the same moment that a method for measuring the entropy of thermodynamic systems—statistical mechanics—provides the mathematical template for an information theory pertaining to communication systems and produces a massive extension of the entropy concept beyond physics, the discourse of cybernetic systems emerges around a functional homology in the homeostasis or self-regulation of mechanical and organic systems. Informatic systems theories are immediately intertwined with cybernetic systems theories. One result of this parallel development is a tendency for informatics and cybernetics to get tangled up, their conceptual differences lost to view. *Neocybernetics and Narrative* disentangles them. It traces the seminal moment of their effective separation to the early 1970s, when second-order cybernetics and autopoietic systems theory converged to posit a noninformatic conception of cognition. We are calling the systems theory that gathers up this conceptual unfolding *second-order systems theory,* or *Neocybernetics* for short.

Self-Regulation

Early in the technological development of the steam engine, a qualitatively different sort of mechanism is invented in conjunction with it, the governor, which automatically stabilizes the rate at which the engine operates. Mechanical self-regulation has arrived. In 1868, leading British physicist James Clerk Maxwell writes up the first theoretical analysis of the governor.[2] He considers it in its status as a dynamical system in which the centrifugal forces spun off of the engine's performance are channeled into mechanical control effects. Coupled to and regulating a thermodynamical system, the mechanical governor uses the steam engine's output of work to operate a valve that regulates its input of fuel. The governor is considered the prototypical cybernetic control system. Cybernetic systems theory takes its name from the Greek root of "governor"—*kybernetes,* meaning "steersman." The governor controls the system it governs through *negative feedback:* it measures a process (constructs information about energy) and feeds that measure back into the process in order to damp its amplification past a set point with a reduction that steers it back to the desired rate. "The first great paper on cybernetics, 'Behavior, Purpose, and Teleology,'" states: "All purposeful behavior may be considered to require negative feed-back. If a goal is to be attained, some signals from the goal are necessary at some time to direct the behavior."[3] Control theory emerges at mid-twentieth century at the confluence of military and civilian interests in communication systems—for instance, the manual and remote control of forces and weapons by means of communications among human operators and mechanical processes. Flanking these cybernetic demands are developments in computation and information technologies that advance the sophistication with which machines from dynamos to computers could be rendered communicable *with*—if not necessarily more intelligent (although that aim was to follow), then at least more perceptive and responsive, more "alive."

Heinz von Foerster captures this analogy to living systems in the statement that the original goal of cybernetic systems theory

> was to characterize a mode of behavior that is fundamentally distinct from the customary perception of the operations of machines with their one-to-one correspondence of cause-effect, stimulus-response, input-output, and so on. The distinction arises from the presence of sensors whose report on the state of the effectors of the system acts on the operation of the system.[4]

Machines with feedback or other automatic control systems between sensors and effectors parallel organisms with sensorimotor systems that self-regulate bodily actions. Or, again, mechanical systems for homeostasis (such as the governor's active regulation of a process within a set range) and organic systems for proprioception—the automatic self-perception of one's movements or actions, enabling the maintenance of balance—are conceptually united in their self-monitoring processes. To that extent, all such systems have the "selves" instantiated by their processes of self-regulation.

Self-Reference

Systems theory catalyzes the emergence of the sciences of emergence. Negative feedback is joined by the concept of negative entropy, self-regulation by the concept of self-organization, by "order from noise," "order from chaos," and "complexity from noise": "*the flow of energy through a system acts to organize that system.*"[5] Niklas Luhmann has summarized the conceptual threshold systems theory is ready to cross by the 1980s: "While this open-systems paradigm has been asserted and accepted within systems theory, a surpassingly radical further step has been taken in the discussions of the last two decades. It concerns contributions to a *theory of self-referential systems.*"[6] Systems theory moves into the later decades of the twentieth century with a multifarious welter of systems discourses, more or less popular or technical as the case may be, but typically too multidisciplinary and/or extrascientific to be placed into traditional pigeonholes. A case in point is the bracing work of Gregory Bateson. Throughout the 1970s, Bateson's lifework, selected in *Steps to an Ecology of Mind,* animates the intellectual counterculture at large, in particular, the audience for the periodical successor to the *Whole Earth Catalog, CoEvolution Quarterly.*

Bateson explains the seminal importance of "Behavior, Purpose, and Teleology" to *CoEvolution Quarterly*'s editor Stewart Brand in a way that forecasts the philosophical stakes of the turn from first-order self-regulation to second-order self-reference. That 1943 report on "the formal character of seeking mechanisms" produced "a solution to the problem of purpose. From Aristotle on, the final cause has always been the mystery. . . . We didn't realize then (at least I didn't realize it, though McCulloch may have) that the whole of logic would have to be reconstructed for recursiveness."[7] Second-order systems theory has pursued that wholesale reconstruction of operational logic. These neocybernetic developments have pressed the analysis of recursive processes beyond organic, mechanical, and computational control processes toward the formal autonomy that endows natural systems with their cognitive capacities. If, in classical cybernetics, circular functions and feedback mechanisms are treated "objectively" as instrumental for the self-regulation of a system, then second-order cybernetics is aimed in particular at that characteristic of natural systems, from cells on up, whereby circular recursion *constitutes the system* in the first place. The logic of self-reference is the abstract counterpart of circular self-constitution.

However, in the milieu of the classical syllogism, self-referential propositions produce paradoxical conclusions. For instance, in the famous liar's paradox, Epimenides the Cretan states: "All Cretans are liars." But since he is also a member of the major class—and this is the form that self-reference takes in this example—the truth value of his claim cannot be determined. If he is lying, then he is telling the truth, and vice versa. But operational processes differ profoundly from logical propositions. In this distinction, we have a clear application of the divergence that Bateson predicts, between the classical humanistic logic that banishes paradox from its calculation of truth values and the posthumanist logic of neocybernetics that sets paradox to work. "In cybernetics you learn that paradox is not bad for you, but it is good for you, if you take the dynamics of the paradox seriously."[8] In the realm of recursive operations, self-referential processes unfold over time to bind those operations into autonomous wholes. Self-referential systems are self-constituting.

Self-Making

The current default sense of the phrase *systems theory* is the body of work associated with German sociologist Niklas Luhmann. The line to Luhmann's development of self-referential systems theory goes directly through Humberto Maturana and Francisco Varela's biological systems concept of autopoiesis and ties to von Foerster's cognitive and epistemological work in second-order cybernetics. Under the regime of self-referential systems, "self-regulation" changes sense from automatic control to autonomous self-constitution, and the polarity between open and closed systems is sublated by a supplementary relation binding openness to the environment to the closure of system operations.

The concept of autopoiesis clarifies what is at stake here. Maturana and Varela introduce the theory of autopoiesis in the context of biological organization. Autopoiesis—literally, "self-making"—names the recognition that a living system, such as a cell or an organism built up from cells, is a self-referential system: it is the processual product of its own production. Autopoietic self-production is thereby, in Maturana and Varela's phrase, "organizationally closed." The autopoietic process turns on itself, recursively: the organization enables the production that maintains the organization, and so on. Open to the material-energetic flux of its environment, an autopoietic system is closed or "information-tight" in the sense that it is self-operating, or autonomous. It self-maintains the continuous production of the components that bind and replenish the system that produces the components that bind and replenish the system.[9]

The concept of autopoiesis has developed along two main lines of application. The first extends its scientific propriety as a biological theory of the organization of living systems. Researchers taking up the work of Maturana and/or Varela have traced the implications of autopoiesis beyond the realm of individuated cells and organisms.[10] Autopoiesis has also been brought up to the level of the biosphere with Earth systems theories of planetary self-regulation, or Gaia theory, as elaborated by microbiologist Lynn Margulis.[11] The second main line of autopoietic developments leads more directly to the matters of subjectivity, mediation, and society inherent in narrative production, by way of Luhmann's systems theory.[12] In this construction, the operational closure of autopoietic self-production demands separate accounts for the separate closures of systems of consciousness and of communication. Media theory then supplements Luhmann's account of the coevolutionary interpenetration of psychic and social systems by foregrounding the technical objects and systems in their midst as additional environmental resources for cognitive operations.

Transporting autopoiesis beyond the organic boundaries of biological systems, Luhmann specifies how the separate operations of psychic and social systems—their differential processing of evanescent event-structures, the elements of consciousness and communication—can produce virtual boundaries for those metabiotic systems. Their metabiotic boundaries are produced and reproduced by the forms of distinction that those same systems construct by making selections within the medium of *meaning*—say, between self and other, between inclusion and exclusion: "Boundaries can be differentiated as specific mechanisms with the specific purpose of separating yet connecting. They assume this function via particular performances of selection."[13] However, from the operational interpenetration of psychic and social systems, those semistable networks we call persons self-organize. Identities coalesce around a system's probable reiteration of the same selections from a given repertoire of possible distinctions, but may be transformed when different selections ramify into a new norm, or new options enter the repertoire of possible distinctions.

Second-order systems theory observes a world so constructed that any single observer's operationally closed cognitive constructions can be rendered stable and pertinent from moment to moment by the structural couplings of, and recursive conversations with, the multiple observers in *its* environment. Just as all nervous systems and all organisms that possess them as subsystems are consortiums of multiple biological autopoietic systems, so are all psychic systems bound into communities, or social systems. Within these social systems, *social* autopoiesis—the ongoing self-production and self-maintenance of communications— produces what von Foerster calls *eigenvalues,* stable yet mobile and multiple recursive consensuses about comparable environments. In this manner, neocybernetic epistemology renders discursively explicit what has always been implicit in the relation of narrative structures to the wider world in which *they* are embedded. Prompting reframing by shifts in embedded levels, inducing oscillations in perspective, the play of narrative forms is a serious rehearsal of the cognitive oscillations of observing systems never out of play in our literal constructions of worldly knowledge.

Media: *Gramophone, Film, Typewriter*

In a neocybernetic view, given the autopoietic multiplicity of living, psychic, and social systems, "the traditional attribution of cognition to 'man' has been done away with."[14] In this description, communication concerns cognitive matters that are not altogether predetermined by nor limited to technological channels. Rather, communication negotiates with forms that are specified from one instance to the next by cognitive systems with variable ratios of autonomy and contingency relative to the compositions of their complex environments, including their media ecologies. In contrast, the media theory of Friedrich Kittler's *Gramophone, Film, Typewriter* is cybernetic tout court.[15] Occupying the intersection of first-order cybernetics and informatics, it humbles the subject of humanistic hermeneutics by interpellation into the discrete material channels of communication: "media determine our situation."[16]

Under the conditions of technological mediation, however, theory remains viable, or inevitable. Media theory has become a hegemonic site within the new academic order of a wired culture. For Kittler, media determine our posthumanity, and they have been doing so in technological earnest at least since the phonograph broke the storage monopoly of writing. As a kind of media theory of history, a requiem and good riddance for the era of "so-called Man," *Gramophone, Film, Typewriter* transmits the tenor of its own historical moment. The German edition appears in 1986, the year after the opening of the Massachusetts Institute of Technology's (MIT's) Media Lab and the Talking Heads' posthermeneutic concert movie album *Stop Making Sense*. Other resonant events in the American culture of that moment include William Gibson's *Neuromancer* (1984), Donna Haraway's "Manifesto for Cyborgs" (1985), and Octavia Butler's *Xenogenesis* trilogy (1987–89). Looming over these three speculative and/or scholarly scenarios published during the final Cold War decade were memories and premonitions of mushroom clouds. Each imagines a posthuman world as the aftermath of a nuclear exchange. *Gramophone, Film, Typewriter* posits its posthumanism on the premise that the Strategic Defense Initiative has already set off the fireworks, that the future is always already a prequel to Star Wars. The text begins with the observation that optical fiber networks are "immune . . . to the bomb. As is well known, nuclear blasts send an electromagnetic pulse (EMP) through the usual copper cables, which would infect all connected computers," and ends with before and after photos of Hiroshima.[17]

Let us read the fabula of *Gramophone, Film, Typewriter,* that is, the story enacted by its narrative of media. Kittler narrates the development of analog media as events leading to an as yet unreached digital climax. The speculative climax of his historical fabula appears at the beginning of his discourse, as an anticipation of an outcome in the making. The tale then reverts to its nineteenth-century preconditions and focuses on readings of the events that push this plot along. In his telling, there are constant shifts of topic, a kaleidoscopic round of detail framed by the gradual chronological progression of the historical argument. However, writ large, his tale occupies an evolving media environment from which particular psychic and social operations have been evacuated.

Kittler's broadband scholarly panoptics afford a sublime technodiscursive vista, and in particular, a point of lucid observation on the ongoing relativization of literary production. Kittler transposes Kant's mathematical sublime into the mechanical transcendence of communications technology over individual subjects, displacing human psychology into machine being, setting off repeated implosions by which so-called Man is apocalypsed into infinite media loops. His high-prophetic meld of Lacan's laconism and Zarathustra's hammer facilitates a neuromantic network of discursive intensities. Kittler's text operates a machine aesthetic tooled to the posthumanist discursivities of his intellectual heroes, but going beyond them to place the stylus of technology onto the groove of inscripted bodies.

Many of Kittler's sublime effects result from a kind of hyperbolic digitality—all-or-nothing assertions pressing seemingly local instances into global histories. For instance, in *Gramophone*, Kittler is fond of audacious chronologies that parody the popular media demand for appearances of journalistic exactitude: "around 1880 poetry turned into literature," or "around 1900, love's wholeness disintegrates into the partial objects of particular drives" (14, 70). A related rhetorical scheme in *Gramophone* mediating the grand transformations of modernism is the *from–to* formation: "Literature defects from erotics to stochastics, from red lips to white noise," or as combined with an audacious chronology: "from imagination to data processing, from the arts to the particulars of information technology and physiology—that is the historic shift of 1900" (51, 73). Again, and as the volume is coming to a conclusion, with the arrival of Turing's universal computer, "the hypothetical determinism of a Laplacian universe, with its humanist loopholes (1795), was replaced by the factual predictability of finite-state machines" (245).

Gramophone, Film, Typewriter is written just as chaos theory is arriving to throw a wrench into such stark digital determinisms, precisely through the operational finitude as well as nonlinear iterations of "finite-state machines." As John von Neumann points out in 1948, although digital computers can produce perfect results, just "as long as the operation of each component produces only fluctuations within its preassigned tolerance limits," computational error is reintroduced by the lack of the infinite digits necessary to carry out all calculations with perfect precision.[18] Kittler melodramatizes Turing's work, it seems to me, because he is captivated by the towering image of an informatic colossus, an all-determining and inescapable imago of media that induces a productive critical paranoia. Media are always already watching *us*, putting their needles into our veins. Already in Nietzsche's response to a prototypical typewriter, the Malling-Hansen writing ball of 1867, according to Kittler, "humans change their position—they turn from the agency of writing to become an inscription surface" (210). *Neuromancer*'s Wintermute is everywhere, or as Kittler phrases it in *Gramophone*, "data flows . . . are disappearing into black holes and . . . bidding us farewell on their way to nameless high commands" (xxxix). We see the particular and pandemic pathologies of modern paranoia precisely as psychic effects driven by the panoptic reach of media technologies in their capacities for surveillance leading to punishment. Not for nothing is the apocalypse according to Schreber's 1903 *Memoirs of My Nervous Illness* (1988)—Schreber having been a schizophrenic autobiographer who recorded his experiences of being the telepathic recipient of divine and demonic rays—a prophetic book of prominent proportions in Kittler's media cosmos.

By operating the cybernetic bridge from the nervous system and its "psychic apparatus" to the *Aufschreibesysteme* or inscription systems of his discourse networks, Kittler reads structural psychoanalysis *into* media theory, redescribing Lacan's triad of real, imaginary, and symbolic as effects drawn from the data channels of phonograph, cinema, and typewriter. Everything that determines the promotion of literary objects into scriptures for modernity's secular humanism—their hallucinatory powers and spiritual effects—derives from the day of its storage-and-transmission monopoly. But literature can only traduce the real and the imaginary, funneling them into the narrow band of the symbolic. For Kittler, the objects of science are also subsumed into the will-to-power of media technology.

By way of theoretical contrast, for Bruno Latour, despite his coinage of "technoscience" to underscore the sociological inextricability of science and technology, the two are granted separate treatments that preserve their disciplinary and epistemological distinctions. However, Kittler does not fall entirely under Latour's blanket indictment of (Baudrillardian) postmodernism: "Instead of moving on to empirical studies of the networks that give meaning to the work of purification it denounces, postmodernism rejects all empirical work as illusory and deceptively scientistic."[19] Rather, in *Gramophone,* Kittler busts open the realm of the real to examine the nonsymbolic and nonimaginary residues of communication technology, everything that cannot be posted: "Bodies themselves generate noise. And the impossible real transpires" (46). Where Latour finds the proliferating quasi-objects of technosocial mediation, Kittler finds the literal networks of communications media.

Kittler's text elides to some extent the history of physics—the crossover from late classical determinism to statistical mechanics, from thermodynamic entropy to information entropy—concurrent with its media history. He scants the ether and electromagnetic field theories, without which no development could have been accomplished—from analog to digital processing, and from preelectrical storage technology (photography, phonography) to broadcast transmission (radio, television), electronic storage and manipulation (tape deck, video camera), and digital computation technologies (microprocessor, fiber-optic cable). Indeed, Kittler runs up against numerous phantasmagorias of energy that emanate from nineteenth-century wave theories connecting the physics of optics and acoustics through an analogy between elastic and vibratory physical media, the air and the purported luminiferous ether, but elides them by metonymic reification in media receivers and inscription devices.

My point is that the multiplicity of the concept of media extends beyond its particular technological instantiations to include both physical and metaphysical registers. A history of media could concern itself as well with the luminiferous ether and the *anima mundi,* the subtle fluids and strange angels that intermingled with the departed souls of phonography and the trick shots of cinema. But for the most part, in *Gramophone,* Kittler displaces such business to premodernist media:

> The invention of the Morse alphabet in 1837 was promptly followed by the tapping specters of spiritistic séances sending their messages from the realm of the dead. Promptly as well, photographic plates—even and especially those taken with the camera shutter closed—furnished reproductions of ghosts or specters. (12)

While the telegraph and daguerreotype remain outside *Gramophone, Film, Typewriter's* primary historical field, Kittler's insistence on the material basis and thus empirical examinability of all media that mediate the cultural imaginary is a crucial theoretical move. Moreover, "The realm of the dead is as extensive as the storage and transmission capabilities of a given culture" (13), and the institutional regimes that sustain the privileges of literary discourse networks (and of us who still inhabit them) are increasingly caught up in the mundane storage functions and media transformations Kittler describes. In its informatic dimension, the daemonic angel of our own history is being driven by the electronic differentiation and digital reintegration of data flows. But, finally, the realm of media in its literal instrumentation is not precisely a realm of the dead. In itself it is a realm of the *abiotic,* a realm for technical affairs that inscribe and memorialize cognitive effects without themselves having been either alive, self-aware, or self-understanding. The *biotic* and *metabiotic* domains of autopoietic contingencies are largely deleted from

Kittler's descriptions. However, if we are to mediate narrative structures and self-referential systems, there are other kinds of systems to bring into focus, other operational dimensions to bring into play. This is why media theory still needs systems theory.[20]

Systems Differentiations

Without systems theory's rigorous account of cognitive operations, our literary and cultural theories fail to progress beyond or tend to slip back toward an earlier cybernetics. They revert to forms of mere informatics that break down proper operational boundaries between narrative and media technologies on the one hand and psychic and social systems on the other. In that case, we tend to float off into fantasies of either hermetic control or incontinent flow rather than holding fast to good neocybernetic differentiations, operational boundaries, and their ineluctable contingencies.

The scheme of systems differentiations presented in Figure 2 is developed directly from Luhmann's social systems theory, but makes explicit some matters that Luhmann leaves unstated or undeveloped.[21] It is based on his definitive appropriation of the concept of autopoiesis put forward by Maturana and Varela for a general systems theory. In their original instance, the concept of autopoiesis provides only an *external* distinction, setting off autopoietic systems as living or biotic systems—those studied by biology—from nonautopoietic systems as nonliving or abiotic systems, for instance, those studied by physics or computer science. As a result, the further development of their approach subsumes psychic and social operations under a generalized notion of living systems. In contrast, Luhmann's extension of autopoiesis beyond the biological instance produces a second distinction, one *internal* to an enlarged concept of autopoiesis, which I have termed that between the *biotic* autopoiesis of living systems and the *metabiotic* autopoiesis of minds and societies.

In this description, autopoiesis is a constitutive process describing the basal self-referential operation of living, psychic, *and* social systems, each of which must operate in the first instance to bind and maintain the system of its own self-production. While the dynamics of biotic systems work on material atoms and molecules, the dynamics of metabiotic systems construct virtual forms and process their distinctions. Luhmann

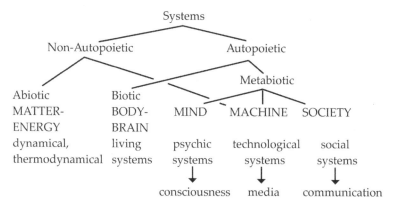

Figure 2. Systems differentiations.

brings psychic and social systems under a general description of auto-poiesis, without collapsing them into living dynamics, by redefining the elements of their production as different kinds of meaning-events. Meaning becomes the medium in which elements of consciousness and communication may interpenetrate while maintaining operational distinction into separate systems. As a result, in this description, psychic and social events also do not collapse into each other but retain an operational level of contingent autonomy.

Metabiotic systems are operationally distinct from living systems. But nevertheless, they emerge only from and exist only in relation to biotic systems. In Luhmann's theory, human psychic and social systems "interpenetrate," that is, while they are operationally distinct, their relative autonomy is coevolutionary, coemergent. Either presents the immediate and indispensable environment of the other. In other words, the extent of their autonomy is strictly internal and operational. Externally, their existence is absolutely contingent on environments that contain other kinds of systems. Moreover, both psychic and social systems participate in the shared medium of meaning.

Let us magnify the content of this second distinction. What Maturana and Varela, carrying forward a mechanistic semantics, term the *dynamics* of an autopoietic system, Luhmann generalizes as the *operations* of such a system.[22] It is the recursive self-operationality of such self-referential ensembles that is proper to autopoietic systems. In each instance—with either the membrane-boundedness of biotic autopoietic systems or the form distinctions of metabiotic autopoietic systems—one confronts the fundamental matter of operational closure. The internal autonomy of any specific autopoietic system of whatever sort—living, psychic, or social—is a necessary condition for the continuation of its dynamics or operations and thus for the self-maintenance of its own life, mind, or communication, as the case may be. Let us now add into the discussion the matters of technology in general and media in particular and theorize the interrelation of autopoietic and technological systems.

We note that machines are not autopoietic: they do not perform either biotic or metabiotic autopoietic operations. However, they emerge only out of environments compounded with the metabiotic autopoietic systems of (not necessarily human) minds and societies. That is, technics is constitutionally paradoxical: it partakes of autopoiesis while not producing it. Here, another distinction emerges that is internal to the concept of the *non*autopoietic system, between abiotic and metabiotic varieties. Abiotic nonautopoietic systems may take straightforward natural forms such as stars and their planets, rivers, or thunderstorms. But machines—nonautopoietic technological systems—are as emergently *meta*biotic as psyches and societies, and therefore are a species of meaning systems in their own right. Technological systems constitute a metabiotic yet nonautopoietic emergence coupled to the interpenetration of psyches and societies. All three kinds of systems, albeit in radically different modes of operation, occupy the plane of metabiotic artifacts.

As we increasingly come to understand from the work of André Leroi-Gourhan, Gilbert Simondon, Michel Serres, Bernard Stiegler, and many others, technics coemerges along with the processes of hominization and is coeval with the human mind and human society. Nevertheless, technical objects are not autopoietic meaning systems: unlike the operations of consciousness and communication, they do not self-(re)produce meaning. Rather, on the plane of metabiotic systems, their particular function is to *convey* meaning, to transmit it. Their production is mediation. Like the trace prior to the sign, they spur the making of meaning, and once made, they make it leap over distances. Relative to the autopoietic realm, then, machines are the externalized receptacles for mentation, socialization, communication, and memorialization, called forth by the continuous metabiotic need to structurally couple together ever-renewed, ever-reproduced psychic and social systems.

The paradox here, again, is that machines are at once both nonauto-poietic and metabiotic. They participate with autopoiesis, while not precisely possessing it. Being so intimate with psychic and social systems, it is as if technological systems feign the status of autopoietic systems. The quest for the self-producing automaton is ongoing. Some would like nothing better than to perfect a cybernetic machine, one that lives, thinks, and communicates. For so they have always already seemed to us. We experience them, or at least, we fantasize them and we fictionalize them as such—as living or thinking or feeling or communicating, as replicants ready at any moment to come to life, to exercise agency, to ache inside, to seek companions. We are so intimate with our machines, it would seem, because in some sense they are not ours; they seem to possess a phantom autonomy. One reason for this, in the idiom of Bruno Latour, is that they are in fact the indispensable *intermediaries* for the operational integration of autopoietic minds and societies, forever verging on a metamorphosis into *mediators,* agents, actors, entities with an autonomous inner life.

One can also place in the nonautopoietic but metabiotic machinic domain certain communications technologies that are easily mistaken as autopoietic meaning systems: writing and narrative. These old media technologies are distinct from yet always in the midst of minds and societies. Placed between and mediating psychic and social systems, like machines in general, texts and narratives are also metabiotic but non-autopoietic superstructures built up out of grammatological and semiotic infrastructures. But it is also worth noting what they are *not:* literary and narrative texts are neither self-organizing nor self-producing systems. Rather, as produced through the coupling of meaning systems to media technologies such as language, writing, printing, phonography, and/or cinematography, they are semiotic structures that mediate self-producing systems. And as the discourse of these significant structures, then, it is appropriate that narrative theory today—narratology—is one of the most viable offshoots of the great wave of structuralism.

How should we organize the signal and noise of narrative structures with regard to the distinct forms taken and produced by their respective observing systems—that is, by the autopoietic cognitions of psychic and social systems? The mainstream model of literary narrative theory drawn after Gérard Genette's *Narrative Discourse* has two layers, *discourse* and *story.* One distinguishes between the given form and sequence of the textual signifiers narrating events in the first instance (the discourse) and the signified space and time, the storyworld and the chronological relations of those narrated events (the story). This model of the narrative object is widely disseminated, and often the straightforward distinction it plies is all that an observer needs to open up a narrative text. However, the problem with it is its equivocal analytical purchase on the location of narrative point of view or perspective—the vital matter of represented subjectivities or, as I prefer to say, signified observing systems put into play by the narrative discourse. Due to this model's indetermination in the location of focalization, its analysis of narrated perspectives tends to slip back and forth, to float somewhere between the discourse layer and the story layer.

For a more rigorous observation of analytical boundaries, Mieke Bal's *Narratology* is an important supplement to Genette's framework. Bal develops a three-layer model of narrative analysis. The *text* is specified as the narrative signifier per se, let us say, the narrative signal that arrives in some manner of potentially noisy but perceptible vehicle, a book or a movie. The *story* in Bal's scheme is the layer of signification at which focalization—or, more broadly, the signified perceptual observation of and within the storyworld—is mobilized by the text. And the *fabula* is then constituted *as* the storyworld and its events, as best as can be reconstructed by a narrative observer of the text and its story. Bal's enhancements fix the problem of floating focalization in the standard model. It is, of course, Genette who introduces the term *focalization* to improve on the equivocal notion of narrative perspective, and Bal picks up from there to develop and refine the specificity of the concept and to assign it to its own layer—the story—within a detailed description of narrative functions. She explains the differential logic of her supplementation of Genette's scheme:

> The speech act of narrating is still different from the vision, the memories, the sense perceptions, thoughts, that are being told. Nor can that vision be conflated with the events they focus, orient, interpret. Consequently, focalization belongs in the story, the layer between the linguistic text and the fabula. (149)

Bal's three-layer scheme confirms for these distinctions of narrative structure (as far as I know, without any contact with or aim to reinforce) a basic correspondence with Luhmann's schemas of operational closures at the level of metabiotic systems, in relation to the environments they constitute as the external obverse of their internal autonomy. Narration corresponds (as structure corresponds to system) to the autopoiesis of communication, while focalization corresponds to the autopoiesis of consciousness. The tricky part of these suggestive parallels, of course, is to keep distinct and negotiate the differences between, as it were, the map presented by narrative structures and the territories of the observing systems that read the map. After all, for all their conceptual resonance, the disciplinary objects of autopoietic systems theory remain external to the disciplinary objects of narratology. Nonetheless, for social systems, the production of narrative texts per se, the narrating instance, is an element in their ongoing productions of communication. For psychic systems, the matter of focalization corresponds to and signifies the productions of specific conscious modalities of perception. And narrative *fabulae* then correspond to the signified environments at large, which, it is good to remind oneself, are the ground of the possibility of both actual and imagined, perceived and intuited systems.

If we put these considerations into a wider view of communications theory, the complexities unified within the narrative signal can be unfolded in the terms of Luhmann's analysis of communication.[23] Here, the narrative *text* as transmitted is the communicative offer, a selection of *information* in a form ready to be processed within a social subsystem. The narrative *story* is the complex of forms through which the narrative information comes to *utterance,* that is to say, in terms of which the signified psyches of narrators and characters come to consciousness and thus to communication. And the fabula, as a recursive selection on the textual information and the story's presentation of perceptual channels, is then *understood* as the environment of the storyworld and the events to be enacted there. From this particular alignment of a suitably complex narrative informatics with a suitably articulated theory of cognitive observation, both the narrative text per se (whatever its story) and the narrative story, in Bal's sense (whatever its text) become two-sided forms, possessing both a structural and a systemic side. This complex relation between story and text offers a structural parallel to Luhmann's technical description of the interpenetration of psychic and social systems. The text is a kind of fractal border or interface. It is both a sign structure, a material object bound up as a structural element in the ongoing self-producing autopoiesis of social-systemic communication—literary, cinematic, or whatever—and also one or more of the possible forms of a discourse attributed to a narrating agency, a literary narrator or a cinematic narration. On the basis of those narrative signs, a reader or viewer may discern the indications of focalization, a specific layer of meaning already encoded within the order of the signified.

For all that, texts do not read themselves. Moreover, when they are read, they are not read alone in systemic isolation. Nothing happens until readers or viewers interpenetrated within some network of social systems—some multiplicity of observing systems—intervene to perceive, to understand, and to respond to the represented orders of conceptual expositions or of storyworld events and the contingencies of the "visions" by which those elements of narrative fabulae come to be constructed on the textual signal. Those orders of meaning do not self-organize per se. Multiple recipients of the textual message operate at once to sort out its signal, to coconstruct the layers of psychic and social effects so represented, to process the irritation of its noise, and to induce from those operations the forms of meaning that then continue the cycles of social autopoiesis.

The Reception of the Trace

In the story "A Sign in Space" from Italo Calvino's collection *Cosmicomics,* after a short epigraph stating a cosmological datum, the metamorphic character Qfwfq begins to narrate the origin of signs:

> *Situated in the external zone of the Milky Way, the Sun takes about two hundred million years to make a complete revolution of the Galaxy.*
>
> Right, that's how long it takes, not a day less,—*Qfwfq said,*—once, as I went past, I drew a sign at a point in space, just so I could find it again two hundred million years later, when we went by the next time around. . . . I conceived the idea of making a sign, that's true enough, or rather, I conceived the idea of considering a sign a something that I felt like making, so when, at that point in space and not in another, I made something, meaning to make a sign, it turned out that I really had made a sign, after all. (31)

Let us imagine another beginning, similar to the one Qfwfq tells, but more down to earth. We can begin not with a sign, exactly, but with the trace that precedes the sign. Our origin myth has two versions. In the first of these, a long time ago, chipped flint in hominid hand, someone confronts a roughly uniform piece of solid matter, say, an outcropping of granite, and, for whatever reason, scratches a mark into the stone. In the second version, equally long ago, if not longer, a meteor falls to Earth sending up a splash of pulverized rock, one shard of which hits the same granite outcropping and leaves an identical if unintentional scratch. For our purposes, the two versions tell the same story: traces arise whether they are intended or not. However it came to be, this trace or mark subsists as a difference etched into its stony medium. It endures for a while, for a thousand or ten million years. Insofar as it endures, it memorializes its making. Persisting as a difference figured onto a ground previously undifferentiated, at least with regard to the presence of marks, the trace marks its own origin. In the first instance, for its observer, the trace refers to itself.[24] The trace refers to its own coming to be as a trace.

But what next? What does it mean for a trace to endure, to cross over the distances and durations that intervene between its coming to be in one place and moment and its itinerary of future destinations? With regard to the temporality of the trace: as long as the trace persists, it never ceases referring to itself. But the trace also marks in an indeterminate manner the datum that time passes and has passed from the moment of its taking place to all the later moments of its being observed, re-marked, received by an observer capable of discerning it as a mark, as a sign of the event that produced it. Qfwfq's account could be taken to indicate that a *sign* comes to be not when its trace is made, but when it is read as such. There will be an interval, however lengthy or infinitesimal, between the production of a trace and its observation as a sign. The time and place to be concerned with intentions is occupied by the observer of the trace.

Placed now in the time of that observer or reader, the trace presents itself to a present reception as a sign. Re-marking the trace, that observer can now intend to understand it, can allow the trace to carry its understanding away, perhaps to reconstruct a notion of the mark's moment of production, or to cross over to whatever other significances that observer can construct or entertain in regard to it. Having imported an observer and all of the systemic baggage that phenomenon brings with it onto the scene, our composite origin scenario is now compounded of: a prior event that makes a trace; a material or technical object capable of tracing; a medium to accept and preserve the trace; the trace itself; intervening space; intervening time; and a later agent to observe and construe the trace as a sign. These contingencies and implications of the trace can be gathered up in the observation that, prior to any intention to code it for communication, the trace transmits itself. The trace is self-mediating.

However, for all that, and this is the crucial link in this argument: *the trace does not receive its own transmission*. Or, again, the trace is not self-observing. Only its observer is in a position to process a trace as a sign conveying the implications that its trace is both self-referential and self-mediating. The simple reason for this is that observations must be performed by systems capable of marking the salient differentiations in a given instance. While the trace is a structure inscribing a difference, it is not yet an observing or self-observing system.

Stepping forward now from these origin stories to our own cultural era, the larger implication of this matter of the heteroreception of the trace is that media systems, in and of themselves in their technological instance, are not self-operating. For all the automation of which they are capable, in the fully systemic instance, they must be operated and observed by—and thus, coupled to—other kinds of systems, specifically those capable of producing cognitions: autopoietic systems. Or, again, in order to have significant effects, traces taken as signs must be embedded in larger networks that include (not necessarily human but) cognitive as well as informatic elements.

I press this issue of heteroreception in order to counter what I perceive as broad but problematic tendencies throughout our own cultural and theoretical moment to off-load the duties of cognitive systems onto informatic structures. If structures, however elaborate, such as signs and their transmission technologies, cannot self-receive at the level of meaning, then this tendency to grant agency and intention directly to them, rather than to the networks within which they may be coupled to cognitive systemic agencies, must be considered not as a literal description but as an allegory of desire or a displacement of responsibility. To bring this home to narrative theory in its literary and cinematic instances, the material mediums for transmitting narrative texts are themselves composed of semiotic elements bound into significant structures. Narrative texts in particular, typically replete with cogitating narrators and characters, come forward as full-blown, self-referential apparatuses for the off-loading of cognition and meaning making onto the media carrying the text. We say, "this text understands itself to be such and such," but we also expect our audience to process such figurations as rhetoric. However, many theories of information and media, despite their purported non-fictionality, deploy narrative figurations to imagine or enact desires to transfer cognitive burdens to mediatic infrastructures. Kittler's media stance is exemplary of this posthuman promotion of informatic structures. It is broadly supposed that in its sheer transmission and storage, in the absence of any cognitive sense making, information is or can be meaningful, its technological processing intentional. However, one need not revert to a prior hermeneutics to insist that meanings result instead from coupled networks of informatic *and* cognitive processes. What a systemic or autopoietic critique of information and media theories can provide is a more precise description of the different systems actually in play when meanings are made.

Semiolepsis

There is an ecology of systems to be brought to bear in any semiotic instance. Cognition collaborates with mediation to produce the psychic and social events about which we think and communicate. So, coming back to the trace, and granting the necessary supplement of an operating observer: in addition to its self-reference, and in addition to whatever may come to be construed as the semantic reference that transforms it into a sign, a trace or mark is also a cue for the intuition of an interval, a duration, and hence a passage in time, if not also in space. If the trace were also an image—an iconic sign—it would already be, even in its stasis, so to speak, a moving image. In its endurance, any trace is already the sign of a passage—certainly from one time to another, potentially from one place to another, and depending on its observer, from one meaning to another. In this sense, writing and telecommunication—as media for the transmission of signals that carry signs—are epiphenomena, further unfoldings, of the originary élan of the trace.

From another important and well-discussed angle, this eventfulness is the *différance* of the trace, its differential structure of multiple deferrals. But I want to emphasize the cognitive kinetics of the situation. *Semiolepsis* picks up this sense by suggesting not the seizure precisely, but by means of the bad pun, the *leap* of the trace. Or, more accurately, the leap that we observers endow on the trace *by* seizing it, yielding the figurative reversal that it has seized us. It may be that we are all constitutionally *semioleptic*, sufferers of *semiolepsy*, in thrall to signs. Nevertheless, and despite that, just as they play us, we also play signs, as I do now. We can game the trace, give signs a spin to see what they can do. There may be no choice but to submit to semiolepsy, but we can still have a go at semiolepsis.

Here is my literary notion: a motivation for displacement is spring-loaded—not into the trace per se—but into the bundle of trace and observer marked by the reception of the trace. After all, for it to jump at and seize us, we must first seize the trace by jumping to it. Between us, human readers, and signs, compounded of traces, is a circuit that is constitutionally jumpy—jumpy in space, jumpy in time, and jumpy in sense. Put another way, the advent of signs is always already eventful. With their mere presentation coupled to their mere observation, a cluster of differences has already occurred, and a story is already ready to continue. My larger thesis is that, in this sense of semiolepsis, any narrative passage is already a virtual allegory of the eventfulness of the sign. Moreover, the mode of deliberate allegory goes beyond the semiotic instance to mark a *figural* semiolepsis, a leap from one level of signification to another. In the Western tradition, as Michel Serres reminds us, this is the mode of Hermes, the psychopomp, messenger of the gods, guide of souls, the maker of passages from one realm of being to another.

Narrative is an allegory of the eventfulness of the observation of the trace. Take, for instance, a particular and perennial form of narrative event, one that is also typically an allegorical event, and one that plays for all it's worth on this spring-loadedness of the sign. This form of narrative fabula literalizes the élan of the sign to induce the depiction of the grandest leap of all, the leap that tops all others—the leap of the soul from one body to another. Its classical Western denomination is *metempsychosis*. I invoke this archaic or hermetic topos to suggest that this mytheme is itself an allegory of the re-marking of the trace, of being carried away by the observation of the trace, the mark, or the sign. The mythos of metempsychosis surely goes all the way back to the scratching of flints on stones. But let us pick up the story with the account of reincarnations that Pythagoras relates in his speech at the end of Ovid's *Metamorphoses:*

> Our souls survive this death; as they depart
> Their local habitations in the flesh,
> They enter new-found bodies that preserve them.

. . . All things change, yet never die,
Or here or there, the spirit takes its way,
To different kinds of being as it chooses,
From beast to man, from man to beast; however.
Or near or far or strange, it travels on. (418–19)

This discourse is, of course, in its attribution to Pythagoras, a sublime pastiche in the service of Ovid's epic comedy of transformations, as he works over a prior millennium of story cycles. Notable nonetheless is the endemic dualism of the Western sensibility, the dichotomy of mortal body and immortal soul, which separation maps so readily onto the dichotomy of material signifier and conceptual signified. It does this so effectively that in his *Course in General Linguistics,* Ferdinand de Saussure has to issue an edict against so construing the composite entity of the linguistic sign:

> The two-sided linguistic unit [of signifier and signified] has often been compared with the human person, made up of the body and the soul. The comparison is hardly satisfactory. A better choice would be a chemical compound like water, a combination of hydrogen and oxygen; taken separately, neither element has any of the properties of water. (103)

Two millennia later than Ovid, roughly contemporary with Saussure, James Joyce, another exiled purveyor of narrative transmigrations, performs a semiolepsis on the signifier *metempsychosis* itself, in *Ulysses* refracting that ponderous sign through Leopold Bloom's interior monologue and recollection of Molly Bloom's literal concretization of its syllables: "Mr. Bloom moved forward raising his troubled eyes. . . . Parallax. I never exactly understood. There's a priest. Could ask him. Par it's Greek: parallel, parallax. Met him pikehoses she called it till I told her about the transmigration. O rocks!" (154). Joyce's retelling of the *Odyssey* in *Ulysses* is, of course, a monumental transfusion of the fabula—that is, not the narrative signifier but the narrative signified, the "soul"—of Homer's epic into a complex tale of linguistic and cultural developments. At the same time, it retains the semioleptic feature of allegorical construction mentioned previously. The world of the Homeric epic is housed in a cosmos, a spatial framework of divine, mundane, and subterranean levels of being, levels mediated or leaped across by Zeus's emissary, Hermes, or by the divine Athena in her metamorphic disguises, as well as, of course, by the vision of the bard transmitting the tale. This leaping among the narrative's diegetic levels returns in Joyce's novel both in its very temporal parallax between the Homeric time of its legendary subtext and the world of Dublin on June 16, 1906, and in its narrator's strenuous shifting between external and internal points of observation.

For one more example of narrativized semiolepsis, you may recall how Carl Sagan's novel *Contact* purveys a contemporary secular mythology by staging a galactic intelligence, its receipt of echoes from the television broadcast of Hitler's opening the 1936 Summer Olympics in Berlin, its retransmission of that broadcast back to us earthlings with an embedded message, its reception on Earth, and its decoding into schematics for the construction of a technological system of some unknown sort. The very name of this fabulation posits the phatic function, the material basis of the contact without which communication as such cannot function. In the movie version, the vehicle at the center of this alien technology supports a single passenger, our heroine Ellie Arroway, played by Jodie Foster. The purpose of the vehicle seems to be the transportation or the transmission of its occupant across the galaxy to a place of cosmic epiphany. But for my reading here, the real crux of this cinematic telling is the drastically extended, viscerally exhausting leap across space itself, as Ellie commits her leap of faith in extraterrestrial intelligence.[25] Down the cosmic wormhole to the system of Vega she goes—or does she? One way or another, the depicted event of her transit draws on the fabled exhilaration of Einstein riding on his thought-experimental light beam. Ellie is our science-fictional Hermes, a cosmic mediator transmitted at the speed of light across a fold in space itself to a moment of sublime reception.

Nonetheless, as a form of *narrative* event, and at the base of all such semantic transmigrations of literary and narrative signs, metempsychosis always was and remains an allegory not so much of the soul but of the technics of the trace. If you want to see a picture of the soul, observe an intentional scratch on a rock. The élan with which we receive the traces of signs is the origin or *Ursprung* of stories that pivot on these radical passages, displacements in space, in time, or in embodiment. Such displaced materialities may also occur with shifts in the literal medium of the narrative text—for instance, the leaping back and forth from verbal to visual signifiers—or with metamorphic shifts in the diegetic body depicted by the signifiers of that text. Breaking this back down to the primal trace: any one mark, when received as a cue for cognitive operations, has multiple implications already built into it. Bound up in any mark is a potential dynamism, a contingent or nonrandom concatenation of signifying events, that is always already on the way to narrative formation. This élan or eventfulness of the trace or mark offers an approach to the connections between signs and their media, a way to further unfold the motivations for displacement, transport, or transmigration built into the power of narrative as a form taken by material mediums, and as a semiotic medium in its own right, within which psychic and social systems construct a significant number of their specific productions.

Telepathy

Telepathy nicely mobilizes all three of our theoretical themes: systems, media, narrative. One approach to telepathy concerns itself with the possible facticity of telepathic phenomena. Here one takes telepathy seriously as an actually or potentially positive event whose reality remains open to determination. It would indeed be a phenomenal event were telepathic communication to be positively verified. For the facticity approach, the issue concerns evidences, theories, judgments, convictions, and beliefs. A debate of this nature happens to run through the discourse of psychoanalysis from its founders to contemporary practitioners.[26] The critical obverse of this, a second approach to telepathy sidesteps the issue of its facticity and reflects instead on the fractures in the discourses generated by the former approach. In this regard, in 1981, Jacques Derrida published the text "Telepathy," which deconstructs Freud's body of commentary on this topic.[27] In Derrida and others, the critical approach offers no judgment on the facticity of telepathy. Instead, "Telepathy" grants that issue free play and stages the paradoxes generated by psychoanalytical writings about telepathy that keep the matter of its reality open.

Another approach transposes the topic of telepathy to narrative form and content. This extracts it from both ontological burdens and philosophical critique. Here, one observes telepathy as coding an epistemological schema at work in literary and cinematic fictions. In this relatively recent line of discussion, the set of relations telepathy posits clarifies some of the ways that stories work. Telepathy comes forward here both as a formal technique of so-called realistic narrative structures and as a highly popular conceit, as content and common event in fantastic and science-fictional storyworlds. The telepathic imaginary is alive and well in the fictional universe, in both obvious and subliminal forms.[28] Finally, I venture a systems theory approach to telepathy that, as far as I know, has not been previously set forth. However telepathic messages would go from mind to mind, were they to do so, their communication would be a sociological matter. Social systems theory could observe telepathy as a sort of phantom sociology.

But let us note the equivocation in its founding statement. The word "telepathy" is coined in 1882 by the British classicist Frederic Myers, who defines it as "the communication of impressions of any kind from one mind to another, independently of the recognized channels of sense."[29] Myers uses "communication" here in the sense of an event of physical contact, as in the communication of motion from one object to another. So the "communication of impressions" precisely concerns the registration of perceptions proper to a psychic system, whereas "from one mind to another" concerns the presence or constitution of a social system. As we will have reason to observe again, from its inception as a concept, the idea of telepathy has been a muddle. And, at the least, unlike discourses with a more strictly psychological or phenomenological orientation, social systems theory is in a position to define this muddle with some specificity: the idea of telepathy muddles together the distinct operations of psychic and social systems.

A venerable habit of thought continues to refer matters of communication, telepathic or otherwise, primarily to minds rather than, as systems theory would do, equally to the social systems constituted by communicative events. Part of the mystique of telepathy is drawn from an exaggerated conception of a communicating psyche. However, this mystification fits with the tradition of Western metaphysics, insofar as the bias of Western thought since Plato has largely run toward idealism—toward *Geist* (mind, reason, or spirit) and toward the phenomenologies of inner experience and private modes of knowledge, at the expense of the worldly materiality of their media, and at the expense of the difference between communication and consciousness. The idea of telepathy both thematizes and mystifies the processes of communication. It follows in the long train of philosophical idealism, and arises at its historical moment from the confrontation of Western notions of spirit with the rise of modern humanism, materialism, and media technologies.

The Narrative Approach

Wim Wenders's angelic fantasy *Wings of Desire* reminds us that the telepathic imaginary is a relatively modern humanization of capacities possessed by the daemons and angels of classical and Christian theology. The film's opening sequence shows an eye, and then its view of the sky over Berlin. At once the angel's and the film's, this supernal view suggests that the cinematic narration is itself located beyond the world of its story. For unlike adult and time-bound humanity, like a timeless child, the cinematic eye can also see the angels, such as Damiel on his aerie overlooking the city. Soon after, either the angel and/or the agency that narrates it flies past a Berlin radio tower and receives its transmissions simultaneously on all frequencies. These sound and film images update the supernatural or divine messenger as a precursor of invisible and seemingly immaterial radio and television broadcasts. As a modern incarnation of daemonic mediation, telepathy concerns matters of transmission and reception modeled on concurrent forms of media technology. It is "mind transmission" from a psychic sender, or "mind reading" on the part of a psychic eavesdropper. For instance, as the angel Damiel invisibly ministers to a flock of lost souls on the subway, the movie renders his telepathic reception through the voice-over narration of their overheard thoughts. Then, visible to us, the angel transmits a moment of spiritual relief to the mind of a tormented passenger.[30]

Nicholas Royle notes that telepathy "is historically linked to numerous other tele-phenomena: it is part of the establishment of tele-culture in general. It is necessarily related to other nineteenth-century forms of communication from a distance through new and often invisible channels, including the railway, telegraphy, photography, the telephone and gramophone."[31] Let us add another channel to this larger history of the modes of mediation and communication, one that Royle's literary account takes for granted—the modern novel. In book form, the novel does not precisely communicate from a distance, but it too is a media technology, for which, at the semiotic level, the signal transmitter is the narrator encoded into the text as encoding its discourse. And broadly speaking, relative to the first-person or character-bound narrator of much traditional storytelling, even before the era of teleculture, the third-person, authorial, or omniscient narrator of so-called realistic prose fiction has been taking some strange liberties. According to Royle: "There is uncanny knowledge. Someone is telling us what someone else is thinking, feeling or perceiving. That someone else may not even be aware of experiencing these thoughts, feelings or perceptions. The history of criticism of the novel is the history of the attempt to deal, or avoid dealing, with this seemingly mad scenario."[32] Some descriptions of different narrative situations in prose fiction can help to clarify the telepathy connection here.

On the one hand, using the terminology of the German narrative theorist Fritz Stanzel, one delineates the *character-bound narrator*. Under the conventions of literary realism, a character-bound narrator provides the self-depiction of a normal person, one having access only to its own thoughts and knowledge. Narrating from within the storyworld that it constructs for the reader as it narrates, about other characters it knows only what it can observe from its own vantage and standard sensory channels. If the story is "realistic," then in whatever manner it proceeds, the reader will expect no "uncanny knowledge" from a character-bound narrator. On the other hand, matters are altogether different with the *authorial narrator,* which is typically presented as the "omniscient narrator." Royle criticizes the notion that such a narrator is "omniscient," noting instead how the authors of a standard reference text of narrative theory "seem to be describing . . . a telepathic logic according to which a narrator—and thus a reader—is 'now looking into this mind,' now into that. Their account motions toward a theory of narrative telepathy, not narrative omniscience."[33]

The notion of telepathy does guide one toward a more precise description of the liberties and limits granted to an authorial narrator: it is not omnipresent but bound to the specific space and time traversed by the narrative discourse it produces. But beyond that, like the cinematic narration of *Wings of Desire,* the authorial narrator operates over and above the storyworld of its construction, and is licensed even by realistic narrative convention to possess potentially unrestricted access to the conscious and unconscious minds of the characters about which it narrates. While not utterly omniscient, then, the authorial narrator is virtually telepathic. And cinematic narration has techniques that easily approximate the virtual telepathy of authorial narration in literature. For instance, in *Wings of Desire*'s subway scene, the direct voice-over rendering of character thought shows the telepathic form not just of the angel's reception but also of the discourse the movie is transmitting.

The virtual telepathy available to the authorial narrator is compounded in an important variant of modern narrative technique, *free indirect discourse*, which Stanzel terms *figural narration*. In the figural narrative situation, a covert authorial narrator renders an overt account from within the character's mind—that is, from the perceptual point of view that the character occupies within the storyworld—and additionally, renders it in the idiom of speech that the character would use, were it narrating itself. The figural narrative situation straddles the border of the storyworld: it suspends or sublates that border by operating on both sides of it at once. In figural narration, the authorial narrator focalizes from within the storyworld through the character, whereas in strict authorial narration, the narrator focalizes as if from above, from its own orbit beyond the storyworld.

We see that "realism" in narrative strictly applies only to the depiction of *characters* and to the matter of their adherence to normal epistemological limitations. Otherwise, even realistic narratives depend on narrators or narrations that stage what in persons would be paranormal or telepathic capacities. When a narrative is ostensibly "mythical," or "fantastic," or "magical," for instance, by presenting characters that are themselves paranormal—angelic or "psychic"—that narrative is, in fact, hiding in plain sight a piece of its own fictive machinery. Or, put another way, a story that presents literally telepathic characters is manifesting a particular form of narrative self-reference. Like a story within a story, it is the case of a technique within a technique. Approached in the narrative dimension, then, the depiction of telepathy is an allegory of the conditions of authorial narration. If narrative altogether is an allegory of the eventfulness of the observation of the trace, the narration of telepathy or telepathic authorial narration concern the occulted construction of traces that seem to have leaped from without into the content of a narrator's discourse.

The Critical Approach

One felicity of the narrative approach to telepathy is that the matter of its facticity is strictly irrelevant. Narratives are free to be fictive constructions. What then about philosophical discourses? Derrida's "Telepathy" is presumably a philosophical discourse, although it actively, albeit obscurely, proceeds in the manner of a literary narration. To credit its initial footnote, this text was meant to be part of the "Envois" section of *The Post Card,* but was inadvertently left out of the manuscript when Derrida sent that book into production. So the form and context of "Telepathy" are familiar to readers of *The Post Card,* where, in short, for several hundred pages in "Envois," a writer much like Jacques Derrida free-associates about Socrates, Plato, philosophy, Freud, Lacan, and psychoanalysis while addressing an absent lover. There is neither linear narrative nor linear argument: this text presents a fictive narrator indiscernible from its actual author on the sending end of an amorous and erudite correspondence. The forty pages of "Telepathy" also proceed in this manner, but are focused quite discernibly on Freud's public and private writings on telepathy.

The single and striking aspect of "Telepathy" that I take up here is the way that Derrida employs a fictional narration for a philosophical examination of the aporias or undecidable gaps within Freud's several efforts to circumscribe or corral the facticity of telepathy, its consideration as an actual or possible phenomenon, within the confines of psychoanalytic discourse. For instance, midway through "Telepathy," the Derrida narrator speaks at length through the unspoken voice of Freud. In other words, for a significant but bounded portion of the text, Sigmund Freud becomes a character whose inner thoughts and motivations regarding the matter of telepathy Derrida's narrator constructs and transmits. Just before that phase of the text begins, with a fictional Derrida on the threshold of straddling a fictional Freud over the actual Freud's efforts to master psychoanalytically the facticity of telepathy, the following passage occurs:

> He [Freud] says that he has changed his views on thought transference. The science called (by others) "mechanistic" will be able one day to give an account of it. . . . The connection between two psychic acts, the immediate warning which one individual can seem to give another, the signal or psychic transfer can be a physical phenomenon. . . . Therefore, the "analogy" with other "transpositions,"

other "conversions" *(Umsetzungen)*, would be indisputable: for example, the analogy with "speaking and listening on the telephone." Between rhetoric and the psycho-physical relation, within each one and from one to the other, there is only translation *(Übersetzung)*, metaphor *(Übertragung)*, "transfers," "transpositions," analogical conversions, and above all transfers of transfers: *über, meta, tele.* (241–42)

With the two voices weaving in and out of each other, through simple indirect discourse, Derrida's narrator summarizes Freud's bids to rationalize the probable facticity of telepathy by analogy to media mechanisms of transmission and reception at a distance. But Derrida's narrator also constructs and participates in Freud's putative anxiety over that same notion, anxiety not so much of overcoming the distances between persons as of operating beyond the bounds of psychic propriety. At least with an actual mechanical telephone, those on either end can hang up! Telepathy in practice could be a continuous nightmare if one could not turn it off or make it stop. Once one mind overcomes or breaks through the boundaries of another mind, or two or more minds do so together for each other, who or what is to determine who is who or what is what?

> But once again, a terrifying telephone (and he, the old man, is frightened, me too); with the telepathic transfer, one could not be sure of being able to cut (no need now to say / *hold on,* / *don't cut,* it is connected day and night, can't you just picture us?) or to isolate the lines. . . . So he is frightened, and rightly so, of what would happen if one could make oneself master and possessor *(habhaft)* of this physical equivalent of the psychic act, in other words . . . if one had at one's disposal a *tekhnē telepathikē.* (242)

The potential anarchy of telepathy transforms matters of mechanical transmission and reception into matters of psychic mastery and submission, or of psychic interference through telepathic noise, or perhaps, too, of jouissance through psychic union. Addressing the absent narratee, the narrator of "Telepathy" elicits the possibility for an endless erotic connection through telepathic intercourse: "(. . . it is connected day and night, can't you just picture us?)." Toward the end of the text, however, the narrator terms this prospect of psychic union "a terrifying consolation. Sometimes I also approach Telepathy as if it were an assurance finally . . . instead of muddling everything up, or complicating the parasitism, as I told you and as I believe, I hope for complete presence *[la toute-présence]* from it, fusional immediacy, a parousia to keep you, at a distance, in order to keep myself within you" (258). Telepathy could be either an abysmal or a glorious muddle. Or yet again, if it could be brought under control, the mastery of a telepathic technology could confer on its possessor power over other minds. What that would entail is also a fearful prospect.

Mind of My Mind

The idea of telepathy is essentially a dream of power with its roots in mythical thinking and the classical daemonic. It is a power, or as one would say in pop parlance, a superpower. Through the narrative approach, we have already taken a measure of the ease of its *tellability*. At the level of narrative construction, all that its fictive depiction needs to involve is the transposition of an authorial narrator's telepathic privilege to a character's capacity. Let us go into a bit more detail on this with a telepathy novel that is not as famous as, say, Bram Stoker's gothic fiction *Dracula* (1897), or Arthur C. Clarke's science fiction *Childhood's End* (1953). An early novel of the late African American feminist author Octavia Butler, published in 1976, *Mind of My Mind* updates *Dracula* to some extent and relocates it: the psychic relationship between the Transylvanian count and the Briton Mina Harker returns in that between the African Doro and the American Mary. The telling of Butler's fiction alternates between authorial and character-bound narrations as it proceeds in sections titled by characters' names. Doro never directly narrates, but the authorial narrator does have selective access to his thoughts. Only Mary narrates, but not all the time; when she does not, the authorial narrator returns to carry the story along. This alternation of narrative situations operates nicely to foreground textual and discursive dynamics in the midst of the telepathic story events.

Doro is an ancient mutant being whose main power is sending his mind serially and irreversibly out from his current body and into a new one. For millennia, he has left a trail of abandoned bodies behind him. A wound-up semioleptic, Doro is metempsychosis personified. He is not telepathic in the sense of having access or exposure to others' minds. Instead, he has a psychic tracking sense. So one could say he is transpsychic: he does not read minds, but he can locate those with psychic powers, and he can snuff them out and take their bodies, reviving himself by "wearing" a fresh one when he needs it or feels like it. His tracking sense receives impressions from "actives," who are, for the most part, the telepathic progeny of his millennia-long breeding program to refine and possess for himself, by proxy, the powers of his offspring. He supplements his lack of telepathy by breeding telepaths. At the outset, one of these actives is a mixed-race and mixed-up nineteen-year-old, the telepath Mary, the novel's protagonist.

All of Doro's actives are born with some variation of psychic power, over which they have no control until they pass successfully through "transition." Many die before they reach it, others die during it. As Butler's *Mind of My Mind* opens, Mary is a telepath prior to transition. She suffers precisely from the problem that Derrida limns from Freud's thoughts about telepathic terror: whenever she receives a random psychic transmission, typically from a nearby nontelepath in some situation of extreme personal harm, she cannot turn it off, she must endure it until it fades out. She relates in her opening section that "I was close to my change, my transition" when "somebody screamed bloody murder inside my head. . . . I was picking up shadows of crazy emotions" (271–75). Mary suffers these psychic muddles especially severely because her potential power is so great. In an effort to preserve her life and special gift, Doro couples her to one of his best post-transition telepaths, the twenty-something Caucasian male Karl. The "Doro" section of chapter 2 informs us of his rationale:

> Doro had never before been able to keep a pair of active telepaths together without killing one of them and taking that one's place. . . . By the time they had been together for a while they would know how hard it was for two actives to be together without losing themselves, merging into each other uncontrollably. They would understand why, always before, actives had been rigidly unwilling to permit such merging—why actives had defended their individuality, why they had killed each other. (282)

Although it is doubtful that Butler would have encountered Derrida's article on telepathy, even if it had been published prior to her composition of *Mind of My Mind,* her depiction of social stress in a society of telepaths matches the one that Derrida's narrator envisions. Compare the narrator of "Telepathy," who writes how

> a life totally transformed, converted, paralyzed by telepathy would await us, given over to its networks and its schemes across the whole surface of its body, in all its angles, tangled up *[embobinée]* in the web of histories and times

without the least resistance on our part. On the contrary, we would take on a zealous participation, the most provocative experimental initiatives. People would no longer have us round, they would avoid us as if we were addicts, we would frighten everybody. (243–44)

Early on in *Mind of My Mind,* Doro describes Mary as "'part of an experiment that's important to me'" (265). And just as the narrator of "Telepathy" writes that "People would no longer have us round," Doro and his people seclude themselves from what they call "mute" society; they settle in their own segregated enclaves. But I will not follow the telling of Mary's tale here any further than to report that by her account, with Karl's help, she has a successful transition. Let us regard the resolution of her particular initiation. It concerns the restoration of psychic autonomy with the emergence of a boundary around her telepathic mind, and with that, the possibility of self-regulation and social participation. Practicing her post-transition telepathic skills, Mary narrates her acquisition of a "shield" in the first moments of its formation:

He had tried so hard to teach me to form my own shield, and I hadn't been able to do it. Apparently I had finally picked up the technique without even realizing it. . . .

So now I had a shield. I examined it curiously. It was a mental wall, a mental globe with me inside. . . . I wondered how I was supposed to open it for him. As I wondered, it began to disintegrate.

It surprised me, scared me. I wanted it back.

And it was back.

Well, that wasn't hard to understand. The shield kept me secure as long as I wanted it to. And there were degrees of security.

I began the disintegration process again, felt the shield grow thinner. I let it become a kind of screen—something I could receive other people's thoughts through. I experimented until I could hold it just heavy enough to keep out the kind of mental noise I had been picking up before and during my transition. It kept out the noise, but it didn't keep me in. (307)

I read Butler's novel here for its foregrounding of telepathy's phantom sociology. It suggests that the precondition for a mind's participation in communication is its own operational autonomy. The conflation or mingling of psychic systems in telepathic relations arises from a supposed usurpation of communicative by psychic functions. The telepathic imaginary constructs a social system between minds and then occults it through an unbinding of psychic boundaries. Telepathy is a swallowing up of the social by the psychic. Its power as an imaginary structure is bound up with the desire for the pleasure of canceling the epistemological closure of the psyche. And yet, in order to function viably as a telepath within society, Mary's transition must restore what her nascent superpower initially overrides. Her transition is thus an allegory of what any "mute" or normal person already has and can never lose without mental derangement, the operational boundaries of a psychic system capable of selecting from and thereby reducing the overwhelming complexity of its environment.

The Systems Theory Approach

Already reading telepathy through social systems theory, we now arrive at the key concepts for this approach. With the first of these concepts—the *operational closure* of an autopoietic or self-referential system—systems theory settles the facticity issue. Telepathy violates autopoietic closure. Minds cannot communicate. Nevertheless, the autopoietic operations of human psychic and social systems also—and this is the second key concept—*interpenetrate*. Luhmann's account of this systemic dynamic is perhaps the most germane and precise text for unraveling the muddle of telepathy. In the chapter "Interpenetration" in *Social Systems,* Luhmann defines interpenetration as "an intersystem relation between systems that are environments for each other. . . . Both systems enable each other by introducing their own already-constituted complexity into each other" (213). Yet they do so without muddle, without compromising each other's closure or autonomy.

How is this possible? How can system boundaries interpenetrate without violating or breaking into each other? The answer Luhmann gives rests on several technical premises of his theory. On the one hand, with regard to both of the two forms taken by metabiotic autopoietic systems—psychic and social systems—their boundaries are not material but virtual. For both kinds of systems, their boundaries are formed by the processing of system-internal system-environment distinctions. But on the other hand, despite this level of formal and operational identity, the particular autopoietic elements of psychic systems (ongoing self-produced moments of consciousness), differ entirely from the elements of social systems (ongoing self-produced events of communication). The kinds of distinctions processed respectively by psychic and social systems are distinct from each other, even while they share the same form of boundedness and a common medium of meanings, as these are carried by the media environments in which both kinds of systems are mutually and always already embedded.

"Decisively," Luhmann writes in *Social Systems,* for the interpenetration of psychic and social systems,

> *the boundaries of one system can be included in the operational domain of the other.* Thus the boundaries of social systems fall within the consciousnesses of psychic systems. Consciousness intervenes and thereby acquires the possibility of drawing boundaries for social systems precisely because these boundaries are not, at the same time, boundaries of consciousness. The same holds conversely: the boundaries of psychic systems fall within the communicative domain of social systems. In the course of orienting itself, communication is constantly forced to use what psychic systems have already assimilated in their consciousnesses and what they have not. This is possible because the boundaries of psychic systems are not also boundaries of communicative possibilities. Every system that participates in interpenetration realizes the other within itself as the other's difference between system and environment, without destroying its own system/environment difference. (217)

As *meaning* systems processing distinct forms of distinction, that is, processing different kinds of difference, the boundaries of psychic and social systems are not materially attached to the internal processes that they bind. This allows such boundaries to interpenetrate with the reciprocal systems in their environments without an accompanying penetration of system processes. The boundaries of metabiotic autopoietic systems are the respective surfaces or two-sided forms where differential system-environment distinctions are put into play and renegotiated from moment to moment. To that extent, the environmental "outside" of one boundary is available to the systemic "inside" of the reciprocal system. The reciprocity of minds and societies in the interpenetration of psychic and social systems could be figured as the reciprocal phantom telepathy by which the ever-renewed impressions of meanings bind consciousnesses to communications even while maintaining the respective systemic closures.

Viewed from here, the ideas of telepathy, mind reading, or thought projection have always been a sort of systemic saturnalia that, by depicted turnings of the operational closure of autopoiesis topsy-turvy or inside out, confirm it as the ultimate contingency for systemic continuation. Observing the telling of telepathy as constructing a kind of hyperdepiction of the typical mishmash of consciousness and communication, we flip it right side out again. Telepathy so observed inverts and remediates the complex topology of structural couplings by which psychic and social systems interpenetrate without operational muddle.

2 COMMUNICATION AND INFORMATION

Noise and Form in Michel Serres and Niklas Luhmann

IN THE CLUSTER OF SYSTEMS discourses that approach issues of cognition, the differences that separate information theory from autopoietic theory are not always observed. Neither of these discursive traditions can be reduced to the other, nor is there sense any longer in seeking a synthesis or merger between them. They are both indispensable but directed toward fundamentally different kinds of systems. As a result, neither theory of systems possesses universal application, although information theory in particular is often treated as if it does. In contrast, as we have argued, only autopoietic systems are cognitive in the first instance. The better course for theory and theory-driven criticism, then, would be to observe and exploit these differences. This chapter approaches such conceptual discrimination from several angles and addresses its wider philosophical stakes.

Within the suite of systems theories derived from information theory, one term in particular has stood out for its heuristic potency and, with some considerable cachet derived from the writings of Michel Serres, its overall intellectual glamour—*noise*. As allied with its thermodynamic elder *entropy* and its younger cousin *chaos,* the concept of noise is a kind of epicenter within postmodernist scientific and cultural paradigms, promising the unpredictable emergence of unforeseen orderings. For some time now, it has been doing catchall duty, injecting the notion of creative flux into media theory and cybernetic systems theory generally.[1] For example, on one page of *Gramophone, Film, Typewriter,* Friedrich Kittler addresses the concept of noise in its native information-theoretic provenance as a contingency of transmissions: "Technological media operate against a background of noise because their data travel along physical channels . . . noise determines their signal-to-noise ratio. . . . Noise is emitted by the channels media have to cross" (45). This is a perspicuous usage. On the next page, however, as noted in chapter 1, Kittler mingles ambient noise into nontechnological materialities aligned (at least in English translation) with a nonspecific or equivocal manifestation of "bodies": "Bodies themselves generate noise. And the impossible real transpires" (46). Is this physics, physiology, or Lacanian theory? All three at once? And, yet, because noise has become a buzzword of such considerable proportions, whatever Kittler is precisely claiming, it lends theoretical plausibility to the unbounded pansystemic application of information-theoretic noise. The universalization of information theory's transmission model draws with it a universalizing of noise.

Terms such as "system," "complexity," "emergence," "information," "noise," and "communication" bounce freely around in interdisciplinary theoretical circles in the humanities and social sciences. All of these system terms take on different meanings depending on the particular theoretical framework at hand. Take the concept of communication. Its *technical* amplification in information theory has been a hugely productive conceptual event. But here in its long aftermath, and due in particular to the emergence of communication in the autopoietic sense, it is time to parse the concept more narrowly once again and reassert for this term and its ensemble of accompanying concepts a framework of systems differentiations otherwise covered over by a broadened usage that is no longer productive.

Specifically, on the one hand, information theory cleared its own conceptual space by redefining communication as a problem of transmission. Transmission involves a suite of processes specific to particular technological assemblages of the sort we now call media systems. For Claude Shannon and Warren Weaver, the social and philosophical weight of communication—the matter of meanings understood and responses produced by the reception of what is communicated—was referred strictly to "the technical problem," or Level A: "How accurately can the symbols of communication be transmitted?"[2] On the other hand, communication is also a primary term in Niklas Luhmann's social systems theory. This theory posits communication as the sole, self-produced, and ever self-reproduced product of the bounded operations of social autopoiesis, as those processes occur alongside but operationally apart from the living processes self-produced by biological autopoiesis, the conscious processes self-produced by psychic systems, and the technological processes of media systems. Communication's autopoietic provenance is quite distinct from and in important ways incommensurable with the information-theoretical definition. To avoid equivocal treatments, one must be ready to shift semantic registers.

At the same time, within the suite of autopoietic or second-order systems theories, other key terms—recursion, self-reference, closure, boundary, and form—are more recondite, less immediately intuitive, and, in their precise stipulations, relative to the concepts of information theory, more hampered by distracting connotations. Moreover, the concept of noise also plays an auxiliary role in autopoietic systems theory, where it is coordinated with systemic reintegration as order or assignment as meaning: "the meaning process lives off disturbances, is nourished by disorder, lets itself be carried by noise, and needs an 'excluded third' for all technically precise, schematized operations."[3] In autopoietic theory, moreover, a fundamentally altered, second-order understanding of *form* steps into the constructive role elsewhere plied by informatic noise. After preliminary discussions separating out concepts of communication from those of media theory and reviewing the concept of noise in those milieus, this chapter proceeds to arguments why the neocybernetic lowering of noise's informatic clamor is not a loss, and why the autopoietic reformulation of form is a gain.

Communication and Media

"She looked down a slope, needing to squint for the sunlight, onto a vast sprawl of houses . . . and she thought of the time she'd opened a transistor radio to replace a battery and seen her first printed circuit. . . . There were to both outward patterns a hieroglyphic sense of concealed meaning, of an intent to communicate" (24). In this key passage from Thomas Pynchon's *The Crying of Lot 49,* as the medium of light allows the communication of images to sight, through the memory of the code-like patterns inscribed on the "printed circuit" of an electronic media device, the protagonist, Oedipa Maas, places herself on the receiving end of an "intent to communicate." Light, (hieroglyphic) writing, print (technologies), telecommunication, meaning: the narration of this transit from physics to phenomenology, from nature to mind to society, also connects concepts of media with concepts of communication. Recent discursive and scholarly developments have registered and reflected on this link: As literacy once came as a literal supplement to orality, and grammatology (the science of writing) as a supplement to linguistics (the science of speech), "media" in the sense that informs media studies has come alongside the study and theory of communication.

In the usage now current, the term *communication* primarily means "the imparting, conveying, or exchange of ideas, knowledge, information, etc." *(Oxford English Dictionary).*[4] Its use to mean the imparting or sharing of material/energetic or organic characteristics—for instance, the communication of motion, or the communication of disease—is now uncommon. But such uses preserve important connotations still underlying its modern informatic sense: its *communality,* and its *materiality.* The communality of communication concerns its complex multiplicity, its conditionality on social grounds prior to individual intentions, whereas the materiality of communication concerns the physical and technical infrastructures necessary for any conveyance of messages or transmission of information. Both of these aspects—social connectivity and material contact—bring "communication" closer to the concept of *media,* as that now names the various technologies for the transport or transmission of communications, and thus to the purchase of media studies.

Outlining "seven traditions of communication theory"—rhetorical, semiotic, phenomenological, cybernetic, sociopsychological, sociocultural, and critical—Robert Craig has also indicated how these thematic disciplinary categories are transected by two formal models, a *transmission model* and a *constitutive model:*

> In the simplistic *transmission model* . . . communication is conceptualized as a process in which meanings, packaged in symbolic messages like bananas in crates, are transported from sender to receiver. Too often the bananas are bruised or spoiled in transport and so we have the ubiquitous problem of *miscommunication.* . . . Communication theorists recently have favored an alternative, *constitutive model.* . . . The elements of communication, rather than being fixed in advance, are reflexively constituted within the act of communication itself.[5]

According to either model, however, communication and media are tightly bound together. The media moment is indispensable to any full consideration of communication: it fills in the potential complexities of

technological mediation often bracketed out of traditional considerations of communicative exchange. What then, broadly considered, distinguishes the topic of communication from the topic of media? The
most abstract way to put this distinction is that communication is ultimately a social phenomenon, whereas in the final instance, media is a
technical phenomenon. One cannot assert such a distinction without
immediately acknowledging the inextricability of the social and the
technological, as Bruno Latour and Donna Haraway have taught us
about the modern proliferation of hybrids, cyborgs, and quasi-objects—
entities that couple together the realms of nature and culture, organism
and machine, the human and the nonhuman. Nonetheless, a neocybernetic approach would suggest that an operational parsing can keep
these relations intact while bringing out strong and analytically useful
distinctions.

So let us at once construct and deconstruct this form of the distinction between communication and media, step forward and look through
it, but also step back and look at it. If we grant for heuristic purposes the
basic distinction of communication and media into the realms of the
social and the technological, we can unfold that distinction further
along two main lines. In the first of these, communication attaches most
directly to the sources and destinations of messages, whereas media
attaches most directly to the means by which messages move from one
to the other. Communication ultimately concerns the sociological context, the relations generated between the information source and the
destination, whereas media concerns the channel of communication
and centers on the technological regimes by which transmission devices
code messages into signals subjected to medium-specific modes of
noise, which are then decoded by receiving devices for delivery to destinations. For instance, in "Linguistics and Poetics," Roman Jakobson
presents an influential translation of communicational into linguistic
functions. His chief concern is to indicate how developments in communication theory driven from the cybernetic human/machine interface can be productively adapted to traditional linguistic and poetic
analyses, presupposing speech or writing as the medium in question.
His "referential" function, for instance, makes explicit the embeddedness of communication within social contexts; it implies that semantic
reference—the ability of language to signify objects in the world—is itself
a function resting on social contracts. His "metalingual" function draws

attention to language (and other kinds of code) as structures through which signifying intentions must be processed, thereby converting "messages" into "signals" fit for the media at hand. And the "phatic" function marks the media moment per se, orienting "communication" once again to the sense of material connection: even in the most "wireless" communication system imaginable, there still must be, as it were, a real material/energetic string tying the tin cans together.

Jakobson's linguistic intervention in communication theory marks a high point in the discourse of structural linguistics, filling in the middle ground occupied by the structures of mediation implemented by events of communication. If we move from here to a poststructuralist position, a short quote from Jacques Derrida's "Differance" offers a deconstructive perspective on the communication/media distinction: "The use of language or the employment of any code which implies a play of forms . . . also presupposes . . . a spacing and temporalizing, a play of traces. This play must be a sort of inscription prior to writing, a protowriting without a present origin, without an archē" (146). Communication (between "source" and "destination," "addresser" and "addressee") is to "the use of language or the employment of any code" as any media technology of transmitted and received signals is to "a spacing and temporalizing, a play of traces." Or, the capacity of a "source" to produce a message is already given by the (linguistic or other) "inscription" of potential forms or distinctions commensurate with the medium available to convey the signals into which messages are transformed in order to be communicated. The medium of signals inevitably feeds back into the form of messages.

Reconstructing the distinction of communication and media into the realms of the social and the technological, let us unfold it along a second line: Communication factors into issues of synchronous and sequential temporality—"real time," the discrete moments of the origination and reception of messages—whereas media technologies generate "virtual time," processes such as inscription, storage, and retrieval, which suspend and/or manipulate the time of communication. Here again, communication is to media as speech is to writing. However, this distinction cuts across the previous one from a different, more deconstructive angle. As Lev Manovich states, it relocates the communication/media distinction within the realm of media itself, subsuming under "media technologies" a distinction between "communication" and "representation":

Modern media technologies have developed along two distinct trajectories. The first is representational technologies—film, audio and video magnetic tape, various digital storage formats. The second is real-time communication technologies, that is, everything that begins with *tele*—telegraph, telephone, telex, television, telepresence. Such new twentieth-century cultural forms as radio and, later, television emerge at the intersections of these two trajectories.[6]

Manovich's approach exemplifies the countertendency in new media discussion to bracket the sociological moment of communication in favor of its media-technological moment. As with the first line of distinction above, Manovich refers the concept of communication most immediately to the sending and receiving of messages, but puts the emphasis on medium-specific differences. Communication technologies—gesture, speech, smoke signals, telegraphy, telephony—transmit and/or broadcast messages without (in the first instance) creating or storing them as media objects. Media technologies per se differ from traditional and modern techniques of communication in that they *inscribe* the information they process: they not only mediate but memorialize—capture and store—their content: thus, writing, drawing, printing, lithography, photography, phonography, and cinema are some of the forms of media. "New media," then, are figured as the *technological* deconstruction through conglomeration of this very distinction between communication and representation: "computers in principle comprehend all other media."[7] Digital platforms typically transmit and store simultaneously. Digital media double once again in binary informatics the prior doubling of the world in sign systems and communicative representations.

Society and System

Theories of communication typically work between concepts of the subject and concepts of society. The goal or effect of communication is said to be the creation of a state of commonality or consensus by which individual differences are set aside. "The central challenge facing all communication theories is the question of how individuality is transcended."[8] The concept of "intersubjectivity" names the implication that certain kinds of communication effectively render exterior and collective what would otherwise remain interior and private, as the self-knowledge of an individual subject enters the public sphere. Such communications would entail the merger or intermingling of inner and outer, psychological and social events. Intersubjectivity is a philosophically palatable guise for what is essentially a telepathic spiritual arrangement.

At the same time, recent conceptions of communication follow what has been termed a "postmetaphysical" trend away from the traditional philosophical focus on mind, reason, or consciousness as having their source solely in the individual. It is precisely the social aspect of the concept of communication that bids to offer an alternative to "the exhaustion of the paradigm of the philosophy of consciousness."[9] The way out of the subjectivist frameworks of idealistic approaches to reason and "the rational subject" becomes "communicative rationality." By this phrase, Jürgen Habermas signifies an account of reason that is constituted through social discourses "oriented to achieving, sustaining and reviewing consensus—and indeed a consensus that rests on the intersubjective recognition of criticizable validity claims" (1:17). Building on Ludwig Wittgenstein's philosophy of language and the speech-act theories of J. L. Austin and John R. Searle, Habermas uses communication theory to move linguistic philosophy toward a social theory of communicative action: "The concept of communicative action presupposes the use of language as the medium for a kind of reaching understanding, in the course of which the participants, through relating to a world, reciprocally raise validity claims that can be accepted or contested" (1:99).

However, such models of social intersubjectivity do not lead out of but rather reinscribe the identity formations of subjective consciousness. In Briankle Chang's analysis, "the conceptualization of communication as the 'transcendence of difference' reflects an implicit subjectivist thesis . . . to which modern communication theories remain heavily mortgaged . . . eventually leading" to an "unquestioned valorization of identity over difference, of the selfsame over alterity" (xi). This is because communication theories built on the concept of intersubjectivity rely on a concept of linguistic *code* (as in Jakobson's "metalingual" function) that smuggles the transmission model of communication back into the theoretical apparatus for the very purpose of providing a medium of social identity that bridges individual differences. In such conceptualizations, Chang continues: "Code is the key to successful communication in that it provides for communicators a standard of translation," which in this context implies a mechanism whereby the content of one mind is effectively "translated" or transferred intact to other minds (58).

The problem is not only that the transmission model is untenable but also that this argument goes in circles: "Intersubjectivity is the key term in explaining how individuality is transcended, and the concept of code is but one of its theoretical representatives . . . The code can guarantee the successful transmission of messages *precisely because it is intersubjective*" (59). Just as Derrida attended to the play of metaphor in the ostensibly nonmetaphorical texts of philosophy, Chang uncovers a circular play of metaphor in the texts of communication theory, where he locates "a *fundamental analogism,* a principle of substitution between intersubjectivity and mediation," by which they "work as paired metaphors" (64–65).

I find Chang's deconstruction of intersubjectivity by eliciting its covert reliance on the transmission model persuasive, but where does that leave the social theory of communication? Luhmann indicates a way beyond this impasse.[10] In his theory, the logical circularity that Chang uncovers in the intersubjective transmission model is replaced by the *operational* circularity or recursive functionality basic to an autopoietic system, a "system that produces and reproduces through the system everything that functions for the system as a unit."[11] From this perspective, the concept of intersubjectivity is incoherent because, akin to telepathy, it blurs the operational boundaries of social systems and psychic systems. The mind (the "subject" of intersubjectivity) is also an autopoietic system that processes perceptions and (re)produces consciousness. By definition, psyches are also operationally closed, and consciousness as such cannot cross directly over to its social environment, while at the same time, there is no way for the communications (re)produced by social systems to cross directly over to the minds within their environment. Rather, they impinge, in the forms properly constituted by the autopoiesis of psychic systems, as internally constructed perceptions and cognitions.

Luhmann's scheme liquidates accounts of social mediation through intersubjective transmission: "A systems-theoretical approach emphasizes the *emergence of communication* itself. Nothing is transferred" (160). Everything is (re)constructed on the fly. Communication obviously occurs, but it is self-constituting and self-perpetuating: "Only communication can communicate" (156), and it does so entirely on the basis of the operational closure of social systems, for which not "subjects" but systems of consciousness, psychic systems, as well as media systems, reside in the environment. In this scheme, language and other semiotic codes (and their technological armatures) remain positioned as mediating structures, but not in the mode of substantial transmission across system boundaries. In every instance, autonomous social and psychic systems construct their own meanings out of their own internal elements. To the extent that these processes can be coordinated, this occurs not by the distribution of shared content but by the structural coupling, of psychic and social systems as coevolutionary phenomena. Their emergence and maintenance is strictly self-referential, but neither would emerge in the first place without being coupled to the other in their respective environments, and mediated by the medium of meaning.

Accounts of the epistemological construction specific to social systems present the strongest extant form of the constitutive model of communication. While Habermas avoids the information-theoretical model of communication, Luhmann provides a radical complexification of it with his account of communication as "a synthesis of three different selections, namely the selection of *information*, the selection of the *utterance [Mitteilung]* of this information, and selective *understanding or misunderstanding* of this utterance and its information" (157). This formulation extracts "source" and "destination" from subjective or psychological implications and reinscribes them as addresses or "connecting position[s]" (163) within the recursive network of a social system's autopoiesis. "The system pulsates, so to speak, with the constant generation of excess and selection" (160). With each cycle or pulsation, the system selects information from its memory or its construction of the environment and then selects the mode of its "utterance," that is, the modality of its coding, for further processing.

The entire scheme loops upon itself like so. According to Luhmann, as an event of social cognition, communication "takes place only when a difference of utterance and information is first understood. This distinguishes it from a mere perception of others' behavior" (157). Perception belongs solely to the psychic systems coupled to but operationally apart from systems of communication. For instance, such a participating consciousness observes in its environment an arm waving: it can construct this occurrence as mere perception, random motion, environmental noise, or as information, as a particular gesture or utterance, of greeting or warning or whatever: understanding must select from its repertoire of possibilities. However, "understanding is never a mere duplication of the utterance in another consciousness but is, rather, in the system of communication itself, a precondition for connection onto further communication, thus a condition of the autopoiesis of the social system" (158). If one waves back, the social system continues. Luhmann differentiates *communicative* understanding from whatever psychic comprehension participating consciousnesses construct from their interpretation of certain perceptions as communicative. This is why misunderstanding—failure of consensus—can as easily spur on as impede communication: the understanding of the social system is sufficient as long as it can connect one communication event to another and so continue its autopoiesis. From this perspective, media ecologies are coevolving environmental spin-offs of open-ended social-systematic evolutions. Their transformations significantly impinge on the changing themes of communication and inflect the forms of social organization, but they do not finally determine how communication will construct its own continuation.

When social cognition is at issue, information theory is best restated in terms of the constitutive model of communication. Information is not an ontological function with an absolute content or quantity, but is relative to the predispositions of the observer that constitutes it and that observer's position along the total channel through which communications must proceed. And the materiality of communication media always determines a potential for discrepancies between the message as meant, as sent, as received, and as understood. Moreover, the distinction of signal from noise depends on the position of the observer. The notion of disorder becomes that much more complex. It can be valorized negatively in the potential confusion of a sender's selection, or in the deterioration of the message in transit, but given an orientation toward the destination of communication, noise and disorder can also be measured positively, converted from uncertainty into new information depending on the reception it receives.

This situation of uncertain reception is brilliantly configured at the conclusion of Pynchon's *The Crying of Lot 49:*

> In the very copper rigging and secular miracle of communication, untroubled by the dumb voltages flickering their miles, the night long, in the thousands of unheard messages. . . . How many shared Tristero's secret, as well as its exile? . . . Who knew? . . . For it was now like walking among matrices of a great digital computer, the zeroes and ones twinned above, hanging like balanced

mobiles right and left, ahead, thick, maybe endless. Behind the hieroglyphic streets there would either be a transcendent meaning, or only the earth. (180–81)

The title of the novel names an event that is to occur only after the novel ends. The story abandons Oedipa Maas still uncertain about the reality of a secret society named the Tristero. The "value" of the information she is to receive when Lot 49 is cried at auction is left suspended somewhere between zero and infinity. More precisely, Pynchon suspends his reader between the inexhaustible desire for a meaning transported from beyond—one no worldly medium could ever communicate—and the transcendence of that desire for transcendence in an acceptance of the immanent value of our improbable world, irrespective of the play of meanings it gives rise to. Information, its utterance through media, and the meanings placed on it are all the cognitive affairs of observers variously positioned along the social and technological networks of communication. They are all constituted in and constructed by the coupled operations of observing systems fated to chase the enigmas that keep them going.

Noise

We are concerned in particular to clarify the interrelations between informatic noise and cognitive form, and more broadly, those between technological and autopoietic systems. The informatic concept of noise has literal and significant purchase when there actually is a signal under transmission for relatively disorderly processes to parasite. The discourse of noise is thus particularly appropriate to the formation and aesthetic critique of artworks, especially those that fold the matter of their own transmission into their semiotic forms. More broadly stated, the concept of noise is proper to the description of material-energetic productions of transmission within media systems, that is, to certain nonautopoietic systems in the machine domain. Nor is the concept overstretched by working it back into the environment at large. The main point for my argument is that informatic noise—like the trace, the signal, or the sign—is a fundamentally abiotic and hence noncognitive concept. Thus, it always also calls for a biotic or metabiotic autopoietic observing system to construe its code and its decoding.

Message

Norbert Wiener channels information theory toward the science of cybernetics, which he defines as the "study of messages, and in particular of the effective messages of control."[12] His immediate aim is to advance computer technology by investigating the functional analogies between organisms and machines. Biological nervous systems and modern electronic devices may both be construed as feeding information from certain sensors back into a processing network. These internal messages enable both the organism and the machine to track and regulate their respective performances. The transmission of signals through communication channels—nerves or phone lines—is analogous to the temporal behavior of closed thermodynamic systems: in both cases, disorder tends to increase over time. In informatics, *noise* can name this increment of systemic evolution over the time of transmission. According to Warren Weaver, in the informatic situation,

> the statistical nature of *messages* is entirely determined by the character of the source. But the statistical character of the *signal* as actually transmitted by a channel, and hence the entropy in the channel, is determined both by what one attempts to feed into the channel and by the capabilities of the channel to handle different signal situations.[13]

The amount of "entropy in the channel," as opposed to the entropy of a message before it is sent, is determined by the degree of noise that impinges on the signal. No real-world channel can be made entirely free of some level of random fluctuation or some bleeding together of concurrent but separate signals introducing noise into the received message, and this circumstance introduces another level of uncertainty into the communication process. By the same token, the process of electronic computation is analogous to the transmission of a message: here, *error* represents the noise of computational transmission. In computation as well as communication, the margin of error as well as the increment of noise is counteracted by the injection of *redundancy* into coding protocols. With some sacrifice of efficiency, redundant coding provides a repetition of crucial calculative steps or message elements and so ensures a reliable if not impeccable level of message integrity at the end of the process.

The significance of noise for the discourse of information becomes clearer if we switch focus from communications systems to media systems, Lev Manovich's "representational technologies"—that is, if we switch from information systems centered on transmission (such as the telegraph and telephone) to those centered on inscription and storage (the photograph and phonograph and their progeny). Graphic and digital systems can do both, of course, but it is important nonetheless to bear in mind this distinction in system functions. We may envision information as perpetually in transit, in social circulation, but in equal degree, the sheer matter of informatic traces accumulates in some actual or virtual location, awaiting retrieval. What the inscription and storage of mediatic differences processable as information also allows is their *manipulation,* an opening beyond utilitarian functions to creative reuses. Stored information becomes a medium out of which various manipulators can produce new orders of form—by editing, cutting, reframing, resequencing, and so forth.

From the standpoint of transmission, any such dallying or meddling with stored information amounts to the in-mixing of noise with its signal. But from the standpoint of art forms instantiated in informatic media (aural sounds, visual images, linguistic signs), the noise *is* the art. For instance, the advent of phonography enabled the discovery, within the otherwise "pure" (Pythagorean) tones of an earlier musical acoustics, of noise: timbre itself is a musical noise derived in the first instance from the material specifics of a given instrument. It allows for instrumental differentiations that then become part of the musical orchestration. The noise of timbre does not physically corrupt, but rather informatically enhances the sound it inhabits.[14] For another example, with the advent of audiotape, time-axis manipulation (TAM) of the recorded signal became a feasible option. The Beatles and Jimi Hendrix famously crafted segments of their popular music by replaying pieces of their studio recordings backward. Media arts remediate information in aesthetic forms sending messages with meaningful noise.

Matter

One of the more problematic legacies of the cybernetic discussion of information is the pervasive oversimplification of its distinction from matter. This result is due not so much to the original expositors, who made a necessary effort to distinguish the object of cybernetics from the object of physics. Rather, the tendency to set matter and information into dialectical antithesis (as if the real and the virtual were antithetical rather than supplementary modalities) follows the engrained dualistic trends of Western thought, intellectual habits that persist despite the efforts of key cyberneticists to cultivate new ways of thinking, for instance, about the emergent productions of system-environment ensembles. A case in point here is Gregory Bateson's seminal discourse on information, summed up in his famous observation that "what we mean by information—the elementary unit of information—is a *difference which makes a difference*."[15]

Bateson brings about a significant relay of cybernetic discourse from the natural to the social sciences. He offers the following comment on "the ancient dichotomy between form and substance" in the context of a protest over the misleading scientism of "the metaphoric use of 'energy' in the behavioral sciences" to schematize psychological events: "The conservative laws for energy and matter concern substance rather than form. But mental process, ideas, communication, organization, differentiation, pattern, and so on, are matters of form rather than substance."[16] Bateson's points are congruent with Saussure's remark in his *Course in General Linguistics* that "in language there are only differences *without positive terms*" (120): the concept of difference is not substantial, but formal or relational. It is "abstract," in the way that mathematics is an abstraction from the world of things enumerated. But seldom does one find consternation over the "immateriality" of language or the "disembodiment" of mathematics. Bateson's point is precisely that information, under its "cybernetic explanation," crosses the form of linguistic differentiation with the form of mathematical probability.

However, the tendency has been to read Bateson's heuristic exclusion of physical quantities from information theory as an ontological exclusion on the mind/nature model that licenses either the pseudoutopian rhetoric of information as liberation from physical constraints or, alternatively, the materialist counterpolemic against information as a discourse of domination. For a sample of the latter tendency, let us briefly unpack another short passage early in Kittler's *Gramophone, Film, Typewriter:* "The technological differentiation of optics, acoustics, and writing exploded Gutenberg's writing monopoly around 1880. . . . And with this differentiation—and not with steam engines and railroads—a clear division occurs between matter and information, the real and the symbolic" (16). As we have seen, Kittler argues provocatively that the "writing monopoly"—print technology as the dominant means of archiving cultural production—broke down in the nineteenth century due to photography and phonography, the new graphic media of that time. In this passage, he aligns literature, information, and the (Lacanian) symbolic. All three involve the imposition of a code by which the world is rearticulated for storage and transmission—moreover, by which the world is informatically rendered into a coded signal. "To record the sound sequences of speech, literature has to arrest them in a system of 26 letters, thereby categorically excluding all noise sequences" (3)—excluding them, it may be, from the *signal,* if not from the *channel.* In contrast, a comparably transcriptive process is not needed when the phonograph records "the sound sequences of speech" or of anything else: the "continuous undulations recorded by the gramophone and the audiotape" are "signatures of the real" (118). If the symbolic is pure signal (and so decipherable by definition), the real is pure noise and—however "recognizable," say, a particular sound sequence may be—always already beyond intelligibility. That would be one reason why the real really is "impossible": we will find a meaning for it despite its inaccessibility.

Kittler's media posthumanism deals a conceptual wild card from the mid-twentieth century that raises the stakes at play between communication and media. Humbly derived from a mathematical-physical treatment of the operation of a communications medium—the telephone system—the discourse of information has bid to subsume both communication and media concepts. In *Gramophone,* the arrival of analog media technologies made possible a "reproduction authenticated by the object itself. . . . It refers to the bodily real, which of necessity escapes all symbolic grids" (12). In this and like remarks, *Gramophone* continues the dualistic treatment of information by rendering the "clear division . . . between matter and information, the real and the symbolic" (16), as a modal opposition on the Lacanian model, if not absolutely on the Cartesian model. Here again, the crucial analytical distinction between matter and information gets reified, with information becoming the technoid signifier for immateriality, dematerialization, or disembodiment. In this way, the concept of information remains available for stigmatization by the spectrum of philosophical and political moralizations attached for millennia to ontological disputes over soul, form, essence, spirit, and their sundry historical avatars.[17]

But if noise is *also* information—and noise is a "signature of the real," as the signal is a signature of the symbolic code—then the concept of information incorporates the unity of the difference between signal and noise. Signal *or* noise, it is all *information*. Or again, the bodies of the technological infrastructures of information systems are always part of the whole message. One gets the kinks out of the concept of information by reentering media environments back into the wider systemic complex under observation, whatever transmissions come across. This prescription is a restatement of the contextual or holistic impetus in the best cybernetic thinking—the imperative to think "organism plus environment," system *and* environment, message together with medium. To do so enables the observer of information to be methodical about factoring the matter of their material couplings and the functional form of their systemic contexts into informatic transactions. In "Cybernetic Explanation," Bateson goes to the heart of this "relationship between *context* and its content," again with an analogy drawn from linguistics:

> A phoneme exists as such only in combination with other phonemes which make up a word. The word is the *context* of the phoneme. But the word only exists as such—only has "meaning"—in the larger context of the utterance, which again has meaning only in a relationship.
>
> This hierarchy of contexts within contexts is universal for the communicational (or "emic") aspect of phenomena and drives the scientist always to seek for explanation in the ever larger units. It may (perhaps) be true in physics that the explanation of the macroscopic is to be sought in the microscopic. The opposite is usually true in cybernetics: without context, there is no communication. (402)

The new relations and distinctions forged at mid-twentieth century between energy and information highlight the crucial difference for systems of all kinds between isolation from, and openness to, their environments. In the cybernetic era, the classical thermodynamic emphasis on the tendency toward equilibrium of closed systems shifts to the nonequilibrium operation of open and multiply coupled biotic and metabiotic ensembles. Even given the assumption of a universal drift toward maximal entropy, biological, psychic, and social systems maintain their autonomous organizations through operational closure hand in hand with environmental openness. For autopoietic systems, worldly perturbations are variously construed as signals or noises—a distinction whose meaning rests on the self-referential binary of meaning-nonmeaning. The point here is that informatic noise always bears "meaning" for the system that construes it, even if for that observer its meaning is to be meaningless, or unintelligible with reference to presently available codes.

Information is defined mathematically as an inverse function of the probability or predictability of a message. From the receiver's perspective, the less certain a message, the more information it produces once it arrives. Because the noise of transmission randomly or unpredictably intrudes into signals, the shape it will take in any given communicative situation will be unknown until it is received. By introducing greater uncertainty into the message, noise goes beyond mere static, a loss of efficiency or clarity, to become a form of information about the media environment. For its observer, noise is the inadvertent self-reference of the medium. It marks a gain in communicative unpredictability with at least the potential to introduce other information of value into the transmission. Bateson famously summed up this situation in "Cybernetic Explanation," using "information" as a whole-for-part synecdoche for *signal:* "All that is not information, not redundancy, not form and not restraints—is noise, the only possible source of *new* patterns" (410).

Noise in Serres

Autopoietic systems theory is focused on differentiations among systems. It goes against the grain of pansystemic identities or mergers:

> One of the most important consequences of the transition to a theory of self-referential systems concerns the operative level, or system processes. . . . [T]o cite an extreme case, no system unity can exist between mechanical and conscious operations, between chemical operations and those that communicate meaning. . . . A human being may appear to himself or to an observer as a unity, but he is not a system. . . . Such assumptions overlook the fact that the human being cannot even observe what occurs within him as physical, chemical, and living processes.[18]

To this passage in *Social Systems,* Luhmann places an endnote, which reads: "Rarely is something so self-evident specifically established and its theoretical relevance recognized. See, however, Michel Serres, 'Le point de vue de la biophysique'" (508). Luhmann must be referring to the passage in which Serres first evokes for any living organism the multitudinous simultaneity of cellular and organ-systemic operations going on at any given moment, and then comments: "From a thermal and information point of view, these movements and transformations necessarily generate background noise. And this noise is certainly tremendous, for the numbers under consideration are gigantic. What prevents us from hearing it? . . . It exists but it goes unperceived."[19] This is indeed a striking moment in Serres's discussion, but he then goes on to explain this nonperception of living processes in a manner fundamentally different from Luhmann.

Elsewhere, Luhmann dissociates his mode of systems theory from the information-theoretical models central to Serres's approach, for the good conceptual reasons we are discussing. It is Serres's acute observation of this pervasive nonperception as "relevant" to theory, not his precise theory regarding it, that corroborates a circumstance for which Luhmann offers a different theory. He selects Serres's observation but not his explanation. The necessary heterogeneity introduced by the operational closure of, as well as the elemental differentiation between, biological and psychic systems would disallow any direct transmission between them. Serres presents quite the opposite thesis, arguing on information-theoretic grounds that such cross-systemic transmissions abound but are at all levels submitted to a "rectification" that mutes the noise while directing it into processes of self-organization. Serres's bioinformatic mentor Henri Atlan transfers von Foerster's physical order-from-noise principle to biological systems in a way that leads Serres himself to envision a comprehensive but questionable unification of system processes. While Luhmann, too, works this same principle for autopoietic systems in general, he maintains their distinct operational differences in the process. Reaching definitive expression in *The Parasite* and *Genesis,* Serres brilliantly exploits the colloquial French term *le parasite* for the technical usage of informatic noise, *le bruit*. I telegraph my own thesis regarding his neocybernetic stance through Serres's own conceptual idiom: his discourse of noise itself parasites a realm of production that goes unnamed because it is unobserved within this system of thought. This realm is the production of cognitive domains by the autopoietic systems that must already be operating in order for informatic interruptions to occur in the first place. Signal or noise, *information parasites autopoiesis.*

Serres is among the first humanistic expositors at the intersection of information theory and postmodern discourse, and I think, still among the best. Two key articles working this broadly cybernetic terrain are "Platonic Dialogue" and "The Origin of Language: Biology, Information Theory, and Thermodynamics," side-by-side chapters of the 1982 volume *Hermes: Literature, Science, Philosophy*. For more than a decade, this text was the main source of Anglophone appreciation of Serres's work. Thus, it entered deeply into the tissue of his American reception, my own included. Serres elegantly captures key elements of information theory and efficiently conveys them so as to pervade ensuing critical discourses engaged with cybernetics, self-organization, chaos and complexity theories, actor-network theory, emergence, and the like. My issue here is not with Serres's texts so much as it is the current overreach and sometime imprecision of the particular informatic models whose premises he so admirably and inventively pursued. My aim is not to diminish Serres's discourse but to delimit its universalizing.

"Platonic Dialogue"

In "Platonic Dialogue," originally published in 1966, Serres is already doing media theory, precisely on the information-theoretic model.[20] That is, he treats written communication as a problem of material transmission. In a manner daring for the 1960s, by adapting a conventional model of writing to the information-theoretic occasion, Serres can shift the stress of the discussion from its semantic and social implications to its material technicities, "the physical appearance of the writing, its graphic form" (65). He is taking up the matter of writing at Level A, treating written communication as a coding regime dependent on a strong signal, a maximal conformation of transmitted signifiers to orthographic protocols. The concept of form enters the discussion as a synonym for a properly coded signal: "Writing is first and foremost a drawing . . . The scribe must execute his drawing as well as possible. What does this mean?" (65–66).

Serres sets up the standard of the form of the written signal in order to proceed to an informatic treatment of its deformation. Orthography— the protocol for well-drawn written signals—is divided from "cacography": "waverings in the graphic forms, failures in the drawing, spelling errors" (66). Speech is brought alongside writing as a comparable transmissions medium, in that it too can suffer formal pathologies: "stammerings, mispronunciations, regional accents, dysphonias, and cacophonies" (66). These naturalized or classical transmission modes are then coordinated with the technical media already lurking as the subtext of the previously unstated information-theoretic approach: "likewise in the technical means of communication: background noise, jamming, static, cut-offs, hysteresis, various interruptions" (66). Introducing the concept of noise into the midst of the classical philosophical discourse of speech and writing, Serres gains two points: he overcomes their classical opposition in a pre-Derridean way, and he prepares for a nonclassical recuperation of noise as part and parcel of an equally nonclassical valorization of the material and the technical.

Serres's immediate definition of noise carries this new note of its essentiality—its nonrandom occurrence, thus meaningfulness as an informatic contingency: "Following scientific tradition, let us call *noise* the set of these phenomena of interference that become obstacles to communication. Thus, cacography is the noise of graphic form or, rather, the latter comprises an essential form *and* a noise that is either essential or occasional" (66). So, here, the information-theoretic signal takes on a "graphic form" whose abstract essence is distinct from a material deformation that may or may not be essential to its transmission. Compare the initial definition Weaver gives as he parses Shannon's famous diagram of a communication system:

> In the process of being transmitted, it is unfortunately characteristic that certain things are added to the signal which were not intended by the information source. These unwanted additions may be distortions of sound (in telephony, for example) or static (in radio), or distortions in shape or shading of picture (television), or errors in transmission (telegraphy or facsimile), etc. All these changes in the transmitted signal are called *noise*.[21]

Weaver presents informatic noise as an interference that enters the channel once the transmission event has begun. That is, he assumes, as it were, a competent scribe, and considers noise to be of the nature of random blots that befall the signal in its transit to the recipient. For Serres, in contrast, the interference may also originate with the graphic or oral transmitter: "spelling errors . . . stammerings." For Serres, in "Platonic Dialogue," what is essential about the noise of writing is not the technical fallibilities or material contingencies of transmission systems so much as the necessary fallibility of information sources and coders. This emphasis on the agent as opposed to the instrument of transmission continues as he presses to his main point: "Simply to write is to risk jumbling a form. In the same way, to communicate orally is to risk losing meaning in noise" (66). Or, again, potentially defeating their efforts to transmit so as to be properly received, communicators run the risk of being overwhelmed by noise simply by submitting their selected forms to the perils of articulation or coding in the first place, and only then, moreover, to the pitfalls of transmission.

Right now, another and justly famous conceptual move is carried out, rapidly and without demarcation from the foregoing. The discourse on communication pegged to Shannon's one-way transmission model morphs through a text from Norbert Wiener into a discourse on dialogue. Implicitly, Serres has shifted from a tightly information-theoretic focus to Wiener's more comprehensive cybernetic orientation regarding a "theory of messages," within which the concept of communication recovers some of its social weight. It is worth quoting Wiener's definition of cybernetics near the beginning of the second edition of *The Human Use of Human Beings:*

> Besides the electrical engineering theory of the transmission of messages, there is a larger field which includes not only the study of language but the study of messages as a means of controlling machinery and society, the development of computing machines and other such automata, certain reflections upon psychology and the nervous system, and a tentative new theory of scientific method. This larger theory of messages is a probabilistic theory. (23)

Serres folds Wiener's theory of messages into his own treatment, but his gambit remains to amplify the concept of noise while bringing cybernetics toward philosophical discourse. In this context, what Wiener gives him is the relocation of information theory away from neutral matters of civilian transmission, such as telephony per se, and back into its former military milieu. Here, noise is not just a random contingency of material technologies; it may also arise among combatants from an active effort on the part of an adversary to defeat the effective reception and decoding of messages.

"Platonic Dialogue" gives a general footnote to chapters 4 and 11 of the 1967 Avon reprint of *The Human Use of Human Beings.*[22] In chapter 11, "Language, Confusion, and Jam," Wiener cites "some very interesting work recently carried out by Dr. Benoit Mandelbrot of Paris and Professor Jakobson of Harvard":

> They consider communication to be a game played in partnership by the speaker and the listener against the forces of confusion, represented by the ordinary difficulties of communication and by some supposed individuals attempting to jam the communication. Literally speaking, the game theory of von Neumann, which is involved in this connection, concerns one team which is deliberately trying to get the message across, and another team which will resort to any strategy to jam the message. (255)

Adding the possibility of intentional noise to the theory of messages makes communication more than a gamble waged against chaos: it can also be a bid for mutual comprehensibility while pitted against a common adversary. Von Neumann's and Wiener's scenarios take up communication as a complex of agonistic relations modeled on a game theory of warfare. We can now observe that Serres's "Platonic Dialogue" has muted what his sources present as the specifically military situation of a potentially literal enemy in favor of a largely civilian scenario.

In this famous passage from "Platonic Dialogue," Serres has resistance to communication arise primarily from the nature of things, as circumambient noises overwhelm the audibility of voices, the thunder and lightning of the world interrupting the clear skies of transmission. Picking up Wiener's explicit reference, Serres declares that for Mandelbrot and Jakobson, dialogue

> is a sort of game played by two interlocutors considered as united against the phenomena of interference and confusion, or against individuals with some stake in interrupting communication. These interlocutors are in no way opposed, as in the traditional conception of the dialectic game; on the contrary, they are on the same side, tied together by a mutual interest: they battle together against noise. . . . *To hold a dialogue is to suppose a third man and to seek to exclude him;* a successful communication is the exclusion of the third man. . . . We might call this third man the *demon,* the prosopopoeia of noise. (66–67)

In Serres's strong deflection of Wiener's text, if dialogue is precarious, the danger is not necessarily due to a human adversary but simply to an adversarial world that always threatens to immerse communication in its random noise. In the remainder of his article, Serres back-reads dialogic noise into the challenges to comprehensibility confronted by Descartes's *Metaphysics* and, at greater length and to epochal Western effect, by the Platonic dialogues.[23]

But while valorizing noise in relation to classical form, Serres's agonistic scenario does not dislodge Platonic ontology, it only submits it to a partial reversal. Unlike the self-referential reformulation of form that will develop in autopoietic systems theory, in "Platonic Dialogue," form remains opposed to matter as the ordered pattern of a message is opposed to its entropic dissolution into random grains of stuff. With Serres, the classical concept of form bifurcates into an ideal and a noisy formation: "To isolate an ideal form is to render it independent of the empirical domain and of noise. Noise is the empirical portion of the message just as the empirical domain is the noise of form" (70). However, despite this daemonic opening of form to a participation in noise, its bifurcation would still adhere to the old ontological pattern. Information theory itself, in the bifurcation of information into signal and noise, replicates in a virtual medium the ontological schism and division of the Platonic cosmos into the ideal and the empirical.[24] To that extent, it does not join in the operational and epistemological transformations to be wrought by second-order systems theory. At the end of this chapter, I return to these matters of form and its theoretical reformation.

"The Origin of Language"

Serres's "The Origin of Language" operates with a synthesis of information theory and first-order cybernetics. It begins with a primer on differentiations among systems, a short course that remains useful both in its presentation and in the pointed deconstruction that Serres then performs on it. However, the article's crucial venture is the promotion of an information-theoretical description of living systems. It opens with the observation that "An organism is a system" (71). To position this statement, Serres distinguishes three kinds of systems in the history of Western ideas—logicomathematical, mechanical, and thermodynamic: "However, the three types all have closure in common" (72). We may observe that the systems enumerated manifest either *logical* or *environmental* closure. Serres then disturbs this same catalog with some midtwentieth-century developments. New thinking about organisms as open, far-from-equilibrium thermodynamic systems and about other lines of implication from thermodynamics to information and communication theory challenges the limits of classical physics: "It was shown, for example, that information (emitted, transmitted, or received) was a form of negentropy.... The system under consideration becomes a system of signs" (73).[25] A concept of information conceived on a par with matter and energy becomes a universal solvent already permeating both the differences and the similarities in Serres's previous catalog of systems: "Right in the middle of the traditional classification of beings, a classification that no longer makes sense since matter, life, and sign are nothing but properties of a system, we find exactly what I want to talk about: the living organism" (73).

This is a realm of discussion well beyond "Platonic Dialogue." But the concept of noise will reappear as part of this information-theoretical modeling of living systems. As we have discussed, information theory is centered on the technical problematics of transmission, or what one could call *signal flow*. In a living system treated as "an information and thermodynamic system" (74), then, matters of signal transmission are remodeled as living flows of energy and information that drive biological evolution "up the entropic stream" (74). The living system

receives, stores, exchanges, and gives off both energy and information—in all forms, from the light of the sun to the flow of matter which passes through it (food, oxygen, heat, signals).... Indeed, due to the energy and information torrent which passes through the system without interruption, it is henceforth impossible to conceive of it as an isolated-closed system, except, perhaps, in its genotypical form. It is an open system ... a river that flows and yet remains stable in the continual collapse of its banks and the irreversible erosion of the mountains around it. (74)

Biological models of this sort derive from a thermodynamic framework focused on the movement of energy (as heat or otherwise) through a physical system. In the statement just cited, offered as a broad physical generalization, no distinction is ventured between processes of structural organization, understood as producing a decrease in the entropy of the system, and processes of *living* organization, which tend to get covered over by an unspecified notion of "negentropy."[26] The universalization of the transmission model could not be clearer than in this image of the informatic leakiness of systems of all sorts.

When living systems are modeled strictly as open thermodynamic-informatic systems, notions of structural self-organization have to patch up the conceptual lacunae that can be properly filled in only by operationally closed autopoietic self-production. In the article at hand, Serres develops the living system as a product of self-organization from the noise of information flows. However, nowhere in Serres's discussion is there a precise explanation of the *forms* of the signifiers that would comprise such a flow of information, such a biological "writing." Here, what are precisely the "symbols of communication" discussed in "Platonic Dialogue," what is the nature of the signal transmitted in the biological instance? A flow of living signs is all very well as a heuristic image, but one can question exactly what the code is here, and what it is that codes and decodes the supposed signal flows of metabolic and physiological functions (as opposed to genetics) conceived on the transmission model.

In fact, in the same period separating Serres's two articles (1966–76), an alternative, noninformatic approach to the cybernetics of living systems was also developing, in work we can center at von Foerster's Biological Computer Laboratory (BCL) at the University of Illinois. Von Foerster's conceptual history is exemplary here. Until the advent of the theory of autopoiesis—thanks in large measure to his own patronage of Maturana's and Varela's early efforts, and in catalytic interaction with his own notions of second-order cybernetics—he was a seminal devotee of information-theoretical systems theory.[27] Von Foerster's 1960 paper "On Self-Organizing Systems and Their Environments," for example, uses a heuristic extension of information theory to develop a model of self-organization conceptualized as the emergence of order from noise—or, more precisely, as von Foerster glosses his usage, from "cheap undirected energy."[28]

I return to von Foerster not only to position him in relation to the writings of Serres but also to recall how, later in the 1960s, his interests went beyond applications of information theory and increasingly toward the operations of cognitive systems. For instance, his 1969 paper "What Is Memory that It May Have Hindsight and Foresight as Well?" expresses impatience over superficial evocations of informatics, along with a critique of storage-and-retrieval metaphors applied to the study of the mental faculty of memory:

Books, tapes, micro-fiches or other documents that are retrieved . . . only when looked upon by a human mind, may yield the desired "information." By confusing *vehicles* for potential information with *information,* one puts the problem of cognition nicely into one's blind spot of intellectual vision, and the problem conveniently disappears. (103)

The problem of cognition brings into play a form of cybernetics not content to dwell with the transmission apparatuses of Level A, but ready to approach, in the title of one of Maturana's key BCL papers, a "Neurophysiology of Cognition." As noted in the introduction, von Foerster's own cognitive turn reaches full statement and maximum compression in the final statements of "Thoughts and Notes on Cognition."[29] Here, the concept of information has its ontological credentials revoked in favor of an epistemological constructivism:

5.6 Cognitive processes create descriptions of, that is information, about the environment.

6 The environment contains no information. The environment is as it is. (189)

Information is no longer the freestanding transmitted input *to* a receiving apparatus—a neuron or whatever—but the outcome *of* self-referential system processes that are cognitive in the first instance. Information has no system-external being; rather, it is the system-internal product of a self-referential cognitive process, which process may then go on to attribute its construction to its environment.[30]

What is afoot here is the emergence of second-order systems theory as a deliberately noninformatic cybernetics of nondesigned systems. To fill in the conceptual framework of this newly arriving discourse of self-referential systems, let us recall the impressively lucid interview given in 1976 by the twenty-eight-year-old Francisco Varela, "On Observing Natural Systems":

Varela: . . . I have come to the conviction that the key to understanding the holism of such systems, the whole-ness of systems, is to understand that they are organized, their parts are organized, in a *circular* form. That is, every part interacts with every other part. That gives us a total self-referential system.

. . . And this is what gives the system its nature. When you have a closed interaction of chemical productions, you can have a cell, and not before that.

When you have a closed interaction of descriptions, you can have self-consciousness, and not before. When you have a closed interaction of species, you have an ecological system, and not before. That is, the closure, the self-referential-ness, seem to be the hinges upon which the emergent properties of a system turn. . . .

Johnson: So any system can be looked at in terms of its closure. . . .

Varela: . . . For instance the understanding of our nervous system, not as an input-output information processing device as is the current understanding in neurophysiology, but rather as a closed unit of perception and action to maintain internally generated reference levels. . . .

Now, a word of caution here. We are *not* saying that such systems are closed for *interactions*. This is a point where there is much semantic confusion; when you say that a natural system has organizational closure, people think that you mean closed for interactions. Nothing of the sort, though this is the common meaning. This connects to your original question; no system is closed for interactions, that is, it is not closed for matter and energy. But it can be organizationally closed, as was said by Ashby many years ago. (26–28)

Turning back to "The Origin of Language," we can compare these two discourses on the issues of the openness and closure of particular kinds of systems. Serres writes about the living system: "Due to the energy and information torrent which passes through the system without interruption, it . . . is an open system." And, as Varela confirms, this statement is correct with regard to the environmental openness of biological systems to fluxes of matter and energy. But still, what precisely is an "information torrent," and what role is this supposed to play in the maintenance of living processes? Does this have to do with the organizational order or form of the living system? This is not clarified. Varela offers a different conceptualization, that the form of natural systems—cellular, psychical, ecosystemic—results from their organizational closure, the circular or self-referential self-processing of their internal dynamics, in a manner orthogonal to their immersion in material-energetic environments.

Some essential differences between the information-theoretic and the autopoietic conceptions may now be tallied. The former conforms to a linear flow model, related to thermodynamics, with a binary state: the system will only be either open or closed. The latter adapts a circular or recursive model related to the discourse of cybernetic feedback, but lifted into a higher dimensionality newly constructed for the biological-cognitive occasion. In the autopoietic conception, thermodynamic matters of open environmental flow are accounted for but not necessarily instrumental for the phenomenon to be explained. As in the classical ecological conception, while energy flows through the system, it is the cyclic forms taken by its elements and their relations that maintain its systemic stability, or the "self" of its self-regulation: "Analysis of the processes that defined ecosystems concentrated on these two ideas, the cycling of chemicals within the system and the flow of energy through the system."[31] The autopoietic system maintains itself as the self-referential product of its own production under the form of an operational closure that cycles rather than flows.

In the following passage from "The Origin of Language," some strain may be observed in Serres's conceptual imagery. I suggest that the informatic systems theory at his disposal does not give him the tools for a clean pass at the form of living organization. He sees that he needs a way to conceptualize the closure of the living organism in the midst of its openness to energy flow, but without some purchase on the circularity or self-reference of such a system, his discourse wobbles between images of openness and closure conceived as occupying the same corporeal plane:

> Within the context of an even more general circulation that goes from the sun to the black depths of space, the organism is a barrier of braided links that leaks like a wicker basket but can still function as a dam. Better yet, it is the quasi-stable turbulence that a flow produces, the eddy closed upon itself for an instant, which finds its balance in the middle of the current and appears to move upstream, but is in fact undone by the flow and re-formed elsewhere. (75)

Serres's resolution is referred instead to the cosmic succession of living and dying beings under the sun rather than to the moment-to-moment maintenance of life by the living. Drawn from Prigogine's dissipative structures and/or the physics of fluid dynamics, these figures do not yield a satisfying model of the bounded stability of cellular or corporeal forms.

In any event, at this point in "The Origin of Language," Serres leaves off discussing the form of the organism in favor of the role that noise may play in this overall description of the living system. He offers the passage to which, as near as I can tell, Luhmann's endnote in *Social Systems* is referring. Here again is the gist of it: "From a thermal and information point of view," living processes "necessarily generate background noise. And this noise is certainly tremendous. . . . What prevents us from hearing it?" (76). Serres's answer to this question hinges on a conceptual term implicit in the previous discussion of noise and widely entrenched in cybernetic discourse—*the observer:* "All of information theory and hence, correlatively, of the theory of noise only makes sense in relation to an observer who happens to be linked to them" (76).

The discourse on cognition in second-order systems theory is also devoted to demarcating the observer, especially to discriminating first- and second-order observers and to marking the observation of observation. In information theory, however, the observer observes but is not observed observing. As a major mode of *first*-order cybernetics, it is precisely a discourse of *observed* systems. For instance, in "Platonic Dialogue," the demon or third man Serres brings forward can certainly be thought of as an observer of transmissions, although as one posited in an adversarial mode. But its cognitive capacity—its ability to observe in the first place, and thus to interfere with, jam, or in some fashion introduce noise into the transmissions of others—is not accounted for, it is simply posited. Similarly with the observer Serres now introduces into his bioinformatic picture, it comes forward in possession of its own channel to the separate channel under its observation. Its capacities to assemble, decode, and rectify the composite of information and noise that it observes there are simply posited.

"Who is the observer here? The simplest answer would be to say that for our own organic system we are the observer or observers in question" (76). Serres identifies the terminal observer here as a kind of composite ego, as a consciousness confronting its awareness of the body from which it emerges. The question remains, when we put the ear of the psyche to the ground of its body, why do we not hear the "background noise" of its living processes?

> We should perceive this noise, the noise of a complex to which a receptor is linked. . . . We should hear this deafening clamor just as we hear the roar of the sea at the edge of the beach. It should deafen us, drown us. . . . But, save for exceptional instances, we perceive almost nothing of this intense chaos which nonetheless exists and functions, as experiments have demonstrated conclusively. We are submerged to our neck, to our eyes, to our hair, in a furiously raging ocean. We are the voice of this hurricane, this thermal howl, and we do not even know it. It exists but it goes unperceived. (76–77)

So Serres pursues a question regarding self-perception: what prevents us from hearing what must be the noise of our own organic processes? However, not at issue are the notions that such transmissions occur and that faculties of perception capable of receiving them are on hand. They are *a priori* assumptions of the informatic model. The question posed is, simply, for the phenomenological self-observer, why is the body's noise turned off rather than turned on?

The answer comes straight out of an informatic biological discourse newly developed at the turn of the 1970s. Directly behind Serres's discussion of the rectification of noise stands Henri Atlan's *L'Organisation biologique et la théorie de l'information*.[32] It must be noted as well that directly behind Atlan's informatic theorization of biological organization stands von Foerster's earlier order-from-noise principle in self-organizing systems.[33] Atlan works with a conceptualization of biological hierarchy in which higher organic levels—say, organ systems—are modeled as *observers* of lower levels—say, cells or tissues. Each organic level is treated as an informatic transmission apparatus generating composites of signal and noise. Each level is to be observable in its totality one level up, from which location the noise below can be added to, rather than subtracted from, the information transmitted by the signal. Here is the famous passage from "The Origin of Language" in which Serres discursively summarizes Atlan's Shannonian biomathematics:

> If one writes the equation expressing the quantity of information exchanged between two stations through a given channel and the equation which provides this quantity for the whole unit (including the two stations and the channel), a change of sign occurs for a certain function entering into the computation. In other words, this function, called ambiguity and resulting from noise, changes when the observer changes his point of observation. Its value depends on whether he is submerged in the first level or whether he examines the entire unit from the next level. In a certain sense, the next level functions as a rectifier, in particular, as a rectifier of noise. What was once an obstacle to all messages is reversed and added to the information. This discovery is all the more important since it is valid for all levels. It is a law of the series which runs through the system of integration. (77–78)

However, Serres's statement is incautious. What he describes here is not a discovery. Atlan does not present it that way. He presents it, quite simply, as a theory. Atlan's discourse offers a heuristic sketch for possible scientific investigation. But in and of itself, much as with von Foerster's scheme of order from noise, Atlan's complexity-from-noise scenario amounts to a theoretical model, a speculative information-theoretical thought-experiment.

The critical question becomes, does this unobserved but posited "thermal howl" actually occur? Or does Serres grant Atlan's model rather more ontology than it merits? Or, instead, does this sound and fury actually signify something else, for instance, the historical and discursive significances of its own self-generation from the premises of the conceptual model at hand? Let me suggest what happens if we bring a different model to bear on this issue of self-perception, one drawn from the discourse of second-order systems theory, in its particular elaboration in social systems theory. Luhmann's late work *Art as a Social System* is centered on the communicative functions of artworks. It begins with a general treatment of perception—the sensory faculty by which artworks are taken up by consciousness—in relation both to communication and to the nervous system. Proceeding on the assumption of operational closure basic to the autopoietic model, for Luhmann, the wonder is not that we seem not to hear the supposed thermal howl of the organism, but rather that, given the respective closures of neurological and psychic processes, brain and mind, we nonetheless do seem to perceive an *outer* world: "It suffices to remain astonished that we see anything 'outside' at all, even if our seeing happens only 'inside'" (5–6).

Second-order systems theory gives noise its due as an unpredictable environmental contingency. But it dismisses the transmission model from its theorization of self-referential system processes. For Luhmann, noise has no primary status for the autopoietic conception of cognitive processes:

> Communication can no longer be understood as a "transmission" of information from an (operatively closed) living being or conscious system to any other such system. Communication is an independent type of formation in the medium of meaning *[Sinn]*, an emergent reality that presupposes living beings capable of consciousness but is irreducible to any of these beings, not even to all of them taken together. (9)

For Serres, I think, the elation with which he celebrates the information-theoretic approach in Atlan's description has to do with the promise he draws from this model to cut right across every level and bind together all systemic formations, from molecules to messages: "I do not need to know who or what the first dispatcher is: whatever it is, it is an island in an ocean of noise, just like me, no matter where I am. . . . A macromolecule, or any given crystallized solid, or the system of the world, or ultimately what I call 'me'—we are all in the same boat."[34] Serres's scientific sublime, akin to Kittler's technosublime, is overtly universalizing. Serres's vision captures a profound desire to recuperate technoscience by getting back from it the means to heal the wounds of modernity. An informatic cybernetics is to heal the cultural incisions it has inherited and continues to inflict upon the modern idea of the human. But it may be that Serres's stance also rests on the overextension of a technological model that in fact does not afford sufficient local autonomies to a world whose wounds are simply a part of its possibility. A world containing autopoietic systems is not a multileveled, hierarchical cosmos but a multifarious farrago of different systems and different kinds of systems. Those capable of observation all construct different if occasionally harmonizable versions of their worldly environments. In the autopoietic vision, no system is entirely in the very same boat with any other, and yet, nonetheless, a lot of nonidentical but sufficiently similar little boats, as it were, can be the medium out of which higher-level systemic formations can certainly emerge—such as organisms from cells, societies from organisms, and perhaps, too, Gaia from the interlocking of the sum of the biota with their coevolved global matrix. In Luhmann's handling, the autopoietic model yields this alternative vision of improbable but evident emergent correspondences, emergent co-observances.

The burden of this model is to factor the differentiations of different kinds of operationally closed systems into the co-observed regularities we nonetheless witness among multifarious autonomous constructions. Regarding system differentiation, Luhmann writes, "perception . . . remains a special competency of consciousness, its essential faculty."[35] That is, perception is the basic if not the only form taken by the autopoiesis of a psychic system. In whatever mode it may be that other kinds of cognitive living or social systems observe, they do not do so in the mode of perception. Borrowing a technical term from von Foerster, Luhmann continues:

> The perceived world is nothing but the sum total of the "eigenvalues" of neurophysiological operations. But information attesting to this state of affairs does not pass from the brain to consciousness. It is filtered out, systematically and

without leaving a trace. . . . The proposition that perception is a special, if not the most crucial, competency of consciousness . . . precludes the view that nervous systems can perceive. . . . Any systems-theoretical analysis must account for the differences in the respective modes of operation pertaining to both kinds of systems and must consequently assume two distinct systems. (6, 8)

Restated through Serres's cybernetics, this is another way to say that even if one were to grant that the organism generates various frequencies of background noise, there is still no channel to transmit the products of those processes directly to those of consciousness, or those of consciousness directly to the organism. And the operational closure of the nervous system applies to all organic systems.

Regarding co-observed regularities, whatever awareness any system of consciousness can produce of the body from which it emerges, it will take a form generated by the psychic system's own operations and manifested in the medium of meaning, not one transmitted to it, the meaning of which it then represents to itself. Nonetheless, we share a common impression that, just as the sun appears to revolve around the Earth, so our perceptions appear to derive from the direct decoding of corporeal or worldly transmissions. Luhmann's discussion of systems differentiations in *Art as a Social System* clarifies the cognitive rationale for our various transcendental illusions:

Consciousness processes perceptions under the impression of their *immediacy,* while the brain is actually executing operations that are highly selective, quantitatively calculating, recursively operative, and hence always mediated. "Immediacy" is nothing primordial, but an impression resulting from the differentiation of the autopoietic systems of the brain and consciousness. (8)

In other words, from within its own self-referential closure, consciousness per se has no choice but to perceive its perceptions as immediate. The ratiocination by which one constructs the understanding that this is *not* the case defies common sense. It must rely heavily on cultural mediations, hard intellectual efforts such as the discourse of second-order systems theory.

Within the realms about which it makes its claims—the natural autopoietic systems of body, mind, and society—Luhmann's systems theory, so to speak, liquidates the ether of communication. The dismissal of the facticity of telepathy is a special case of this general premise. Yet we in the West have still hoped to discover a medium of continuity through which dynamic waves, informatic flows, or even spiritual ripples may be transmitted so as to bind together bodies to bodies, to meld minds to minds or groups to groups. But this is not to be observed. Communication happens, of course, and forms ever new or renewed emerge from the granular medium of worldly differences, but when these things happen, it is for reasons other than the ability of living organisms to rectify informatically the thermal howl of the cosmos. Several decades and many technological generations and cyborg fantasies further on from Serres's initial formulations, we can now appreciate more fully why the celebration of informatic totality is as unwise as it is unreal. We can celebrate instead the likelihood that, for all their possibilities of effective coupling, the incommensurable competencies of informatic and autopoietic systems place an operational firewall between the mergers of mechanical and living systems, or computational and psychic systems. What appeared to be homogeneous totalities are to be reobserved as heterogeneous networks of systems.

The Reformation of Form

The autopoietic concept of form stands out against the long tradition that it supersedes. The classical form-matter binary corresponds to a subject-object binary that provides no accounting for either the operational boundedness or the temporal contingency of the subject in relation to its purportedly given objects. Due to this nonobservation of systemic constraints, in Plato's day, it was not difficult or unreasonable to imagine or speculate regarding the necessity of an unbounded and atemporal entity called the soul. The idea of form was coordinated then with the subject or soul in opposition to the matter or content of its objects. Kittler is correct to say that the "wheel of media technology cannot be turned back to retrieve the soul."[36] However, that wheel can now turn toward the contingencies of *systemic* form. The very possibility of systemic form is the availability of a viable medium contiguous to an autopoietic system. The unity of the system-environment distinction already brings with it a necessary relation between environmental medium and systemic form and, in addition, a third term absent from classical accounts—a *boundary*. By the very nature of its operation such a system necessarily produces its own boundary, always and only in time and never forever, the boundary that cuts such a system out of its environment. This is systemic form.

The medium of the operational distinguishing that brings about systemic forms is the previously unmarked plenum of its occurrence—in short, its environment. The environmental medium is not antithetical to the concept of systemic form, but rather, the contingent horizon within which such forms manifest their possibilities. Whereas the classical form-matter binary presented a static ontological polarity, the systemic form-medium binary is not ontological but operational, emergent, self-referential. The form-medium distinction loops back upon itself to include what it excludes. A self-referential system can maintain its forms of self-distinction and operation only in viable relation to an environment that supplies and maintains its medium:

> The shift toward difference-theoretical analyses will affect and radically alter the concept of world. This alteration can perhaps best be demonstrated in conjunction with the concept of form. Until recently, form was conceptualized (without much effort, for there were practically no alternatives) in terms of an ordered nexus between elements. . . . Form, in this [prior] sense . . . corresponds to the possibility of perceiving form as a unity directly and without analysis.[37]

Luhmann's passage provides an example of the larger point that in first-order observation, consciousness has no choice but to perceive its perceptions as immediate. He continues in *Art as a Social System* to note that perceptions of classical form also partake of this immediacy effect, which promotes the notion that form stands apart from the mediations of matter and process:

> Chance is [classical form's] counterconcept in the sense that the simultaneous appearance of elements not bound by form was believed to be random. Earlier versions of information theory and cybernetics were still working from within this traditional understanding of form when searching for ways to quantitatively compute improbability in terms of a link between redundancy and information. Such theories thematized form in relation to a recipient of information—that is, to an observer—but the only determining counterconcept available was the idea of chance. (27)

Compare Serres's peroration in "The Origin of Language," a hymn to ontological nondifferentiation derived from a cosmic positioning of the recipient of worldly noise and form, modeled precisely as chance and necessity:

> Nothing distinguishes me ontologically from a crystal, a plant, an animal, or the order of the world; we are drifting together toward the noise and the black depths of the universe, and our diverse systemic complexions are flowing up the entropic stream, toward the solar origin, itself adrift. Knowledge is at most the reversal of drifting, that strange conversion of times, always paid for by additional drift; but this is complexity itself, which was once called being. Virtually stable turbulence within the flow. To be or to know from now on will be translated by: see the islands, rare or fortunate, the work of chance or of necessity. (83)

I confess that I rather value my differentiation from a crystal, while I am also happy to understand that my animal body is, in fact, a symbiogenetic consortium of bacteria that are already, in their minimal but utterly definitive autopoietic natures, cognitive systems in their own right. In any event, in *Art as a Social System,* Luhmann gives the matter a completely abstract formulation: "A difference-theoretical reconstruction of the concept of form shifts the emphasis from the (ordered) content of form to the difference it makes. It extends and places on the 'other side' of form the realm of what used to be considered chance and thereby subsumes under the concept of form any difference that marks a unity" (27).

We see one more time how noise is rectified within the autopoietic cosmos. Whereas, in "Platonic Dialogue," one may question Serres's promotion of the adversary of military transmissions into the third man of any dialogue whatsoever, his workup there of the noise of written and oral communications is perfectly cogent. However, with regard not only to Serres but also to the various hypertrophies of cybertheory yet abroad on the conceptual landscape, what still demands critical pressure is the unrestricted extension of the informatic model beyond the technological occasion. When, in distinction from that occasion, the system at hand is a self-referential, cognitive system, such as a body or a mind, noise functions as an unpredictable component of its environment, as a percolation of the medium from which that system assembles its forms, or as the unmarked state on the other side of its self-generated indications. "One of communication's most important achievements is sensitizing the system to chance, disturbances, and 'noise' of all kinds. In communication one can make understandable what is unexpected, unwelcome, and disappointing."[38] Noise is thus accorded a productive if not overarching role in system formation and maintenance. Autopoietic systems are not hardened structures but dynamic entities interacting with their environment, characterized by a necessary instability that makes them responsive to perturbations and open to change. Well-advanced theories of form and medium are available and already coordinated now with the theory of self-referential systems.[39] Thus, it would be more productive in most instances not to ask from noise more than it can give, but to operate with second-order form and system theories and to further develop the descriptive powers of their denotative vocabularies.

Cognitive operations are neither transmissions nor receptions. Under the regime of the operational closures of observing systems necessarily orthogonal to thermodynamic flows, cognitions—and hence information, whether signal or noise—derive from an infinite play of forms. These forms are infinitely differentiated by systemic autonomies, which bring forth the worlds of which they are capable and, by that very bounded construction, throw what remains for them uncognized into their own shadows. This argues for the wisdom of a certain epistemological humility. However, from what I can see of it, the big world made up of these little worlds is reasonably sociable and has effective ways of rising both to continuities and to improbable formations.

⊐ FEEDBACK LOOPS

Media Embedding and Narrative Time from Jimi Hendrix to Eternal Sunshine and Memento

CNN showed a picture of a TV tuned to CNN.
—*NEW YORKER*

Loopings

Let us pick up the matter of self-reference and unfold it further into some of its significant patterns—loops, embedding, and reentry—on the way to an encounter with metalepsis, the self-referential reentry or feedback of narrative form. In chapter 1, we treated the self-reference and heteroreception of the trace, noting how a trace marks its own origination for the observer that constitutes it. We could now add: any trace also marks its own reorigination. The original origin recedes beyond recovery, but if a trace endures, its observation can occur or recur at any time. The trace and its observer are inseparable even in their necessary distinction. The self of self-reference is a composite of structure and system unfolding out of the observation of the trace. Self-observation divides the self into observer and observed:

> At least one distinction is involved in the presence of self-reference. The self appears, and an indication of that self that can be seen as separate from the self. Any distinction involves the self-reference of "the one who distinguishes." Therefore, self-reference and the idea of distinction are inseparable (hence conceptually identical). . . . The self is the whole space including the mark and its observer.[1]

In "Self-Reference and Recursive Forms," Louis Kauffman diagrams this dynamism of self-reference with an arrow intended as a pointer—the

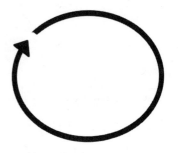

Figure 3. A self-pointing arrow, after Louis H. Kauffman, "Self-Reference and Recursive Forms" (1987).

graphical arrow as the literal icon of an indexical reference—by analyzing the arrow into its body or tail and its barb or pointer (Figure 3). Then, "when we turn the arrow on itself we achieve self-reference with the whole as the arrow itself, and the barb and tail as 'parts.'"

"The self-pointing arrow becomes self-referential only through the agreement of an observer. . . . It is a symbol for the condition of observation in which the self appears to divide itself into that which sees and that which is seen" (54). We have another occasion to reflect on the dynamism of self-reference, the engine of epistemological operation. Knowing the other is the operation of a self that knows itself through the other, the other through itself. As they loop upon themselves, the rhythms of knowing, the operations of observation, alternate and exchange phases of merger and separation.

The next loop shows a group of people on a field in California at the Whole Earth Jamboree of 1978, playing the lap game, assembling themselves into so-called unsupported circles (Figure 4). These ephemeral structures capture a form of social interaction intended to symbolize the formation of social wholes or systemic unities out of individual parts (participating persons). People drawn into a circle sit down on the knees of the one behind them. If the queue does not loop back upon itself like a self-pointing arrow, the circle will be broken.

The unsupported circle has no foundation, no strongest link. But in closing upon its own form, its momentary integrity arises from a collective structural coordination that transforms its individuals into emblematic system elements swept into a precarious emergent whole. The unsupported circle is a form of social rhetoric: it idealizes how a society should operate. Its observer is both out of play—excluded from the circle of inclusion—and in the game at the same time, insofar as in refer-

Figure 4. Concentric lap games with an Earth ball at the Whole Earth Jamboree, Gerbode Valley, California, August 26–28, 1978, *CoEvolution Quarterly* (Winter 1978).

ring to the assembled icon as a self-referential sign of social unity it also refers to itself, and so enters another circle looped into those observed. In this image, two social rites interlock: Bouncing an Earth ball around the circle affirms spiritual solidarity with the natural world, while two massive and concentric lap games affirm communal solidarity with each other. The doubling of this social structure embeds that affirmation.

For one more example in this current series of loopings, cybernetics as the science of control mechanisms has cultivated the concept of feedback. Many kinds of designed and natural systems maintain or steer their own output through feedback loops. They regulate themselves by reintroducing information drawn from their output into their operations as supplemental input, maintaining their behaviors within preset or effective ranges. As noted in chapter 1, in a standard feedback circuit, the feedback is negative if its reintroduction stabilizes, tamps rather than increases, the output of the process. This is the desired function in the case of servomechanisms or neural circuits for homeostasis, holding the system's behavior within an acceptable range of operational limits. However, with positive feedback, the signal that is fed back compounds rather than subtracts itself, amplifies rather than damps down the output of the system.

Negative feedback is thus the cybernetic norm, the control function, whereas positive feedback is the aberration, the system setting itself into a wild state. But then, the wild state is not always an aberration, and especially not in the electronic mediation of artistic performances. Consider a case of positive feedback within electronic audio amplification, in the wider context of its exploitation within popular music. Here the message is a source signal—say, from a guitar pickup—that the audio system registers, codes, decodes, and boosts into speakers. Audio feedback in an amplified circuit is produced when some of the aural output from the speaker of an amplifier reenters a microphone or an electric pickup. This can generate unwanted noise, a distorted signal, the screech of runaway feedback in a microphone too close to its speakers. However, when audio feedback is properly calibrated by an operator balancing the amount of output fed back, a kind of harmonic equilibrium can evolve. In a sort of fragile positive homeostasis, sound crystals emerge and condense to reveal the angularities of overtones and chord harmonics—islands of order emerging in the chaos of amplified noise. This momentary system effect can itself be modulated within various limits and sustained to form a beam of sound. For instance, at the beginning of "Foxey Lady," Jimi Hendrix lays down his classic feedback signature as he rattles his electric guitar string with his fretting hand into an overdriven amp until it generates enough input/output to loop into a feedback beam.

Rock feedback is a musical medium created by rodeo riding a cascade of recursive noise. Emerging full-blown in the mid-1960s, guitar feedback unleashed a new world of unheard-of sounds. A natural technical consequence of overdriving an amplifier to fill up a room too big for it, feedback was gradually recognized as a sonic resource that could be both tonally and melodically controlled. Rock feedback was anticipated by Chicago-style electrified blues guitarists exploiting the pleasingly gritty sound of overdriven vacuum-tube amplifiers. That electric-blues signature was later reprocessed by British guitar heroes of the mid-sixties such as Clapton, Richards, Beck, and Page, who also found fuzzy or wavery feedback tones effective for signifying the mind-bending effects of pot and LSD. But one performer literally embodied the *social* feedback of feedback—the export of American electric blues to British rock and roll and its cultural reentry or reimportation into the States as the sound of psychedelia. The London-incubated American rocker Hendrix raised blues-based rock guitar feedback to an art form, playing feedback like a violin.

Hendrix especially perfected the spacey feel of psychedelic rock through ingenious ways of looping and relayering a noisy feedback signal to produce a sonic density or depth effect. He made guitar feedback sing through a rig assembled from a Fender Stratocaster, his signature stacked quartet of Marshall amplifiers, and an unprecedented repertoire of newly created guitar-effects pedals, especially the fuzztone, which jacked up the volume of the electric guitar while simultaneously enabling sustained feedback tones at the punch of a floor pedal. Hendrix added to this the wah-wah pedal, the Octavia octave splitter, and the Uni-Vibe that simulates the tremolo effect of the revolving tweeters in the sound box of a Hammond B3 electric organ—giving his feedback sounds a further range of stunning effects. For instance, in "Third Stone from the Sun," Hendrix comes out of a spacey jam to reassert the head of the melody by capturing a feedback beam and using it to sing the tune, while rippling the aural solidity of the beam with the guitar's whammy bar. A few years later, Hendrix distilled this form of guitar attack in his monumental performance of "Machine Gun" on New Year's Eve, 1969, the day the sixties turned into the seventies. Here, after the first set of verses, at the beginning of the main instrumental break, Jimi condensed the horror of jungle warfare into a long-sustained, perfectly tuned, single-pitched scream of feedback, its octaves split by the Octavia and eerily lashed by the jungle helicopter-like rotations of the Uni-Vibe.

In the informatics of rock feedback, musical art is formed out of noise by reprocessing not a stored signal but one produced on the fly, in the moment of improvisatory performance. If the pioneers of cybernetics and information theory studied the formal parallels between electronic circuitry and organic systems, Hendrix showed how to couple the electric guitar and its amplification and sound-processing technologies *to* the body *in* performance, communicating his own cybernetic fusion to his actual live and virtual mediated audiences. Playing on the cutting edge of this human-machine interface, Jimi's rock persona embodied the "Body Electric" seen in the poetic ether a century earlier by America's first rock prophet, Walt Whitman. He transformed that romantic body into a cybernetic body sustained by the potentially infinite singing of a feedback loop.

Embedding Media

On the February 10, 2004, edition of the cable news show *Hardball with Chris Matthews,* discussing the results of the Virginia and Tennessee

Democratic primaries, the regular political commentators in the studio were joined by a field report from Ron Reagan, the one-time rebellious son of the former president, then a thirty- or forty-something person of indeterminate credentials. That he was there to provide a perspective "on the Left" may have been confirmed when the window containing his talking head, framed within the full screen, carried the caption "Ron Reagan, Culture Wars Embed." Credit *Hardball* with at least one playful moment satirizing what was, at that moment, a media matter of some seriousness.

The singular form "media" in "embedded media" names a proxy witness for a mass audience, an observer of news in the making who forms and circulates mass communications. As such a media observer, "David Bloom, of NBC, stood before the camera in Karbala last Tuesday, a couple of hours before sunset, wearing goggles in the gloom and holding light sticks."[2] News reporters are assumed to be distinct from news makers. News makers—such as U.S. soldiers in Iraq—are to be the first-order observers: they confront the things they do head-on. Only through the observation of that distinction can media witnesses remain in a position to observe at second-order the observations of the historical actors. However, just a few days later, broadcasting from a troop carrier careering north to Baghdad, David Bloom made news. He died in the field from a pulmonary embolism, and then became the object of another reporter's report.

Of course, the mass media has no ultimate autonomy and is contingent on a manifold of other technical, corporate, state, and social systems. It forms a differentiated subsystem contiguous to other such systems, all of which share the immediate worldly environment of this social embeddedness. But embedded war reporting covers over its hypermediated status with a raw feed that reeks of immediacy. As the sand and grit blow by, the video seethes and the audio crackles with the noise of mobile transmission to satellite links. The operational boundaries that would maintain the media system distinct from its objects oscillate in and out of functional phase. The equivocal apparatus of nested, interembedded systems induces the remediated (in)authenticity of embedded media. But in any event, the reporters are not there to reflect on the paradoxicality of their situations. Rather, they collude with a mass audience in failing to see or tell how their embedded status gives their reportage a self-referential twist and turns their reports away from ostensible detachment, merging them with the military itself and boxing them up inside its machine. "Embedded media" is a covert euphemism for a co-opted and co-opting observer, one observing itself in bed with the thing to be observed, one for which the distinction between maker and mediator, actor and witness, is constantly collapsing and reforming. The military can now usurp the location of second-order observation and self-mediate the form of embedded media reports. In the idiom of narrative theory, the war reporter as embedded mediator is now not *authorial* or external but *character-bound* to a delimited horizon.

From a *New York Times* column of December 28, 2003, alphabetically breaking down the year's biggest buzzwords, we learn that: "E is for embed—a journalist placed in a military unit during the American take-over of Iraq to cover its activities."[3] Two days earlier, CNN ran the following Reuters story:

> Web Site Picks Year's Top Word. . . . A U.S. Web site specializing in language named what it called the top word, phrase and name of the year on Thursday, picking them all from the war in Iraq. "Embedded," as in the reporters assigned to accompany military units during the war, beat out "blog" and "SARS" as the top word of 2003.[4]

In "Embedded for Life," a July 4, 2003, piece on his war coverage in the First Battalion, Seventh Marines, CNN journalist Martin Savidge contemplated the brevity of the Iraq conflict:

> The officers used to tell the journalists planning to embed in their weekly briefings before the war: "You will be embedded for life. You won't go home until after your unit has its victory parade down Main Street." Of course it didn't last anywhere near that long. Most of the embed journalists never made it past Baghdad, if they made it that far. Like me, many were told to break free and begin covering the liberation of the capital without the embed restraints. . . . I will carry those memories inside of me long after this conflict is past. They are embedded for life.[5]

When persons are embedded in material frames such as combat units, to be embedded is also to be constrained, subordinated to the operations of the embedding system. A journalist embedded with a military unit is necessarily incorporated into the apparatus of military self-observation and self-description, an apparatus for the self-construction of its publicized image. And yet, as Savidge unfolds the military metaphor of embedded morale, his account affirms that once one has been embedded in the unit, one cannot altogether "break free" into independence or recover autonomy or "objectivity" with the ostensible return of a severely curtailed self-determination. The rhetorical appeal of *embedding* links up with the participatory ideal of the war machine and emerges from the romance of the organic metaphor it elicits. In the figural physiology of embedded media, what is embedded in memory ends up, as it were, on the inside of the soul, along with the heart and its feelings, where the essences of things are inscribed in their permanence.

Moreover, the military embedding of media reporters has the narrative effect of embedding them, sometimes lethally, into their own stories. As a self-narrated character inside his own reports, only in death does David Bloom live on in the world of someone else's story. But paradoxically, this self-referential mediation of embedded media makes its war journalism seem more literary, at once more subjective (up close and personal) *and* more objective (rough and tumble). The embedded reporter has crossed over from the authorial to the character-bound narrative attitude, from the third- to the first-person, and potentially from narrator-focalizer to character-focalizer altogether. We expect the independent media witness to maintain the role of an authorial narrator—one that remains on the other side of an observational border from the sphere of action being narrated—thus retaining authority to select the frames through which it observes the characters acting out the story, and to select the terms by which it reports the news. To that extent, "authorial" media observers are not embedded, but embedding. Whatever their specific tilt, if they are to offer independent perspectives, media frames must encompass and embed the frames that contain the actors and events. "Embedded media" are, by definition, narrated elsewhere. But at least they make glaringly obvious the self-reference of the media system, normally erased by the authorial or "objective" stance. In mediatic self-reference, as in dramatic self-reference, as David Roberts has written, "The paradox of the second re-entry of form is this: the play, which is contained and framed within the play, *contains and frames at the same time the play which contains it.* The form *in* the form is the form of the (containing) form."[6]

Jay Bolter and Richard Grusin ground a related duplicity of media in "a double logic of *remediation.* Our culture wants both to multiply its media and to erase all traces of mediation: ideally, it wants to erase its media in the very act of multiplying them."[7] As they explain, remediation also concerns the propensity of newer media to embed the forms of older media, as cinema embeds photography, then television embeds cinema, then the Internet embeds television, and so on, but typically and apparently seamlessly, by placing the boundaries of these differential embeddings out of sight. The military embedding of Iraq War news coverage is an example of remediation in action, constructing hypermediated images of events that appeared to a mass audience as less mediated and more immediate. Much as the writers of fantastic tales from Homer to Borges and beyond have done, news producers use embedded or hypermediated forms to induce the effect of immediacy and the often unwitting nonobservation of the rhetorical constructedness of these deeply framed narrations. Media embeddings of various sorts are at once manifest and latent, explicit and self-erasing. Embedded reporting owes its recent glamour as a media technique at least in part to this figurative power, but at the same time, its rhetorical oscillation underscores the paradoxical operation of embedded frames.

Systems

Embedding is not only a matter where media and narrative intersect: embeddedness is the necessary status of all systems relative to their environments. We are materially and virtually as well as cognitively embedded within the worlds our observing systems construct for us. Bound by these necessities, we take pleasure in creating scenarios that put us in charge of them. For instance, in the same 2003 *New York Times* column saying that "E is for embed," it is also reported that "Z is for zorbing—a new sport . . . from New Zealand. In zorbing, a person is strapped inside a large sphere, which is itself held inside a larger sphere by a cushion of air . . . and then rolled along the ground or, better yet, downhill."[8] The playful zorber rolling along in concentric spheres may seem to reside quite a distance from the media person embedded in a war machine, but they are nonetheless in comparable formal situations. The journalist as media embed is literally embedded in a troop carrier in a military battalion, and systematically in layers of logistical and informatic mediation, including and culminating in the subordination of his or her civilian status to a military command structure. The zorber is also literally embedded in a material apparatus, but social-systemically, the zorber is allied only to a civilian athletic subculture that has reified embeddedness within a material apparatus for physical kicks.[9]

As Gregory Bateson might say, the zorber has embedded embeddedness within a "play frame." In "A Theory of Play and Fantasy," Bateson explores how social play marks itself off from nonplay by suspending the literal denotation of playful acts, by framing or embedding its actions inside virtual or operational boundaries, such as a demarcated field of play during a match with a demarcated duration.[10] Play puts itself inside a box, stages itself within a field cut out as a play space. For certain games, such as teasing, animals including humans must maintain the communication of the play frame to other players by signaling that their current behaviors are not to be taken seriously. These various examples of communicative embedding expose a paradox at the heart of any meaningful proposition. In the first instance, the significations of things depend not on those things but, like "Ron Reagan, Culture Wars Embed," on the stipulations attached to the box one finds them in. Most James Brown songs are variations of the same basic song structure, but declaring that "Papa's Got a Brand New Bag" makes that particular incremental variation seem especially shiny and new. Besides, whatever box something is currently in, that box is always also embedded within other, more-encompassing boxes, demarcated according to different logics. Meanings are always contingent on this potential for oscillation in context. As Gertrude Stein remarked in *Wars I Have Seen*, "Money is always there but the pockets change."[11]

Systems theory from Bateson to Niklas Luhmann explicitly factors this basal paradoxicality of embedding or observational framing into its epistemological constructions. Neocybernetic epistemology renders discursively explicit what has always been implicit in the relation of literary narratives to the wider world they are embedded in. Narratives are paradoxical play frames that constantly reframe themselves. Second-order systems theory begins precisely when cybernetic discourse embeds itself within its own discourse. For instance, in the 1976 conversation with Stewart Brand, Bateson and Margaret Mead reflect on the recursive turn in cybernetic thinking. Recalling that the engineering phenomenon at the root of cybernetics is the circular recursion of operational feedback in governors and servomechanisms, Brand gets Bateson and Mead to recall how they and their colleagues at the multiyear cross-disciplinary annual forum known as the Macy Conferences were engaged in extending the explanatory range of circular recursion in feedback control devices from mechanical to natural systems. With this broader appreciation of goal-oriented self-reference, the conceptual way is clear to the operational reentry or self-embedding of psychic and social systems.

Cognitive forms proceed from an emergent, ever-shifting, ever-evolving overlapping of living, psychic, and social systems. The philosophical debate over systems theory and its epistemological implications is really about the crisis of classical logic confronted with the chaotic yet deterministic anomalies of circular recursion. Can our intellectual culture supplement or transcend its traditional logical frames so as to factor, in the title of Luhmann's article, "the paradox of observing systems" into its ways of knowing? Are we ready yet to own the constructedness of the real, that is, the self-reference that embeds every observer, not just media embeds, within their observations of the other? Perhaps this epistemological constructivism remains a minority view because it posits a leveling of cognitive authority. The modern scientific observer was precisely *not* embedded in the realm of its objects, and was thus taken to be immunized from self-reference. As Bruno Latour famously argues, the increasing polarization of object and subject distracted modern epistemology from taking due notice of all the embeddedness always already at hand and whose notice is now inescapable in the implosion of "hybrids, half object and half subject, that we call machines and facts."[12] Perhaps the epistemological empire consecrated under modernity still fears to lose its colonies.

The media embed is a late-modern hybrid of machines and facts, a colonized observer maintaining a façade of independence covering the absence of its idealized autonomy. But when it comes to the cognition of the real, we are all epistemological embeds at once inside and outside the stories we tell about the world, at once the subject and the object of our cognitive narrations. I take this to be the gist of some remarks that Bateson makes later in the interview with Stewart Brand. To clarify the development of cybernetic insight into the logic of recursion in observing systems, Bateson sketches a diagram that contrasts "computer science"—first-order cybernetic control theory—with the second-order cybernetic recognition of cognitive embeddedness (Figure 5). Contributing the psychological and anthropological insights of social cyberneticists,

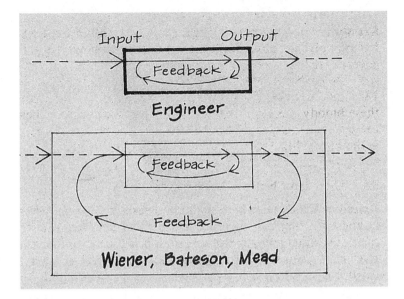

Figure 5. Feedback and the recursion of observation, from Stewart Brand's interview with Gregory Bateson and Margaret Mead, *CoEvolution Quarterly* (Summer 1976).

Bateson and Mead affirm that the observer is to be contained within the frame containing the object to be observed:

> Bateson: Computer science is input-output. You've got a box, and you've got this line enclosing the box, and the science is the science of these boxes. Now, the essence of Wiener's cybernetics was that the science is the science of the whole circuit. . . . Now, there may be boxes inside here, like this, of all sorts, but essentially your ecosystem, your organism-plus-environment, is to be considered as a single circuit.
>
> SB: The bigger circle there . . . .
>
> Bateson: And you're not really concerned with an input-output, but with the events within the bigger circuit, and you are *part of* the bigger circuit. . . .
>
> SB: . . . The engineer is outside the box . . . and Wiener is inside the box.
>
> Bateson: And Wiener is inside the box; I'm inside the box . . .
>
> Mead: I'm inside the box.[13]

Brand's rendering of Bateson's diagram circles around Heinz von Foerster's recently dubbed "cybernetics of cybernetics." First-order cybernetics has already cognized the profundity of feedback mechanisms.

Both mechanical and organic systems with negative feedback circuits can control and regulate their own behaviors. However, when output is coded to be fed back as input, to that extent, output becomes input, and the distinction between them breaks down. A looping circularity reshapes a strictly linear flow. Feedback's paradoxical circularity prefigures another, higher-order recursive circuit, the one that embeds the observer within his or her observations. Bateson's second box shows how second-order systems theory develops from the feedback of feedback as that results from locating the observer both within and without the system to be observed. In true cybernetic observation the border between observing and observed systems shifts to the holistic frame. And to return to matters of popular rhetoric, as a form of systemic embedding, the term *feedback* was grounded in cybernetic discourse long before the current media canonization of *embedding* for their own lexicon. As a popular cybernetic operator providing a general marker of the circular recursion of systems operation, the concept of feedback preceded that of embedding and made explicit the operationality implicit in the latter.

So the current semantic mobility of *embedded* and the *embed* follows from the general form of relation exposed by systemic embeddedness. The epistemological significance of this form is given in the first instance by the differentiation of systems from environments. The forms and processes of embedding differ as one shifts systems reference from biological to psychic to social to technological organizations, and from nonhuman modes of cognition and communication to linguistic, narrative, and digital computational operations. And the general form of relation posited by the embeddedness of systems within their environments is reproduced again *within* systems, within any system complex enough to differentiate itself into subsystems, and then to differentiate its differentiations. Embedding is operationally (not ontologically) fundamental: it names perennial abstract relations of contextualization and containment that determine the very possibility of systems arising, self-maintaining, and reproducing themselves. For psychic and social systems, it names basic operations and relations of sense, cognition, and communication. The embed arrives on the contemporary rhetorical scene directly at the interface of mechanical, organic, and social operations, already invested with the cachet of technoscience. Beyond its media buzz, embedding resonates as a cybernetic trope, a figure ready for narrative duty and preinscribed with systems-theoretical content.

Reentry and Time

In its treatment of cognition as construction, second-order systems theory's claims for the autonomous emergence of knowledge—as opposed to its direct representation—rest on the premise that self-referential closure is the necessary condition of any system capable of producing an observation of its environment. Operational closure is the cognitive loop you do not see—unless you extract it from your blind spot. Put another way, observing systems are always already looped by their own self-referential circularity of operation. Cognitive operations are not linear affairs because the environment contains no transparent medium or mediation, and while there are endless possibilities for connectedness, there is no possible relation of immediacy between minds and messages. But, clearly, there are blind spots into which these contingencies of mediation and cognition easily slip. As with the seeming immediacy of perceptions per se, let alone hypermediated images, such cognitive slips can produce convincing illusions of transparency, of direct reception from without. These experiences can be pleasant and they can be profound, but still, they are seductions. Any corresponding and critical theory of media has to negotiate the operational closures and hence partial blindnesses of every observing system. This evacuation of immediacy—a removal of the ether of cognitive continuity from the constructivist cosmos—may be understood, in a second sense, as a withdrawal of notions of *instantaneity.* Media must also negotiate the contingencies of operational durations, the observing systems' processing times.

Discussions of temporality in second-order systems theory often operate with algorithms devised by British mathematician and logician George Spencer-Brown in *Laws of Form.* This text develops a symbolic calculus of indications enabling an extreme compression of complex worldly affairs into succinct expressions of their formal essentials. It has become a primary text in the line of second-order systems theory extending from von Foerster through Francisco Varela to Luhmann.[14] Our interest here in *Laws of Form* concerns how its consideration of time emerges in tandem with the operation of *reentry,* the self-referential embedding of a form of distinction back into its own indicational space. Luhmann later develops Spencer-Brown's concept of reentry as a cognitive operation specific to psychic and social systems, which must not only develop frames for making distinctions between self and other, but also temporalize their complexity—that is, unfold the density of their operations along temporal axes. They do so by constructing markers that set off past and future time, again following Spencer-Brown, through the interplay of a *memory function* and an *oscillator function.*

The following sections of this chapter walk this neocybernetic line to redescribe certain observations of narrative form—in Gérard Genette's scheme, some matters of *order* and *voice,* in particular, analepsis (flashbacks in story time) and metalepsis (the transgressive looping of narrative levels). Drawing examples from the novel *Mrs. Dalloway* and the film *Eternal Sunshine of the Spotless Mind,* I distinguish and describe how both formal reentries and systemic reentries structure the operations of narrative observation. This approach to narrative mediation aligns the reception and experience of narrative with the wider epistemological constructivism that continues to renovate our general understanding of observation as a creative act. As von Foerster, the thinker who most closely connects Spencer-Brown and Luhmann, observes in 1973 and states properly in the social-systemic plural: "When we perceive our environment, it is we who invent it."[15]

Let us proceed to the densest thicket of *Laws of Form,* chapter 11, "Equations of the Second Degree." Chapter 11 introduces both reentry and time into the operations of the formal calculus. In his famous review first placed in the spring 1970 iteration of the *Whole Earth Catalog,* von Foerster summarizes the chapter as follows:

> In Chapter 11, Spencer Brown tackles the problem of infinite expressions by allowing an expression to re-enter its own space. This calls for trouble, and one anticipates now the emergence of antinomies. Not so! In his notation the classical clash between a simultaneous Nay and Yea never occurs, the system becomes "bi-stable," flipping from one to the other of the two values as a consequence of previous values, and thus generates time! Amongst the many gems in this book, this may turn out to be the shiniest.[16]

The chapter opens by recounting that all the expressions of the calculus discussed so far have been *determinate.* That is, for all prior expressions, a value could be calculated, yielding one and only one of the two possible solutions of the calculus up to this point: the marked state ($\daleth$), which constructs a distinction, or the unmarked state ( ), which suspends or holds open the matter of marking. Solutions of such first-order equations, those without reentry, may be demonstrated "in a finite number of steps" (54). Being finite, every previously permissible function of the calculus comes to a definite and definitive stop at one or the other solution.

Consider this first-order, hence finite, expression in *Laws of Form*, verbalized as "a-cross-b-cross-all." $\overline{\overline{a}\,b}$ It may be taken to encapsulate a situation for which the indication generated by one distinction is embedded in the indication of a second distinction, such that the two distinctions mutually specify each other. Its solution may either preserve or annul the marked states at hand, but cannot yield both states at once. This expression may also be allowed to "generate a step-sequence" so as to be expanded into any number of ever-larger expressions, each an "echelon of alternating a's and b's" of equivalent value (55). Nonetheless, despite their differences in size and detail, all such expressions will still be finite and so determinate. Significantly, in such cases, since their values in the calculus are predetermined and will never change from an initial, determinate value, operational duration does not factor into their outcome.

However, Spencer-Brown asks: "Let us imagine, if we can, that the order to begin the step-sequence is never countermanded, so that the process continues timelessly" (55). His locution already intimates that we are on the verge of mathematical paradox, in that one result of initiating this "timeless" or infinitely recurring process is precisely the advent of time. Jumping slightly ahead of ourselves, we will understand this advent as announcing operational time, the indeterminate duration in which a recursive process unfolds its potentially endless and indefinite cycles. "Now, since this form, being endless, cannot be reached in a finite number of steps . . . we do not expect it to express, necessarily, the same value" (56). An "excursion to infinity" has turned Spencer-Brown's form calculus into a nontrivial machine, a calculator potentially capable of incalculable solutions.

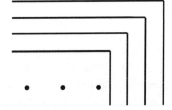

Figure 6. A second-order (infinite) expression from the calculus of distinctions in George Spencer-Brown, *Laws of Form*, chapter 11 (1969).

In the generalized expression given in Figure 6, reentry has entered the picture: "The key is to see that the crossed part of the expression at every even depth is identical with the whole expression, which can thus be regarded as re-entering its own inner space at any even depth" (56). Like Epimenides the Cretan crashing one of Aristotle's logic seminars and smuggling in the possibility of contradictory conclusions, self-reference has entered the calculus in the form of reentry. As a result, "the excursion to infinity . . . has denied us our former access to a complete knowledge of where we are in the form" (58).[17] The previously definitive distinction between the marked and the unmarked states that obtained with the solution of finite expressions has now collapsed. Stated in form notation, this paradox is ¬ = ¬̇, or the marked state equals the unmarked state, which may be restated as: ¬ = . Linguistic analogues to this paradoxical form-calculation are statements such as: "This sentence is false," or "The truth is a lie."

How does Spencer-Brown finesse the self-generated, self-referential dilemma he has placed his calculus into by the excursion to infinity? Right here is where the text of *Laws of Form* lifts off from the inspired plodding of the finite calculus and goes into mathematical orbit, precisely in its determination to stay within the form of the form. As with the invention of imaginary numbers a century earlier to solve the dilemma posed by the need to derive i, the $\sqrt{-1}$, Spencer-Brown proposes to allow an imaginary state of the form. And the upshot of this permission is to make the tacit operation of time within his formal system *explicit*—the time necessary for the subsequent, potentially endless oscillatory loop to flip between marked and unmarked states:

Since ¬ and   represent the only states of the form hitherto envisaged, if we pretend that [¬ =] has a solution, we must allow it to have a solution representing an imaginary state, not hitherto envisaged, of the form.

Time

Since we do not wish, if we can avoid it, to leave the form, the state we envisage is not in space but in time. (It being possible to enter a state of time without leaving the state of space in which one is already lodged.) (58–59)

By adding a temporal dimension to the calculus, one declines the entire formal paradigm of *Laws of Form* into the syntax of operational time.

One brings forth a world primed for the temporalized complexity formulated in the neocybernetic description of observing systems.

Building on *Laws of Form,* the discourse of systems theory has further unfolded the formal repertoire of reentry, the imaginary state, and operational time. One could say that the transit from a classical to a constructivist orientation brings about a comparable declension from static to dynamic form, from ontological being to operational process, supplementing reversible space with irreversible time. To observe observations as ongoing recursions—self-looping processes—demystifies the seductions of immediate or unmediated being. Second-order systems theory has relinquished an epistemology rooted in the metaphysical distinction between subject and object for one based on a corresponding but infinitely richer, decidedly nonmetaphysical distinction between system and environment. The system–environment relation is the product of a specific history, which must be maintained by the system's continuous—and for it, endless—production of its boundary relative to its environment.

Luhmann describes psychic and social systems as interpenetrated in the medium of meaning. Meaning systems self-embed the *form* of their distinction *from* their environment. Put another way, through reentry, both the form–medium and system–environment distinctions recur on the inside of these systems, which can now undergo differentiations into subsystems, forms whose environmental medium is the system as a whole. Such a system can now produce for itself an imaginary state, a heteroreferential invention it calls the environment. Reentering the form of their distinction from their environmental medium, these systems self-constitute an internal medium of meanings from which to produce more complex forms of cognition. This higher complexity is marked precisely by the possibility of distinguishing between self-reference and heteroreference. In addition, the medium of *time* can now be produced within the system and attributed to its environment as well as to its own operations.

Let us confirm this point: the reentry of the form of the system–environment distinction into the cognitive operations of psychic and social systems establishes an internal schema by which they can now construct distinctions between self-referential and heteroreferential observations, and alternate between internal and external and past and future attributions of those cognitive events. Psychic and social systems in which the reentry of form occurs through the processing of linguistic distinctions can now construct their observations as forms placed on a common medium of meanings. In this way, systems theory provides an operational account of both the possibility and the contingency of knowing a world beyond the self. Only by constructing a code through which to cognize a distinction between self and world do we invent for ourselves the form and the experience of a world. In sum, self-referential reentry producing heteroreferential cognition is to second-order systems theory what feedback control was to its first-order cybernetic precursors—the indispensable form of recursive operation on which the new conceptual apparatus pivots.

Luhmann's late essay "The Control of Intransparency" deploys Spencer-Brown's formal repertoire of reentry, time, memory, and oscillation as operational modes for self-referential systems. The essay addresses both a major contingency of reentry—"self-produced indeterminacy"—for those systems that can perform it, and the operational resolution of that contingency through the production of time. "Self-produced indeterminacy" is the systemic analogue to Spencer-Brown's "excursion to infinity," as reentry leads to a loss of "access to a complete knowledge of where we are in the form":

> Translated into system-theoretical terminology, the result of such a re-entry into the system of the distinction between system and environment is that such systems operate in the mode of *self-produced indeterminacy*. As such they reproduce this mode in all they do—as it were as a medium which they have to presume. . . .
>
> Self-produced indeterminacy should only mean that the system operates recursively, and in doing so has to fall back upon past states which it cannot fully remember, and has to anticipate future states about which decisions may be taken only in future presents.
>
> . . . It seems that for the solution of the problem of self-produced indeterminacy and intransparency a *temporalization* of the situation of the system is required.
>
> . . . After the introduction of the re-entry of the distinction into itself, the system, in order to be able to carry on, has to dispose of a memory function and an oscillator function. . . . The system has to identify the state into which it has brought itself, to be able to start from there; and it has to oscillate its indications between marked and unmarked space because it must allow for indeterminacy.[18]

Closely following Spencer-Brown's text, Luhmann treats reentry here as generating self-produced indeterminacy in the observation of *time*. This form of intransparency is, so to speak, the temporal counterpart of spatial or positional intransparency in the respective closures of psychic and social cognitions, the background of indetermination or unmarked states against which we have to select between self- and heteroreferential observations. In the remainder of this chapter, I show that this set of processes and problematics specifically associated with formal and systemic reentry can be closely mapped onto narrative forms and events. Reentry in systems that observe in the mode of meaning is our key for elaborating a neocybernetic redescription of narrative forms and mediums. The reentry of form into the form, the subsequent processing of intransparent distinctions into self and other, memory and oscillator functions, all have their avatars within the narrative realm.

Narrative Observation in *Mrs. Dalloway*

Starting from the structure of the narrative text as its given disciplinary object, narratology proceeds to analyze it through primary distinctions between discourse and diegesis, or text, story, and *fabula*. The discursive and diegetic faces of the narrative sign encode the real conditions of meaning production under which their observing systems—minds and societies—operate. But at the same time, and especially in their fictive or artistic forms, narrative fictions supplement their rehearsals of mundane cognitive events by promising forms of ecstatic release from the enclosure of their actual operations. As with the virtual telepathy of the authorial narrator, narrative signs typically replicate their readers' limits of knowing precisely in order to surpass them. This is where the connection of narrative to formal and systemic reentry comes in. The reader or viewer of a narrative text, as the actual observer of this discursive structure, is invited by the very genre to enter an imaginary cognitive state. Narratives beckon us to reconstruct their virtual structures as the actual traces of other observers, to experience those narrations as observing systems and not just as sequential semiotic structures. For narrative structures to be declined into psychic and social operations, we must accept the invitation to complete their communicative offers, to perform their fictive traces as observing systems under our own, now second-order, observation. Just as its readers or viewers construct a *fabula* and so construe a storyworld *as* a world, so do the text's significations of saying and seeing constitute intuitions of both real and imaginary values, possible and impossible systems of observation. This happy production of a playful excess of observation is, so to speak, the *jouissance* of narrative.

For a short initial example of this manifold of narrative signs for both the indication and the transgression of system operations, let us take the authorial narrator of Virginia Woolf's *Mrs. Dalloway* as the signification of an observing system in spirited but typical excess of mundane operational closures. The novel begins:

> Mrs. Dalloway said she would buy the flowers herself.
>
> For Lucy had her work cut out for her. The doors would be taken off their hinges; Rumpelmayer's men were coming. And then, thought Clarissa Dalloway, what a morning—fresh as if issued to children on a beach.
>
> What a lark! What a plunge! For so it had always seemed to her, when, with a little squeak of the hinges, which she could hear now, she had burst open the French windows and plunged at Bourton into the open air. How fresh, how calm, stiller than this of course, the air was in the early morning; like the flap of a wave; chill and sharp and yet (for a girl of eighteen as she was then) solemn, feeling as she did, standing there at the open window, that something awful was about to happen.[19]

To construct the narrator of this literary text as an observing system is, first, to construct its shifting between self- and heteroreference, and second, to mark how its heteroreference to the storyworld crosses impossibly into the psychic enclosures of its characters. In its self-reference, Woolf's narrator operates as a freestanding external observer, an authorial narrator—the originary producer of a text allowing the construction of a *fabula* from which the narrator stands apart. Then, in its heteroreference, this authorial narrator transgresses psychic closure to render an indirect transcript, more or less transparently or telepathically, of Mrs. Dalloway's thoughts, her fabled "stream of consciousness."

This particular fictive ecstasy—the authorial narrator's discursive oscillations across the border between its self-reference (to its own agency external to the storyworld) and its heteroreference (to characters inside the storyworld)—constitutes the figural narrative situation, or in other words, free indirect discourse.[20] With "Lucy had her work cut out for her," and then, "What a lark! . . . How fresh, how calm," we get externally rendered reports of Clarissa's internal thought stream, largely in her own words, "of course." At once, however, the figural situation commences to fluctuate within its authorial framework between free-indirect and indirect discourse, as when the narrator interpolates parenthetically the external comment "(for a girl of eighteen as she was then)." The parentheses provide literal marks of distinction that indicate the border over which the authorial-figural or self- and heteroreferential shiftings in focalization move between the reporting of external witness and internal thought.

As we reader-observers construe the text so as to burst into its storyworld, our vicarious transit resonates within a complex tableau of virtual boundaries, refracted through the spatial and temporal thresholds of the storyworld. The fluctuations of observational attitude (that is, focalization) just detailed in the story layer continue on, independently of a second oscillation, this time in the time-signatures of those thoughts. The memory of a squeaky hinge carries Clarissa's thoughts back to a late-adolescent summer morning in the town of Bourton. Clarissa Dalloway's plunge out of doors into the fresh morning air of London calls up her once having burst open the French windows at Bourton. A form of past feeling—a feeling then, as now, of heightened anticipation and future possibilities—reenters her present system, as she pulses at the threshold of the (un)knowable developments just around the existential corners of both her past and present moments. In both the text and the fabula of these opening lines, narrative time commences to cascade out of an overlapping and reinforcing set of vigorous formal crossings and recrossings. At the same time that the discursive shifting between authorial and figural situations produces spatial alternations in focalization between external and internal perceptions of the storyworld, the shifting of diegetic locations between Clarissa's London present and Bourton past plays on the chronological order of the story. It initiates a series of analepses, flashbacks seemingly external to the London day of the first or main narrative, to a bygone time of which we will get further partial glimpses and from which we will always return to adjacent moments of *Mrs. Dalloway*'s ongoing day.

But we should also note that, irrespective of the character currently under the narrator's observation, the analepses or time leaps of this novel are always figural-internal rather than authorial-external. We could say that they proceed from and occupy the cognitive subsystems constituted by the characters' signified minds. These flashbacks are programmatically *intra*diegetic, that is, located entirely within the *characters'* memories as internal reconstructions of past experiences. Just as, even during its figural or free-indirect shifts across borders that distinguish characters' psyches, the narration never formally leaves its ultimate closure within the observing frame of the authorial situation, so too that narration never formally displaces the reader from its continuous witness of the ongoing London day of Clarissa Dalloway and her fellow characters.

With some further assistance from Spencer-Brown's *Laws of Form,* let us return to the epistemological implications of these narrative forms. In particular, with free-indirect discourse—or, the figural mode of authorial narration—*textual reentry* enters the narrative situation. Figural narration is produced by reentering the form of authorial narration back into the authorial situation but on the inside of the storyworld; this formal cross momentarily suspends or renders indeterminate the distinction between external narrator and internal character. In the figural narrative situation, authorial narrators seem to abscond from their own narration in favor of the minds of the characters they continue to observe covertly. This impersonal narrator is rendered covert (yet, paradoxically, all the more all-encompassing) by straddling or merging with the two-sided frame between their narrative level and the storyworld over which they narrate. That is, a narration already external to the storyworld is reentered *into* the storyworld as the voicing of a character's unvoiced observations. The storyworld has not been enlarged; the external cognitive boundaries of character and authorial narrator have not changed. Instead, those boundaries have imploded *on the inside.* The space of the storyworld has become thicker with a kind of distributed cognition.

Franco Moretti has noted that, "placed as it is halfway between social *doxa* and the individual voice, free indirect style is a good indicator of their changing balance of forces."[21] Postmodern conditions have further imploded the infolded space of narrative representation, and the development of the cinematic medium has radically altered the forms of narrative voice. Film scholar David Bordwell importantly points out that because "film's lack of deictics (person, tense, mode, etc.) makes it difficult to account systematically for the speaker, situation, and means of enunciation," with film, he prefers "to give the narrational process the power to signal under certain circumstances that the spectator should construct a narrator. . . . [In cinema] the narration . . . creates the narrator."[22] In the midst of these differences in narrative production, however, the cinematic medium has not bypassed but reformed and remediated devices of narrative reentry. Indeed, the modes of narrative reentry show us those aspects of literary and cinematic discourse that are most comparable: flashbacks and flash-forwards, oscillations of external and internal text and *fabula,* fluctuations of narrative level.

Eternal Sunshine of the Spotless Mind

In *Eternal Sunshine of the Spotless Mind,* the form of cinematic narration fully reenters the diegetic space of this quite loopy storyworld. In this romantic technoscience fantasy, at the Lacuna Clinic, unhappy lovers Clementine Kruczynski and Joel Barish have all of their memories of each other—bad and good—wiped out once and for all, or so the clinic claims. In this narration, the cinematic apparatus cuts across the multiple boundaries of the outer storyworld, the waking mind of Joel Barish, and the inner memory world to which he gains increasing access the more he unconsciously fights against the erasures to which he had thought he wanted to submit himself. Cinematic metafiction for the masses, *Eternal Sunshine* pushes the multiple reentries of its multiple levels toward a series of metalepses, moments when Joel's inner and outer worlds both intrude on the other. Textual reentry in the modernist figural narration of a work such as *Mrs. Dalloway* can be thought of as a station on the way to the techniques of diegetic reentry brought to bear on the cinematic text of *Eternal Sunshine.*

With the movie's opening frames and then for several episodes, Joel comes forward as a character and a character-bound voice-over narrator with no temporal distance from his waking actions. That is, his voice-over commentaries are simultaneous with the film's nonverbal narration of his external activities within the waking storyworld. A habitual writer and illustrator of personal diaries, Joel provides self-commentaries in the mode of diary entries concurrent with their content. Over an initial two-day period of outer story time, alongside subjective glimpses of his perceptions, he comments simultaneously with and from within the cinematic presentation of his waking actions. One comes to understand that Joel's conscious grasp of his immediate situation has been suspended by the Lacuna procedure he has just undergone. The larger story begins to unfold with the long-delayed movie credits, which start to roll directly over what we retrospectively recognize as the cinematic narration's first abrupt analepsis, to the prior evening when Joel began undergoing that nightlong procedure. Eventually we re-mark the previous chronological sequence, from the moment Joel awakes, as taking place the morning *after* the completion of the procedure now beginning. From this point onward, rolling forward on the momentum of its first analeptic loop, the narration implodes on the inside of its forms.

Using our laws of narrative forms, we can say that the cinematic narration begins, as it must, by marking the formal distinction that creates the narrative space of its primary mise-en-scène. Within that initial observing frame, Joel wakes up and comes forward as main character and sole voice-over narrator. Several episodes then ensue through an unremarkable set of normal cinematic forms. All this is broadly comparable to the literary presentation of characters by an authorial narrator that can cross over into its characters' thoughts. Initially, the two diegetic levels of the cinematic situation shift back and forth in a normal way between external observations and character-centered thoughts and perceptions, and a single boundary forms between them, the border between the external narration of the storyworld within which Joel is a character and the internal voice-over narration or cinematic soliloquy running in Joel's head. But then, as we noted, the cinematic text folds over the temporal order of its storyworld with an external analepsis that reaches back to the evening before the previous scene of awakening. Crossing its own initial temporal boundary, the text cancels for the moment its initial time frame. The form of this external cross then begins to reverberate within Joel's inner world, as Joel is now in a drug-induced stupor having his brain invaded and specific memories wiped out by the Lacuna procedure. The mise-en-scènes begin to cross between the outer events within Joel's apartment—his currently present environment within his storyworld—and the realized dream and memory events of his unconscious mind, the internal diegesis I am calling Joel's memory world.

The form calculation of this narration now resembles that of the figural narrative situation, in that the boundary between the external cinematic observer and the observed character has been reentered into the narrative.[23] But there is a crucial difference corresponding to the cinematic rather than literary contingencies of the current medium. In this instance, the reentry occurs not on the inside of an external literary narrator's storyworld, but on the inside of the character-narrator created by the cinematic narration. While remaining character-bound, Joel's observations and voice-over narration shift to an extradiegetic situation relative to his memory world, and to a position of increasing temporal distance from the diegetic locations of the memories embedded within his increasingly lucid dream of those memories. While he is voice-over narrating the events of his memory world, Joel is in his external present relative to their internal past.

In one scene of diegetic interaction between his drug-induced dream state and the Lacuna-provoked memory world interspersed with it, a moment of metaleptic overload is wonderfully staged by the remediation within the cinematic screen of a TV screen whose embedded image is sutured directly to its embedding frame. Specifically, with a dream of his memory world set in his apartment currently occupying the full cinematic frame, the picture on the TV set merges almost seamlessly into the picture on the screen of the room containing the set. This is not the last moment of cinematic metalepsis in *Eternal Sunshine* that induces diegetic merger rather than interference.

Concurrent with and reaching backward from Joel's ongoing Lacuna procedure, all further analepses are staged internally—within the memory world of Joel's dream state—rather than, as with the initial loop from his morning after to his evening before, externally by the cinematic narration per se. With wild oscillations amplifying the authorial-figural model we examined in *Mrs. Dalloway,* the cinematic text cross-cuts the narration of the Lacuna procedure with the narration of the events leading up to his decision to have the procedure done. And from there, we are led along as Joel follows the procedure's analeptic itinerary, working backward from the least to most distant memories of the love affair, from the painful incidents of the recent breakup to the earlier, sunnier moments.

To reiterate, in the literary medium, figural narration defaults to the gap or blind spot in the diegesis between the character and the authorial narrator, and results when the form of authorial narration is reentered into the authorial situation. But in this cinematic instance, a comparable situation of discursive interference occupies instead a gap in the memory world within the main character's mind, such that the form of the distinction between his outer environment and psychic system is *reentered into his psychic system.* In other words, once Joel is under the Lacuna procedure, a third narrative level emerges as a second boundary develops *inside* his mind, the boundary between his inner awareness of being presently under the procedure and his increasingly interactive witness of the past memories that the procedure is currently mapping in order to delete. The cinematic narration—the outermost inside of the narrative forms at play—gathers all this together and plays with diegesis interference at two different levels: (1) the spillover of present outer events into Joel's inner recollections, and (2) the spillover of Joel's inner awareness of his outer predicament into the past events of his memory world. However, these narrative reentries are not infinite; the paradoxes at play are not bottomless. And thus we can hold onto a sense of where we are in their procession.

One payoff for tracking these borders carefully comes in the scene from his memory world in which Joel and Clem wander happily through fallen leaves of a field in autumn, while Joel converses with her lucidly about the dilemma his entire memory of her faces from the ongoing Lacuna procedure. On a dare from this dream Clem, dreaming Joel pulls back his eyelids and induces a metalepsis that doubles his present cognition and carries it fully across from the inner memory world of their autumn stroll to the outer storyworld of his apartment, where he lies now blinking his eyes—like a patient whose surgical anesthesia wears off too soon—semiconscious of the Lacuna process he is undergoing, before snapping back to the leafy fields of dream.

To add this up: first, the external cinematic observing system produces Joel as a character within the *fabula*. Then, depicted as an observing system in its own right, the psychic system coordinated with the character Joel replicates the machinery of cinematic observation. Joel is now virtually an embedded systemic replication of the cinematic apparatus. And on the outside of this inner recursion, the Lacuna technology itself is a mirror reversal of the cinematic apparatus, a machine for erasing rather than producing memory images. Then, within Joel, as he undergoes the Lacuna procedure, another movie starts to roll, one in which he works to reverse or delete the procedure's deletions. He becomes lucid within the procedure, that is, he becomes conscious of being unconscious. It is as if another subsystem has differentiated itself, one for which Joel is now the observer dwelling in *its* environment, and over which, as the director of his own movie, it becomes possible for him to exert some control. Like Mary, in Octavia Butler's *Mind of My Mind,* learning how to control her newly emergent psychic shield, Joel learns on the fly how to double-cross the operation he is under. His awareness shifts between inner and outer environments with present lucidity regarding both his dreaming state and the Lacuna procedure's ongoing attack on his Clementine memories.

In the end, Joel's fantastic ability to observe at both inner and outer psychic boundaries allows him to solicit the assistance of his good memories of Clementine toward their own preservation from the effects of the Lacuna procedure, which he had initiated not out of desire, it would now seem, but out of despair in reaction to the discovery that Clem had already erased *him*. By doubling Clem's earlier desperate gesture, he stumbles on the rediscovery of why he fell in love with her in the first place. We come to realize that his impulse to skip work and go to Montauk that first morning already signifies the breakdown and failure of the Lacuna procedure and the eventual success of a plan for evading it, a plan that his lucid unconscious had hatched while undergoing it the night before. In the end, the love story spirals around on itself and starts over at a different place. The return of the discourse to a dream memory of its own point of origin is an emblem either of thoughtless lovers perpetually chasing each other's tails, or perhaps, of Joel's having gotten the kinks out of his own feelings.

I prefer the latter, sentimental but hopefully recuperative reading of *Eternal Sunshine*'s love story as itself an allegory of my larger thesis regarding second-order systems theory's epistemological, perhaps epochal, recuperation of self-reference and recursive forms. Ever since the first oral or epic poet told a story that embedded one storytelling character inside a story told by yet another character, forms of narrative self-reference have been hiding in plain sight. The recent development of concepts by which to recognize the self-referential nature of cognition altogether would seem to resonate with the equally recent recognition of narrative art as a medium for the staging of recursive forms. The multiplication of such narrative intricacies in postmodern texts runs parallel with the rise of a systems-theoretical discourse of observation that is actually adequate to the complexity of the art. Once the discourse of cybernetic feedback was set in place at mid-twentieth century, another stage was set, both formally and historically, for the neocybernetic discourse of reentry. Thus, metafictional and neocybernetic wisdoms go hand in hand. Loopings are the way we move forward in this world, by turning about in feedback circuits until we generate a cognitive excess and get somewhere else.

Narrative Time

Systemic operations entrain the notion of time. Whereas structures are temporally indeterminate, autopoietic systems take time, they operate in time. Moreover, they *make* time: as the product of their own productions, observing systems construct the time of their own observations. In Luhmann's terminology, they temporalize their own complexity.[24] For systems capable of observing time, time emerges in the first place as a repercussion or contingency of their own self-referential operations. Systems time, in short, is an emergent construction specific to the system that produces it and bound up with the recursive self-production of that system. For instance, this operational dynamic can account for the standard distinction between subjective and objective time, "experienced time" and "clock time." At any given moment, time consciousness registers the present phenomenal state of a psychic system whose very ongoing product is the self-perception of consciousness. Clock time is no less a systemic production, but one that social systems generate and communicate through technological mediations, through a broadcasting of collective temporal standards allowing the social synchronization of psychic systems. But as we are all aware, any psychic system is at liberty, at its own social peril, to desynchronize itself from the collective clock.

This distinction between phenomenological and social time has affinities with the narratological distinction between discourse and diegesis, between the reversible time of the telling and the irreversible chronology of the *fabula*—the tale as embedded in the forward temporality of its storyworld. The analogy holds enough to bridge our discussion back to narrative theory proper, but starts to unravel if we consider that, over and above the order and time play of a narrative discourse, the temporality imputed to a *fabula* or storyworld is ultimately not social time but natural time, time abstracted from social and psychic mediations—time per se in its simple vacuity. But while thermodynamic entropy sends time forward for physical systems, autopoietic systems generate their own time. "Real time" is precisely and merely what we blindly indicate nowadays by casual uses of that phrase: the thoroughly mediated experience of pseudosimultaneity constructed by the momentary synchronization of psychic, social, and technological systems.

How can we bring these operational matters of systems time to bear on matters of narrative time? Genette comments: "The narrative text, like every other text, has no other temporality than what it borrows, metonymically, from its own reading."[25] Indeed, observations of a text's temporal and other significations come to pass only in its reading—*reading* being the standard term under which the systemic operationality of the observation of narrative structures is unknowingly acknowledged and thereby removed from critical awareness. The operating of narrative (that is, of narrative structures) by narrative observers (that is, by observing systems turned toward narrative structures) and the systemic contingencies of reading as the particular operation of an observing system—indeed, of multiple and multiply interpenetrated observing systems—are often not observed. Let us briefly remove the brackets from the operationality of narrative observation, and redescribe systems-theoretically what occurs when reading. What sorts of things occur when the ongoing observing of a psychic system capable of taking its time to produce perceptions, intuitions, interpretations, and so forth, posits a narrative text—a complex semiotic structure circulating within the literary subsystem of a social system, within which it stands as a communicative offer of a narrative kind—as an environmental entity immediately adjacent to itself and so available for sustained scrutiny?

A *narrative* text will carry a selection and sequence of signifiers intended to represent temporal durations and relations of certain sorts. On the face of it, this just means that whatever the events under narration may be and however their narration proceeds, a narrative text automatically thematizes temporality. We already assume that in order to be imagined to have occurred, those events will be thought to *take time* of some sort. These structures of represented time are the proper terrain of Genette's structural narratology, in which narrative temporality is generated as an article of analytical specification with regard to order, duration, and frequency precisely by dividing observation of the text by the fundamental theoretical distinction into discourse and diegesis, narrative signifiers and narrative signifieds. But as Brian Richardson points out, this distinction is "mimetically grounded."[26] It presupposes that such textual signifiers represent rather than trigger the reader's construction of the storyworld. Notwithstanding the utility of the standard discourse/ story distinction, its conceptual integrity rests on the possibility of stabilizing a temporally coherent representation of the story. But that representation must emerge from the processing of a narrative discourse that is typically far from consistent in its temporal ordering of narrated events.

Standard narratological procedures with regard to story time confront the structural regress of their own semiotic representationalism.

But as with Nicholas Royle's offer to deconstruct the structural descriptions of narration and focalization, the mere deconstruction of narrative time is all too easy, and does not displace the structuralist nexus that it deconstructs.[27] A more productive move is to redescribe the narrative text systems-theoretically as a semiotic structure embedded in a nexus of systemic considerations. From this angle, narrative time is a particular epiphenomenon of systems time, first of all, the time of reading. In whatever way things stand with the structure of its temporal significations, reading a narrative text will take a certain amount of time—enough time at least that the duration of its observing system's engagement with it will take on a significance of its own. With reference to Genette's mode of analyzing narrative duration, this is neither "narrative time" (the quantity of discursive signifiers) nor "story time" (the signified duration of the diegetic events), but *reading time,* the operative temporality or "real duration" of an observing system in contiguous processual simultaneity with the narrative discourse its observations construct.

In the reception of a narrative text, much will depend on how its observing system perceives its time of reading alongside and as informing the signified times of the text. One measure of the text's aesthetic efficacy with a particular reader will be the extent to which his or her perception of reading time is canceled out or written over by the individual's *intuition*— the "imagined perception, that is, the self-induced simulation of perception"—of the story.[28] The reading mind crosses over from its own systems time and into the intuition of the narrative time of the storyworld induced by the text under observation. In *Art as a Social System,* Luhmann notes regarding this embeddedness of aesthetic intuition within the operations of psychic systems: "Only in the form of intuition does art acquire the possibility of constructing imaginary worlds within the life-world while remaining dependent on triggering perceptions (not least, the reading of texts)" (7). So we have a recursion of temporal frames: narrative time always occurs as embedded within the systems time of its observer. The construction of the reading system's own temporality frames the narrative observer's construction of the *fabula*—the story time of the storyworld. The systemic structure of this epistemological framing suggests that narrative time constitutes an allegory of reading time. The structures of narrative time compose an allegory of the operations of systems time.

Luhmann develops an "operative approach to the temporality of systems."[29] A few passages of this discussion can suggest how narrative time thematizes systems time. To begin with, Luhmann states: "In complex systems, time is the basis of the pressure to select. . . . Selection enlists time in order to maintain itself in an already temporalized environment" (42). Let us narrow our systems reference to the psychic system. In this case, its production—consciousness—demands an ongoing selection of evanescent events, a "train of thought" that must proceed along (by selecting) a path of differentiations: "An action does not remain an information; an event does not remain an event. Temporalized elements cannot be reinforced by repetition; they are determined from the outset to connect to *something different*" (47). That the operation of systems demands an ongoing selection of differential elements that enable the connection of event to event from moment to moment suggests another level of appeal or allure exercised by narrative structures for the psychic system (besides, as we have previously noted, the *jouissance* of imagining the opening up of psychic closure). Narrative texts—stories of any sort—come to the mind preprogrammed with a sequence of differential semiotic selections. The literary narrator already renders into discourse a train of signified observations that reading can process with no further ado (as attested by phenomenological criticism) as an intuition of consciousness. Cinematic narration only augments the fascination felt in the psychic system by compounding the layers of semiotic text (its multiple visual, aural, and textual bands) and automating its temporal unfolding of narrative communication.

Luhmann's discussion of autopoietic temporality in *Social Systems* includes this proviso regarding the temporality of structures self-organized by systems:

> The actual temporality of structures and processes requires a more precise determination. It would be wrong simply to understand structures as atemporal and processes as temporal. The oppositions of static versus dynamic or constant versus changing are equally unsuitable. The difference between structure and process reconstructs the original (= environmentally conditioned) difference between reversibility and irreversibility within a time that is ordered irreversibly.
>
> Structures capture the reversibility of time because they hold open a limited repertoire of possibilities for choice. One can negate structures, or change

them, or with their aid gain security for changes in other respects. Processes, by contrast, mark the irreversibility of time. They are composed of irreversible events. They cannot run backwards. . . . Processes (and this defines the concept of process) result from the fact that concrete selective events build one upon the other temporally. (44)

It would strain our adaptation of systems theory to narratology to insist that *reading* "can negate structures, or change them." Crossing out or revising the text in hand is always possible, but unless one is the author of that text in the process of composing its form, doing so flouts the rules of the narrative game. We reach a threshold where we would need to change our systems reference from the psychic systematics of the temporality of reading to the social systematics of the temporality of narrative productions and of the circulation of narrative communications. At the level of social systematics, the narrative observer can always "negate structures, or change them" by drawing up a different syllabus, rejecting one narrative's communicative offer or selecting it over another. Systems theory easily comprehends and encompasses shifts of that sort, but they would take us entirely out of narratology.

However, if we maintain our framing of Luhmann's theoretical abstractions within the context of narrative reading, we would say that the systems time of reading is irreversible. A narrative text can be read only in the irreversible time of the event of that contemplation. But at the same time, because the text is itself an extended structure, the irreversible temporal sequence of events constituting its observing can always turn back to a previous passage, reattend to a prior selection of its discursive structure, and jump forward once again. The reading system can emplot its analytical course by choosing the sequence of its attention. And all of these processual options for the reading system can and do reenter the form of the narrative text itself through the play of anachrony at the level of narrative discourse. Textual anachrony is the narrative allegory of the reversible time of structures, while the chronology of the *fabula* is the narrative allegory of the irreversible time of processes and systems operation.

Certain narratives are especially apt at lifting this systemic operation on reversible structures and irreversible processes up to the letter of the text. Seymour Chatman has analyzed how sustained backward narratives proceed either episodically, like *Memento,* or continuously, like

Time's Arrow or "Spiegelgeschichte."[30] In normal analeptic passages or flashback scenes, time reversals of lesser or greater extent are usually framed episodes, and thus subordinated to the "frame tale" or first narrative within which the analepses are embedded, and which anchors the progressive temporality of the *fabula*. However, with *Memento*, the analeptic movement is sustained through multiple temporal recursions following each other systematically and without superordinate framing. The reverse narrative *is* the first narrative.

Embedded within and subordinated to *Memento*'s first narrative, being the reverse sequence of color episodes, the black-and-white scenes move forward in past story time from scene to scene. But taken altogether, relative to the time and extent of the reverse first narrative, the black-and-white scenes are all analeptic, chronologically prior to the point when they connect to the story time of the *fabula*-in-reverse. Nevertheless, the sequence of these embedded scenes marks the reassertion of the systems time of the *viewing* of the reversal of first-narrative time. Per Krogh Hansen has introduced the notion of "virtual fabula" to name the forward temporality of the reader's or viewer's construction of reverse narratives.[31] We could say that the portion of the narrative *fabula* embedded in the black-and-white scenes of *Memento* encodes or alludes to, without precisely representing, the virtual *fabula* or irreversible system time of cognizing *Memento*'s predominantly reversed discourse. Sometimes it takes an unnatural narrative device such as reverse narration to assist the diagnosis or delineation of otherwise unconscious or unobserved processes of narrative observation. As Lenny says at the end, or is it the beginning, of *Memento:* "We all need mirrors to remind us who we are."

4 OBSERVING *ARAMIS,*

OR THE LOVE OF TECHNOLOGY

Objects and Projects in Gilbert Simondon and Bruno Latour

The Technical Object

Due in part to the theoretical attentions of Gilles Deleuze and Bernard Stiegler, Gilbert Simondon's secondary doctoral thesis, *On the Mode of Existence of Technical Objects,* published in 1958, has been resuscitated in recent years.[1] At midcentury, Simondon presents a philosophy of technology with what may be retrospectively identified as a postmodern ethical bent: "Recognition of the modes of existence of technical objects must be the result of philosophic consideration; what philosophy has to achieve in this respect is analogous to what the abolition of slavery achieved in affirming the worth of the individual human being."[2] Simondon's nonideological materialism, his orientation to concrete technical objects, is in pointed contrast to the dystopian tones one finds in the more famous contemporary work of Jacques Ellul, *The Technological Society,* published in France in 1954. A Christian philosopher and social critic, Ellul develops cautionary arguments against technological domination by constructing an ineluctable ahuman spirit to inveigh against, called *technique,* defined as "the *totality of methods rationally arrived at and having absolute efficiency.* . . . Technique must reduce man to a technical animal, the king of the slaves of technique."[3] In an odd clash of master-slave scenarios, Simondon would liberate the subject status of technical objects, whereas Ellul would deliver humanity from enslavement to the principle of their modern proliferation.

Releasing nonhuman objects from merely instrumental or utilitarian consideration, as well as from totalizing allegories of machinic tyranny, Simondon also prefigures what Michel Serres and Bruno Latour will develop under the terms *quasi-object* and *quasi-subject*—a rigorous loosening and renetworking of ontological relations previously cordoned off by classical notions of human subjects and nonhuman objects.[4] In keeping with an enlarged ethics of the technical quasi-object, Simondon's thesis posits something like a technological afterlife: "Many abandoned technical objects are incomplete inventions which remain as an open-ended virtuality and could be taken up once more and given new life in another field according to the profound intention which informs them, that is, their technical essence."[5] The notion that abandoned technical objects persist in a state of virtual suspension, awaiting "new life in another field," strongly brings to mind Bruno Latour's singular writing practice in a book originally published in 1993, *Aramis, or the Love of Technology.*

This "Aramis" is an acronym for *Agencement en Rames Automatisées de Modules Indépendants dans les Stations,* "arrangement in automated trains of independent modules in stations." "Aramis" names the failed prototype for a Parisian PRT, a personal rapid transit system to supplement the Métro by crossing the subway with the automobile. The regional authority that supervised the Aramis project commissioned Professor Latour to produce a sociotechnical analysis of Aramis's on-again, off-again development and sudden end.[6] After completing that commission, Latour compiled *Aramis* in part out of materials—copious historical and technical documents and numerous interviews—gathered for the official report. But he went much further, performing not a technological but a discursive and novelized resurrection of this abandoned project. Briefly put, Latour runs a concrete test on actor-network theory (ANT) and on his wider argument that *society* should be observed as composed not just of human persons but also of nonhuman things—quasi-objects corresponding to quasi-subjects—and that natural objects as well as technological artifacts deserve social representation, a place at the table alongside human beings. As a kind of exploded sociotechnical novel, *Aramis* takes this test through the mode of literary narrative.

Aramis frequently elicits two nineteenth-century British literary works involving the development and dismantling of technologies, Mary Shelley's *Frankenstein* and Samuel Butler's *Erewhon.* It constructs a series of literary frames through which its historical and theoretical materials are raised to another level altogether. In his preface, Latour sketches some of how *Aramis* is to accomplish this literary elevation. The invented narrative proceeds as "a young engineer is describing his research project and his sociotechnological initiation. His professor offers a running commentary" (x). It is important to register this reading instruction, that not Latour himself but his fictional alter ego, Professor Norbert H., is to be taken as the author of the text's sociotechnical commentaries. The author Latour places Norbert as character-bound internal mouthpiece next to the novel's nominal character-bound narrator, the anonymous Young Engineer. Conversations between Norbert and the young engineer are always reported by this student narrator; however, the sociotechnical commentaries are always set apart from that narration. Latour arranges to have it several ways—to be at once the literary author of a fictional narrative and the scholarly author of a fictional nonfictional discourse. Norbert displaces as well as voices Latour's own analyses of the Aramis affair. Norbert's segmented commentaries render theoretical interventions both internal to and broadly detachable from the narrative: they are at once invented meditations to be read against the young engineer's skeptical remarks and entries for a general primer in ANT. This innovative refraction of the kind of professional writing Latour does elsewhere in his proper persona licenses these passages for melodramatic heightening over and above Latour's own propensity for rhetorical indulgence. Embedded within and so contextualized by the young engineer's first-person accounts, these simulacra of "academese" give Latour's own lyrical moments of high theorizing further poetic license. Through Norbert, he both mimes and transcends the "objective" commentary of regular scholarship.

The reading instructions of the preface continue: "The (invisible) author adds verbatim accounts of real-life interviews along with genuine documents, gathered in a field study carried out from December 1987 to January 1989. Mysterious voices also chime in and, drawing from time to time on the privileges of prosopopoeia, allow Aramis to speak" (x). With these devices, Latour gives Aramis a lease on a literary afterlife, manifested in the volatile medium of narrative writing. He succeeds in producing a veritable work of literature in the grand tradition of baggy monsters, as it were, a *Moby Dick* for urban transit systems. I do not attempt to unfold *Aramis* in all its multifarious detail, but I track its opening movements up to the point that Aramis the PRT system is granted voice, while describing some of the narrative and figurative considerations mobilized by Latour's authorial gambits. In the spirit of Latour's insistence on the heterogeneity of social ensembles, I conclude with some methodological and systems-theoretical issues for the philosophy and sociology of technology.

Objects and Projects

Further parallels between the Simondon and Latour texts concern their mutual placing of the interrelations of machines and humans on the same plane of being.[7] The ostensible similarities in their respective philosophies of technology are immediately noticeable in a comparison of programmatic statements made in Latour's preface and Simondon's introduction, respectively. In the preface to *Aramis,* for instance, Latour asks: "Can we make the human sciences capable of comprehending the machines they view as inhuman, and thus reconcile the educated pubic with bodies it deems foreign to the social realm?" He then frames the text of *Aramis* accordingly: "I have sought to offer humanists a detailed analysis of a technology sufficiently magnificent and spiritual to convince them that the machines by which they are surrounded are cultural objects worthy of their attention and respect" (vii–viii). In a comparable passage from the introduction to his text on the technical object, Simondon declares: "The opposition established between the cultural and the technical and between man and machine is wrong and has no foundation. . . . It uses a mask of facile humanism to blind us to a reality that is full of human striving and rich in natural forces. This reality is the world of technical objects, the mediators between man and nature" (11). Writing a generation earlier than Latour, Simondon is, if anything, harder on traditional humanists for their bigotry against technology. But he, too, as Latour does, fashions himself as an intercessor on behalf of technical beings, as an advocate "who can achieve an understanding of technical reality and introduce it to our culture . . . an organization engineer who is, as it were, a sociologist or psychologist of machines, a person living in the midst of this society of technical beings as its responsible and creative conscience" (14).

Viewed in large strokes, Latour's *Aramis* would seem to run on the rails of Simondon's philosophy of technology. But when the letter of Simondon appears in *Aramis*, which happens precisely once, a third of the way through the text, it serves instead to highlight a fundamental discrepancy between the primary topics of their respective attention.

The passage in question occurs in the midst of one of Norbert's commentaries (the significance of its sans serif font is explained below). The reference to Simondon comes in a footnote placed on Norbert's terminology:

> **In the first place, a project isn't one project. It's taken as a whole or as a set of disconnected parts, depending on whether circumstances are favorable or unfavorable.**
>
> **In the first place it's abstract,* since each element, once drawn in, once "interested," pursues its own goals and tries to conform as little as possible to the common translation. It becomes concrete only gradually, if it can count as one in the eyes of all its users. . . .**
>
> ***In Gilbert Simondon's sense; see Du mode d'existence des objets techniques (Paris: Aubier, 1958; rpt. 1989).** (106)

This passage stands out in *Aramis* as an odd moment. For one, Simondon's technical terms of *abstract* and *concrete,* through which he builds his primary discourse regarding the increasing *concretization* of the technical object as a measure of its technical refinement, never recur in the text of *Aramis* and have no ongoing purchase. Norbert briefly transposes Simondon's categories for the technical object to the considerations that control the discourse of *Aramis,* but they are not really appropriate. The rigor of Simondon's terms is lost by that transposition.

The Simondon reference instead underscores Latour's reformulation of the Aramis system as a technological topic. In short, the system that Aramis is meant to become never gains existence as an *object.* Rather, "Aramis" is a perfunctory name by which to gather up a disjointed *project* for the creation of an object or ensemble of objects, but one that never succeeds in becoming realized, that is, fully operational as a working transport system under Paris. In other words, Latour's *Aramis* is devoted to a thorough description of the mode of existence of the technical *project.*[8] Moreover, by giving a sole footnote to Simondon on the basis of a passing glance at his technical terminology, the text of *Aramis* may imply that Simondon's discourse on the technical object is itself an "incomplete invention," and that what it needs for its further development is a transfusion of the sociology that the text of *Aramis* will bring to the issue. So Simondon's *Mode* also counts as "an open-ended virtuality" that "could be taken up once more and given new life in another field according to the profound intention which informs" it. But for this to happen, Simondon's notion of "technical essence"—the soul of the abandoned technical object that would persist awaiting reincarnation in a new machine—will have to submit to some doctrinal deprogramming.

Norbert's commentary is quite blunt on this point: **"There is no such thing as the essence of a project. Only finished products have an essence. For technology, too, 'existence precedes essence'"** (48). This is an important matter of debate between Norbert and the young engineer, who is at first content to believe in technical essences as a way to resolve the question they are pursuing together regarding whether the Aramis system as originally conceived was ever feasible. At one point, Norbert barks at the young engineer, "You aren't born feasible or infeasible; you become so" (122). In comparing the Aramis project to its successful if relatively simpleminded brother, VAL—a semiautomated transportation system developed by the same firm, which does succeed in becoming an operational object—the young engineer reverts to the notion of technical essence in narrating his resistance to Norbert's thesis against it:

> On the one hand, the engineers didn't want Aramis to be downgraded; they held to its essence come hell or high water—though they had progressively improved the essence of VAL. On the other hand Norbert, a perfectly preserved existentialist in the year 1988, was asserting that existence preceded essence; the absolute cynicism of his translation model looked to him like the only source of certainty and morality. (122)

In staging these philosophical debates within *Aramis*, the wider point is that in order to bring technical essences into some mode of objective existence, sociotechnical networks of human and nonhuman actors must carry out negotiations *with each other* to construct them as such. This "translation model" of technical being is cynical only in the eyes of an observer, such as Jacques Ellul, subscribed to a technological essentialism. *Aramis* aims to demystify the misplaced concreteness of the alternative "diffusion model," by which technologies are thought to be conceived of full-blown, autonomous, and self-propelling essences. Ellul argues that "technique is autonomous with respect to economics and politics. . . . Technique's own internal necessities are determinative. Technique has become a reality in itself, self-sufficient . . . . There can be no human autonomy in the face of technical autonomy."[9] In *Aramis*, Norbert sarcastically invokes Ellul as a chief perpetrator of the diffusion model: **"The project engineers would light candles to Saint Ellul—never**

mind that he's a Protestant—if it would help Aramis lose a little of its discouraging reversibility" (127).

At the same time, *Aramis* attempts to enchant science and technology studies by a detour through the mode of literary creation. The vigorous repartee of Norbert and the young engineer is one of the conceits through which Latour dramatizes serious methodological and ontological points. Norbert makes one of these points early in the text:

> In the beginning, there is no distinction between projects and objects. The two circulate from office to office in the form of paper, plans, departmental memos, speeches, scale models, and occasional synopses. . . . The observer of technologies has to be very careful not to differentiate too hastily between signs and things, between projects and objects, between fiction and reality. (24)

From this it follows that the reality of the failure of Aramis to become real can be most effectively conveyed by translating the virtual fictions and other inscribed traces of its project phase into the medium of the deliberate fiction Latour elaborates to frame his scientifictional tale.

The Orchestration of *Aramis*

Reviving or reinventing a locution coined by American publisher Hugo Gernsback in the 1920s, Latour notes that the "hybrid genre I have devised for a hybrid task is what I call *scientifiction*" (ix).[10] Conversant in a multitude of scholarly, technical, and theoretical idioms, Latour's scholarship transcends disciplinary boundaries and reductive categorizations. Among his competencies is a considerable preparation in literary matters. The preface to *Aramis* explicitly engages with narrative issues: "Can we turn a technological object into the central character of a narrative, restoring to literature the vast territories it should never have given up—namely, science and technology?" (vii). Underscoring his academic collaborations with and writings on American novelist Richard Powers, Latour notes that *Aramis* "was published too soon for me to use the treasure trove of narrative resources developed by Richard Powers" (x) in *Galatea 2.2,* published in 1995.[11] Nonetheless, "Helen," the sentient artificial intelligence, the digital Galatea that centers Powers's novel, "is Aramis' unexpected cousin" (x).

As we have noted, as a hybrid work of discursive art, *Aramis* describes itself to some extent and, through the character of Norbert H., provides its own gloss. Nonetheless, Latour himself and those few critics who have addressed its literary aspects have focused largely on matters of *genre*: is *Aramis* worthy of being called a novel? If so, is it a work of science fiction, a detective story, a hybrid genre called "scientifiction," or a postmodern pastiche? Whatever the case, narrative theory would suggest a shift of focus to matters of *mode* and ask instead what may be said about the structure of its discourse, the line of its *fabula,* and the stylistic innovations that punctuate the text. At the least, *Aramis* is a not merely an academic exposition but a *narrative.* As such, it proceeds in a mode of composition potentially indifferent to the distinction between fiction and nonfiction. How may the narrative forms of *Aramis* be described?

First of all, the text of *Aramis* is woven from ten distinct elements that provide different kinds of discursive content. Three are *historical:* (1) documents, (2) interview excerpts, and (3) photographs. Five are *expository:* (4) the preface, giving the author's description and justification of the text; (5) figures, illustrating various processes of the Aramis system and phases of the project; (6) the glossary, which elucidates actual persons, events, firms and organizations, and technical objects and processes; (7) footnotes; and (8) the "running commentary," what Norbert terms "a little sociology manual" (11). Although these passages of commentary are to be read as voiced by a fictional character, their matter is to be taken, by and large, as straightforward scholarly argument. The remaining two elements are properly *fictive:* (9) the young engineer's character-bound (first-person) account of his internship with Norbert, and (10) the "mysterious voices" scripted to various quasi-objects of the project.

In addition to these ten discursive elements, the text employs typographical devices to sort out the "discursive modes [that] have to be kept separate if the scientifiction is to be maintained" (x). Whereas the historical and expository elements are largely given in sans serif fonts or Courier typefaces, the fictive elements are presented in serifed fonts— the young engineer in roman, the mysterious voices in italics. Three elements are one-offs, set apart as single sections: the preface, the photographs, and the glossary; the figures float above, the footnotes below, whatever text is proceeding at the moment. The more significant elements of the discourse are the other five, labeled here for future convenience— interviews (I), documents (D), and commentaries (C) interspersed with narrations (N) and the mysterious voices (M). These five discursive elements—I, D, C, N, and M—arrive in segments arranged in chapter-long sequences.

As distinct from its discourse, *Aramis*'s fabula—the explicit and implicit series of narrated events comprising its story, returned as much as possible to chronological order and causal sequence—is nonfictional before it is fictional. It begins in the historical world and only later enters the storyworld concurrent with the actions of its fictional characters. At that point, the fabula alternates between historical and fictional times and places. The text outlines the historical component of its fabula with a D (documentary) segment, a project chronology running from 1969 to 1987 (12–15). While this history is complicated, the historical story (or nonfictional fabula) gets complex only in the years when Latour and Nathaniel Herzberg conduct and compose the sociotechnical analysis of the Aramis system. Once Latour goes on to construct the hybrid non/fictional text of *Aramis,* its composition, publication, and ongoing reception continue the history of the Aramis project, as well as partially reconstruct it through the story told within its covers.

Over and above its real-world locations, the storyworld of *Aramis* collects a series of discrete fictive spaces. Some are determinate—such as the fictive U.S. Senate chambers visited in an early M (mysterious voice) segment. Others are indeterminate—the nonplaces from which some of the other mysterious voices utter their dialogues and Aramis voices its soliloquies. But the matrix of the storyworld is the fictive office at the real École des Mines de Paris, to which the young engineer and his professor repair after commuting around Paris and over to Lille between 1987 and 1988. From this paraspace adjacent to the historical world, the text establishes its first narrative or primary diegesis, rendered through the young engineer's character-bound narration. These N (narrative) segments construct the frame tale within which the other segments of the discourse are embedded, just as all the events of *Frankenstein* are embedded within the frame narrative rendered by Walton's epistolary account. The fantastic M segments represent the amplification of the fictive N segments, raising the literary stakes of Latour's narrative gambits.

However, regarding the frame structure of its discourse, we should recall—although this is not mentioned in *Aramis*—the uncanny moment toward the end of *Frankenstein,* when Walton confides:

> Frankenstein discovered that I made notes concerning his history: he asked to see them, and then himself corrected and augmented them in many places; but

principally in giving the life and spirit to the conversations he held with his enemy. "Since you have preserved my narration," said he, "I would not that a mutilated one should go down to posterity." (232)

Looping its discourse back on itself, that text now refers within itself to its own self-"correction." In this moment, Walton's account mutilates itself, places itself *en abyme.* The first-, second-, and third-degree narrators—Walton, Frankenstein, and the Monster—and the distinctions between their respective narrative levels, blur into an undecidable composite of unreliable voices within overlapping frames. Somewhat less vertiginously, neither does the young engineer—the Walton of *Aramis*—have control of the content or the sequence of the discourse of *Aramis.* The "(invisible) author" orchestrates it from the base of scholarly operations established in the paratextual preface, supplementing the various expertises of the fictional characters with his own academic and disciplinary credentials. The metalepsis perpetrated by *Aramis* concerns the point made above: the published book enters the future of its own story about the afterlife of Aramis. This is more akin to the unfolding of *Don Quixote,* when the actual publication of Book 1 is noted in the fictional continuation of Book 2.[12]

Crucially for the orchestration of *Aramis* as a scientifiction, every major division of the text—the prologue, seven chapters, and the epilogue—begins and ends with an N segment, uttered from within the storyworld of the first narrative. Specifically, each of these divisions begins with a piece of the young engineer's account, proceeding in chronological sequence; each division ends either with another, later piece of that narrative or, from chapter 2 onward, with an M segment rendering a prosopopoeia of Aramis. In this manner—either on the primary, realistic level of its first narrative, or shifted up to the fantastic or oneiric level on which Aramis is given utterance—the text of *Aramis* maintains the fictional matrix of the invented component of its fabula. Despite the abundance of historical and documentary materials, the consistent construction of this fictive framing of the discourse wins *Aramis* its spurs as a novel.

As with the sequence and simultaneous-narrative (serial present-tense) construction of Walton's epistolary frame in *Frankenstein,* in *Aramis* the frame narrative itself presents little or no anachrony, no major kinks in its timeline. Until a certain epiphany achieved late in the narrative, as a character-bound narrator, the young engineer is distinctly unliterary and literalistic, straightforward, both chronologically and intellectually. He begins as an objectivistic and linear fellow whose scripted role is to be the straight man, typically exasperated with and skeptical of Norbert's **"variable-ontology world"** (173) of reticulated networks and methodological detours. Nonetheless, due to the heterogeneous orchestration of the historical and expository materials, the discourse of *Aramis* taken altogether is vigorously anachronic. From the time of the frame narrative of its storyworld, between 1987 and 1990, otherwise undated interviews (I segments) and commentaries (C segments) are interspersed with the sequential if vaguely dated segments of the first narrative (N), with mysterious voices (M segments) having either fictive or nonexistent dates, and with documents (D segments) whose dates range from the late 1960s to 1987. While the particular sequence of the historical I and D elements has a chronological drift corresponding to the factual component of the fabula, it is by no means linear. From segment to segment, the reader is whisked back and forth from one year to another, from one decade to another, or in and out of time altogether. For instance, chapter 2 ranges over a hybrid factual-fictive fabula that extends from 1972 to 1988. Its entire discursive sequence runs: N, D, I, M, I, C, M, N, D, C, I, M, N, I, C, I, C, N, I, C, N, C, D, C, M, N. The variably (in)determinate temporality and largely unpredictable sequentiality of the *Aramis* discourse supplies a great deal of the exhilaration available to its determined reader.

Mysterious Voices

In "X-Morphizing," Laurier and Philo note about *Aramis* that despite this "remarkably hybrid style of writing . . . what is perhaps most surprising . . . is that the result is still a *readerly* rather than a *writerly* text. In other words, a large part of the labor of assembling the text is *not* left to the reader" (1051). While I agree with this observation for much of the text, in that there is no great difficulty in grasping either Latour's intentions or most of his narrative procedures, the mysterious voices near the outset of the narrative undercut that relative transparency. This particular orchestration keeps the reader slightly off balance in the early going. Several of these fantastic segments force the reader to construct their sense, either by surmising their larger significance or by forming an attribution. Laurier and Philo are not the only published readers of

Aramis who seem to interpret Latour's remark above—"Mysterious voices also chime in and . . . allow Aramis to speak"—to mean that *every* unattributed M segment is to be read as Aramis speaking. In the first quarter of the text, this is not the case. During a particular concentration of enigmatic M segments in chapter 2, *Aramis* is mildly writerly. Getting these attributions right enables a stronger reading of Latour's discursive art.

Prior to that particular patch in chapter 2, however, in the first two M segments, which occur in chapter 1, the voices are curious but rather less than mysterious. As with an evening speaker warming up a professional audience, the first two M instances are voiced by scholars in science and technology studies and are essentially in-jokes for the benefit of Latour's colleagues. A supposed Senate hearing on PRTs is peopled by "Senator Don MacKenzie" and "Senator Tom 'Network' Hughes" (19–20).[13] Similarly, a few pages later, the second M segment presents an obviously fictitious account of the already-dead Aramis's triumphant debut at the 1989 World's Fair, bylined "Reuters, September 10, 1989, from our special correspondent Bernard Joerges" (22).[14] However, when these initial M segments are read against their adjacent segments, these relatively unproblematic initiations of the M device implicitly provide the needed reading instruction. The connection or attribution to be constructed will be a metonymy of some immediately preceding or following textual component, off of which the mysterious voice is a fictive riff.

For instance, these initial M segments are interspersed with short I (interview) and N segments and immediately framed by the first two C (commentary) segments in the text. When cut out of the chapter as a whole, this sequence runs: C, I, M, I, N, M, C (18–25). The second C segment, following hard on the second M segment, begins by introducing an important new expository predication: **"By definition, a technological project is a *fiction*, since at the outset it does not exist, and there is no way it can exist yet because it is in the project phase"** (23; my italics). The fanciful M fictions, then, are deployed in part to underscore as well as offset the earnest theoretical formulations delivered in the C segments. In the immediate context, the text of *Aramis* is arguing both rhetorically (M) and discursively (C) for the propriety of treating technological projects such as Aramis as narrative fictions in their own right. Such projects are thus significantly comparable to literary productions. At the same time, they seek to take on the reality properly granted to those technical *objects*—steam engines, telephones, space shuttles— that actually do enter and, for some historical duration, operate within the world materially and not just semiotically.

Chapter 2 climaxes with the arrival of the voice of Aramis proper. All subsequent M segments are mysterious only insofar as they continue to voice the florid prosopopoeias of the disgruntled ghost of a failed PRT project. However, at the outset of this chapter, it is important that Aramis does *not* yet speak because Aramis does not yet exist, even as a proto- type. Within the fabula currently unfolding, Aramis is as yet only an idea for a technological character in search of the design specifications nec- essary for its "realization" of sufficient cybernetic autonomy. The full story follows this halting technical gestation to the bitter end of its run. Only at the end of chapter 2 will the provisional success of an early prototype provide a nucleus of realization sufficient to allow its voice to coalesce to utterance. The care taken with this staging of Aramis as a literary character reflects how meticulously the fictive narrative observes the historical chronology of the Aramis project.

Chapter 2 thus contains the largest concentration of M segments that are actually mysterious. As we have established, they riff on the concep- tual resonances of their immediate historical or expository contexts in each case. Preparing for but also delaying the voice of Aramis, once again clustered within a concentrated sequence, this second batch of M segments now occupies the same sociotechnical limbo as that from which the voice of Aramis will proceed. Of the three M segments in this sequence, the second one introduces the device of prosopopoeia in a comic register. It is set up by a C segment that concludes:

> **So if you don't want the transportation system to turn back into a beet field, you have to add to the task of interesting humans the task of interesting and attaching nonhumans. To the sociogram, which charts human interests and translations, you have to add the technogram, which charts the interests and attachments of nonhumans.**

> *"For my part," the motor declares, "I won't put up with nonmaterial cou- pling. Never, do you hear me? Never will I allow acceleration and deceleration to be regulated down to the millisecond!"*
>
> *"Well, as for me," says the chip, "I bug the CEO and his journalists."* (58–59)

Instead of Aesop's or La Fontaine's talking animals, we have Latour's talking mechanical components. While this use of the device is mildly comical, it is only seemingly ingenuous. For one, it motivates significant dialogue in the immediately following N segment. The young engineer vents his frustration with what he still considers to be Norbert's childish or irrational position:

> "It's a confusion of genres," I said, forgetting my place. "Chips don't talk any more than Chanticleer's hens do. People make them talk—we do, we're the real engineers. They're just puppets. Just ordinary things in our hands."
>
> "Then you've never talked to puppeteers." (59)

Norbert's canny retort implies the availability of puppeteer testimony corroborating the semiautonomy possessed by the quasi-objects at the ends of their strings. And for another, this issue of the attribution of "voice"—and with it, agency and interests—to nonhumans corresponds to the larger strategy mobilized in *Aramis,* its *symmetry,* putting literary and sociotechnical discourse on the same plane. This is not at all "a confusion of genres": the resources of literary criticism and theory are being brought to bear on the analysis of a nonliterary phenomenon that nonetheless begins as novels, poems, and plays do, as invented forms, verbal images of things without objective referents, responding instead to some set of needs or desires, sketched on a blank page or screen. In a prior C segment, Norbert notes: **"A fiction with 'variable geometry': this is what needs to be invented, if we are to track the variations of a technological project that has the potential to become an object"** (24–25).

The other two M segments in this cluster resonate with related literary and metaphysical issues, but in a more mysterious way, in that the fictive voices are constructed through conceits only obliquely related to their historical antecedents. The key to these proceedings is withheld until the last moment and, thus, is somewhat easy to miss or misconstrue. The interpretive constructions of other commentators have been too impatient. Contra Laurier and Philo, these M segments do *not* record Aramis speaking out, nor do they present, in Bould and Vint's initially plausible reading, a moment when "Aramis itself criticizes the author of *Aramis.*"[15] Rather, these voices are spoken from the perspective of the project engineers charged with the development the Aramis system. The voices at hand refract an engineering debate over the project's design directives, over *the extent of the operational autonomy to be engineered into it.* This issue of technological autonomy resonates on several levels throughout the entire narrative. At the moment, raising the issue of autonomy connects the cybernetic aspect of the technological project to design a driverless, self-regulating subway car to the ontological issues foregrounded by the attribution of agency and interests to fictive as well as factual nonhumans. The immediate context of the dialogue given in this M segment (in italics below) is an interview excerpt. The following extract cites an editorial caption heading the interviewer's question and the interviewee's response, then proceeds across a bar to the M segment proper:

M. Berger, former RATP engineer who was acquainted with the project at the time, responding to questions: . . .

"*Switching isn't done on the ground, then?*"

"No, it's done on board. The big challenge with Aramis is that the cars are autonomous; they don't touch each other, yet they work together as if they were part of a train. They have nonmaterial couplings—nothing but calculations. . . .

". . . Each car has to calculate its own speed and position; it has to know where it's going; it has to be able to be leader or follower; it has to know when to stop at a station, open its doors, and . . . take off again . . . at 25 kilometers per hour, even in rain or snow, all day, all night, thousands of times, without breaking down."

"*I find your characters one-dimensional. They seem flat. They're just ideas, words on paper. They need to be animated; you have to make them move, give them depth and consistency. More than anything, they have to be autonomous; that's the whole secret. . . . Your characters are just sacks of potatoes. Give them a little breathing space, a little autonomy. Make them cars with minds of their own. . . .*"

"*But what if they start moving around on their own, taking their lives in their own hands? Maybe they'll get ahead of us!*"

"*And what are you getting paid for, may I ask, if it's not to come up with a transportation system that has a life of its own and can get along without us? . . . We're doing business, you know, not writing novels; . . . These characters have to live on their own, do you hear me? They have to. You figure it out.*" (54–56)

This passage introduces a motif that goes throughout *Aramis:* the individual capacities to be incorporated into self-regulating technical components are "characters" partaking of the mode of existence of *literary* characters. A significant C segment coming a few pages later makes this connection explicit: **"When our engineers cross the qualities of drivers with the qualities of automatic pilots and central computers, they're embarking on the definition of a *character*. An autonomous being or an omniscient system? What minimum number of human qualities does that character have to bring along?"** (62). At the same time, in line with Bould and Vint's intuition, the voice saying, " *'I find your characters one-dimensional'* " is also ventriloquizing the invisible author's *self*-critique of his scientifiction's novelistic pretensions. Nonetheless, the significant antecedent of that first voice—the historical element off of which it is riffing—is not the author, Bruno Latour, addressing himself in the second person, but the system engineer, M. Lamoureux, speaking to a colleague, M. Berger. Lamoureux's factual report is cited in a nearby D segment, "defining the character" an Aramis car must have if the system is to work. According to "the Aramis principle, an Aramis car must be able to: . . . *follow* . . . stop . . . connect . . . approach . . . *supervise* itself" (60). And the technological matter of *Aramis* at the moment lies adjacent to the cybernetic issues of machinic agency being dramatized during the same period of the seventies and eighties in ostensible cyberfictions and aired in their theoretical reflections. What is the possible autonomy of an automaton, the possible self-determination of an autopilot, the metaphysics available to a mechanical or computational device? In the same C segment cited above, Norbert continues: **"Yes, we're actually dealing with metaphysics, and the anthropomorphic expressions must be taken not figuratively but literally: it really is a matter of defining the human (*anthropos*) form (*morphos*) of a nonhuman, and deciding on the limits to its freedom"** (62).

This mention of metaphysics is followed immediately by an interview excerpt quoting M. Berger responding to a reading of Lamoureux's document just cited by saying, " 'Yes, I have to admit that our discussions sometimes took on theological dimensions' " (62). Hard on this comes another extended segment of M dialogue couched in theological phrases, along the lines of this sample: *"Let's give Aramis more autonomy, as befits a divine creature, after all; for won't God's work be judged all the more beautiful to the extent that His creatures are more free?"* (63). These mysterious voices—now enacting a satire of theological conversation between engineer-monks debating how to cultivate the souls of machines—once again refract the historical engineering duo of Lamoureux and Berger presented in the immediately preceding I and D segments. The author slips in the readerly key to the immediate proceedings on the next page:

> *"Forgive me, Father, I did get carried away, but the questions of freedom and predestination are ones I care deeply about."*
>
> *"Where is this chapter on the preaffectation of [Metro] stations?"*
>
> *"Oh—sorry, Lamoureux, I was thinking about grace."* (64)

Soliloquy

I have been detailing the literary-discursive texture of the deliberate and drawn-out buildup to the moment when Aramis itself is granted voice. This device will be the most memorable in the text, and will license some of its most imaginative rhetorical flights. Latour has accorded the stakes at play the weighty labels of essence and existence, spirituality, ontology, metaphysics, and theology—in other words, the sorts of philosophical substance we typically claim for serious literary work. But whether a critical reader will be convinced to take this all that seriously hangs, in the end, by a literary thread. So let us move now to the final two segments of chapter 2. The chapter as a whole is titled, "Is Aramis Feasible?" One could take the subtext of this title to be the text's own self-interrogation: given that it will hinge on its reader's generosity in accepting the repeated soliloquies of an aborted technical project, is *Aramis* feasible?

The penultimate segment is a passage of Norbert's commentary that begins, **"To study a technological project, one must constantly move from signs to things, and *vice versa*"** (80). In this initial phase of indeterminate ontology, technological projects correspond to and partake of the media of literary construction and, more broadly, artistic creation. Within this oscillation between signs and things, however, the creative mode of the project phase is distinctly *narrative:* **"In 1973 Aramis is a *narrative program*, a story that is told to the decisionmakers, to stockholders, to local officials, to future passengers to 'bring them on board,' but it is also a work program, a flow chart, and a distribution of tasks"** (80). Against reactionaries such as Jacques Ellul—who overstate the technological case by demonizing it as *irreversible,* a kind of inhuman juggernaut—Latour is insisting (as in the *vice versa* above) on the mundane reversibility of the projects by which anything technical does or does not come into existence. Signs and stories in the project phase lead to preliminary *things*, materializations in the form of experimental prototypes, which, succeed or fail as they may, then lead back once again to the drawing board.

This same C segment compounds the appeal to narrative and story by specifying narrative *fiction*. But this time, the analogical relation of the literary object to the technical project is tempered by including the observer in the observation. The topic now is not fiction per se but the "account of a fiction," which **"is generally easy to follow; you never depart from its textual form and subject matter"** (81). What it takes to follow the nonfictional account of a fiction is now distinguished from following the account of a project. In the former, the critical or interpretive account of the text demands no departure from a shared semiotic medium, whereas in the latter, as is the case with Aramis, the account must account for the metamorphoses of the actors in the network, as signs transform to things and vice versa: **"The account of a *fabrication* is somewhat more difficult, since any one of the figures may move from text to object or object to text while passing through every imaginable ontological stage. In order to follow a technological project, we have to follow simultaneously both the narrative program and the degree of 'realization' of each of the actions"** (81). Norbert's argument here is far from watertight (note the efficacy of Latour's positing it through a fictive mouthpiece, thus allowing himself a level of plausible "theoretical deniability"). But whatever its merits, it does possess the virtue of prompting an analogous consideration of the social metamorphoses of *textual* objects. For instance, the communicative products of social systems circulate and occasionally coalesce to literary narratives that give rise to cinematic treatments or even to vastly disseminated sociotechnical developments. From a neologism coined for a technoscience fantasy enacted in 1984 in William Gibson's *Neuromancer,* "cyberspace" (6) migrated to virtual thinghood in the virtual reality (VR) boom of the nineties and to an abiding abode called the Internet.

This C segment concludes with Norbert's issuing a summary exclamation lamenting the frustrating reversibility, the utter precariousness, of technical projects. Just across the bar, in the M segment prompted by Norbert's designation of the Aramis project as a "narrative program," Aramis speaks for the first time. Its utterance reverberates with an exclamatory tension comparable to Norbert's:

If only we always went from signs to things! But we also go in the other direction; and we soon find ourselves not in a subway train but in a conference room, once again among signs speaking to humans—as if there were subjects!

Alas, VAL speaks well for itself, holds up all by itself. Why can't I? . . . Proceed in a train! Move ahead! Split up! Behave! Go! Stop! Merge! Haven't I carried out all these orders? What more do you want? . . . Why, oh why have you abandoned me, people? What do I have to do with prosopopoeia? Will you ever console me for remaining a phantom destined for a work of fiction when I wanted to be— when you wanted me to be—the sweet reality of twenty-first-century urban transportation? (81–82)

Aramis nominates itself metafictively as a character in the scientifiction within which what is left of its virtual but unrealized ontology as a technical object is being carried forward. Now that Aramis has been set forth as capable of self-representation, it speaks both from the limbo of its unfulfilled technical gestation and from beyond the grave of its ultimate demise. As with the condemnation Mary Shelley's monster launches at its feckless creator, Victor Frankenstein, to whom Aramis explicitly alludes in the continuation of its initial plaint, the primary passion marking the voice of Aramis is its inconsolable, unconsummated yearning to exist. But even as a narrative conceit, such a consummation could come about only through a social ratification that never comes. Aramis can be spoken for, and Norbert will imagine it as conversing (see 294–95), but the invisible author never extends the fantasy such that Aramis is reached or conversed with. The poignancy of soliloquy is that its audience understands that the voice crying out to it is not really audible. In soliloquy, the internal verbal spinning of a psychic system is rendered social through narrative's prerogative to construct and transmit an imaginary audibility. Soliloquy grants social connection only on the condition that it is simultaneously withdrawn. In this regard, Latour's consistent literary construction of the character of Aramis as forever enclosed on itself is superbly rendered.

Autonomy

The extension of organismal descriptions beyond the biological occasion has been a long-standing motif of cybernetic research. For instance, the organic systems for physiological homeostasis—regulated constancies of heart rate, body temperature, locomotive balance, and so on—are seized as analogues for cybernetic mechanisms, governors, thermostats, and other technological servomechanisms. However, at *its* outset in cybernetic discourse, the concept of autopoiesis returns the technological development of homeostasis back to the biological realm. This premier event in the emergence of second-order cybernetics involves a kind of reentering of operational closure back into its previous organismal conditions. In *Principles of Biological Autonomy,* Francisco Varela remarks:

> The idea of autopoiesis capitalizes on the idea of homeostasis, and extends it in two significant directions: first, by making every reference for homeostasis internal to the system itself through mutual interconnection of processes; and secondly, by positing this interdependence as the very sources of the system's identity as a concrete unity which we can distinguish. (13–14)

Humberto Maturana and Varela have largely confined the concept of autopoiesis to biological application. For Varela, in *Principles,* "the idea of autopoiesis . . . refers to topological boundaries," specifically, the membranes of cellular systems. In this description, autopoiesis is the capital principle of *biological* autonomy; moreover, one should not "confuse autopoiesis with autonomy" (54–55).

However, Varela develops a general definition of systemic autonomy that lifts that concept beyond biological specificity: "We can take the lessons offered by the autonomy of living systems and convert them into an operational characterization of autonomy in general, living and otherwise" (55). As we have discussed, Niklas Luhmann develops a conceptual move parallel to Varela's, one that generalizes the concept of autopoiesis itself to allow for its application to systems—in particular, social systems—with formal or virtual rather than material elements and boundaries. Accepting that extension allows Varela's generalization of autonomy to rejoin the generalization of autopoiesis when its mode of self-maintenance out of self-produced elements is properly maintained in the manner indicated by Luhmann's theory. To return to Varela's discussion, he treats both autopoiesis and autonomy under the idea of organizational *closure:* "We shall say that autonomous systems are organizationally closed. . . . Autopoiesis is a case of, and not synonymous with, organizational closure, and the autonomy of living systems is a case of, and not synonymous with, autonomy in general" (55, 57).

I rehearse this chapter of the history of systems theory in order to gain some wider purchase on the ways that Latour's *Aramis* interrogates ideas of autonomy. It does this on several different levels. But importantly, I think, it does so *without explicit coordination with a notion of operational or organizational closure.* Latour's actor-network concept has great structural flexibility, but precisely because the concept crosses organizationally *open* network structures with momentary or enduring actor relations, the matter of autonomy becomes problematic in relation to it. In this instance, the indetermination between Aramis as actor-network and Aramis as failed system induces a certain equivocation in its conceptual description. At the same time, if it is proper to treat Aramis as having a kind of self, then it is also proper to treat Aramis as the system defined by the self-binding of that self, and thus as both needing and possessing some form of organizational closure. This lacuna in the text might be considered as a blind spot of Latour's treatment, or alternatively, as an irony suitable to the treatment of something that never existed as something that also *did* exist, accentuating Aramis's ghostly signature as, in Simondon's phrase cited above, "an open-ended virtuality." And as a sort of unconscious driver, this nonobservance of closure is certainly effective for Latour's project of narrativization. At the level of the composition of *Aramis* as a narrative structure itself, this open project for a closed object is a most productive conceptual slippage.

One level on which *Aramis* explicitly treats the matter of autonomy, then, is that of the individual (human or nonhuman) actor among other interdependent actors. As we have noted in working through the mysterious voices derived from the Aramis engineers Berger and Lamoureux, the technological starting point and engineering challenge for the achieved Aramis system is the way that its passenger vehicles are to combine both collective automation and individual autonomy. As a systemic ensemble, they are to be automatic in the sense of driverless, and yet self-determining in the responses necessary for their moment-to-moment interoperation. Here, the notion of autonomy has a positive valence in relation to an ultimate systemic subordination: such autonomies are produced as relative contingencies by the total operation of the Aramis system. During an important dialogue in which Norbert and the young engineer model and ventriloquize the interplay of the Aramis actors, the young engineer plays the role of an individual mobile unit or Aramis car and gives it this declaration: "'I go too fast—you can't send me enough information fast enough. You have to let me have an autonomous personality. I have to drive myself'" (231).

A second level on which *Aramis* treats the matter of autonomy is also one we have previously encountered, for it pervades the text—that of a deleterious philosophy of technology. Here, the notion of autonomy is deprecated in a manner similar to vague impugnings of "the system," any system, as a faceless demonic force. One wonders whether Latour is blurring a cryptotheological notion such as Jacques Ellul's approach to the social autonomy of technique together with the properly neocybernetic notion of the relative autonomy specific to operationally or organizationally closed systems. Latour repeatedly rips as a misbegotten metaphysical totalization the sociological (but decidedly not systems-theoretical) notion that technological autonomy is a collective runaway machine. Norbert harangues the young engineer: "There can't be an intrinsic idea of Aramis; that would mean returning to a diffusion model, to the autonomy of technologies, to their irreversibility, their inhumanity" (120–21). In a later commentary, Norbert composes a sarcastic passage mocking this unfortunate cultural stereotype: **"They're really fun, those people who write books in which they think they're castigating technology with adjectives like smooth, cold, profitable, efficient, inhuman, irreversible, autonomous! These insults are qualities with which the engineers would be delighted indeed to endow their hybrid beings. They rarely succeed in doing so"** (174). And again, for good measure, during Norbert's final restitution before his audience of bewildered Parisian technocrats: "You had a hypersensitive project, and you treated it as if you could get it through under its own steam. . . . You believed in the autonomy of technology" (292).

And yet, on another, more recondite level of this narrative, *Aramis* dramatizes the possible but abandoned autonomy of which this specific technological system, through its closed couplings of human and nonhuman actors, could have been capable. This individualized achievement is played out between the account of Aramis's computerization in its final phases, as the system prototype unfolded out of the Aramis project closes in on its constitution as a self-operating object, and the young engineer's assumption of intellectual independence from his overbearing mentor. This transformation occurs in a long passage in which the young engineer renders a transcript of his dialogue with Norbert in the form of a dramatic script. To prepare for this play, they first survey the four-level architecture of the Aramis system, from Level

1 of the mobile units to Level 4, "'the central command post, which sees, understands, feels, decides, acts, orders, and manages the entire flow, but which would crash if all the information from each mobile unit were to come back to the center'" (230). The young engineer contends: "'You need a minimum of democracy—that is, delegation of tasks: the mobile units have to fend for themselves, in part.'" He will play "ME"—a mobile unit at Level 1, while Norbert will play "HIM"—the central command post: "'So this time we're doing politics again for real—politics in things. I'm playing the dictator, you're playing the democrat,' said Norbert, whose choice did not surprise me. And we replayed the software in order to test Aramis' viability" (230).

ME: "I go too fast—you can't send me enough information fast enough. You have to let me have an autonomous personality. I have to drive myself."

HIM: "Well then, take care of things yourself, if you're so smart. But since you're not human, I'd be surprised if you were capable of doing much."

```
A pair of cars has two redundant UGE's [control units],
one per car.
```

ME: "If one of them breaks down, the other one takes over. I am a pair of nonhumans. Pilot and copilot. I'm not asking you for very much; that's the condition for being autonomous."

HIM: "Okay, but two nonhumans don't yet make one human."

```
—An electronic interface between the UGE and the subsys-
tems has to be controlled in the car (doors, brakes,
traction, steering). . . .
```

ME: "No one will open the doors; it's too dangerous—someone nonhuman has to open them. No one will put on the brakes—someone nonhuman has to put them on and make sure they're working in synch with the car's speed. . . ."

Little by little I was becoming the Aramis mobile unit. I understood how it worked and, like it, I was taking on confidence and personality. I no longer wanted to be a lowly student constantly lorded over by his mentor-master. . . . I was the one, now, who was dictating my own technological choices. I had fought hard to win the right to recognize myself as autonomous. I was no longer afraid. (231–36)

"Men and things exchange properties and replace one another; this is what gives technological projects their full savor" (61). We arrive at the beginning of the climax of the bildungsroman Latour has tucked into the young engineer's intellectual autobiography. As the detail of the Aramis prototype's operational autonomies is rendered in increasingly technical terms and arcane program codes, the young engineer hits his stride. Meanwhile, confronted with technical complexities beyond his ken and spooked by the convergence of human and nonhuman systems that mutually no longer need him around, the Norbert persona starts to recede. Norbert complains to his increasingly liberated companion:

> "But the farther we go, the more crowded it is. Every part of the system is as complicated as the system as a whole. Every plate we unfold is itself made up of plates to be unfolded!"
>
> "Pure Borges, my dear mentor. Why let it upset you? You love literature, after all—and you love folds. . . . The only question is whether the details are strategic or not. And these particular ones are important; they're at the heart of Aramis's autonomy, the adjustable mobile unit. If it can do that, it's an autonomous being, a real automobilist. It can exist."
>
> "A heteromobilist, still, we're the ones who give it its laws."
>
> "No, it becomes autonomous for real; we've given it its laws for all time."
>
> "But it's like us," Norbert snapped back furiously. "If we were characters in novels, we wouldn't escape our author." (243)

The passing Borgesian mise en abyme of the fiction offers to draw us away from the immediate dialogue and back to the level at which the narrative has been constructed. It reminds us that both of these characters are quasi-autobiographical projections of the implied author's comprehensive deliberations, the dramatically enacted devil's advocacy through which a sociotechnical philosopher-critic is self-interrogating each fold of his argument.

ANT and Systems Theory

I add in one more theoretical element, this time from the outside of the text, a supplementary sociological discourse. On the one hand, Latour's *Aramis* does repair certain deficiencies in the sociological witness of Simondon's text on the technical object. Despite Simondon's critique of humanism in *On the Mode of Existence of Technical Objects,* the social element appears largely in the indistinct collective singular, "man," and the invention and genesis of technical beings corresponds more to the human "essence" than to heterogeneous social forms:

> We are able to create technical beings because we have within ourselves an interplay of relationships and a matter-form association which is remarkably analogous to that which we establish in the technical object. The relationship between thought and life is analogous to the relationship between a structured technical object and the natural environment. The individualized technical object is an invented object, one that is a product of the interplay of recurrent causality between life and thought in man.[16]

This observation has its virtues as a kind of technological humanism. But on a comparable issue of technical invention, contrast to this a passage of Norbert's commentary at the point that the Aramis project has reached its final phase in the mid 1980s:

> **The microprocessors become the center of the new Aramis.... Five years ago they didn't exist; now they are making Aramis possible at last.**
>
> **Where is this being, the microprocessor, to be situated? ... The object, the real thing, the thing that acts, exists only provided that it *holds humans and nonhumans together, continuously.* ... For the thing we are looking for is not a human thing, nor is it an inhuman thing. It offers, rather, a continuous passage, a commerce, an *interchange,* between what humans inscribe in it and what it prescribes to humans. It translates the one into the other. ... Neither object nor subject. An instituted object, quasi-object, quasi-subject, a thing that possesses body and soul indissolubly. ... We have been mistaken. What we had called the "technological object" is what lies on the garbage heap, in the scrap pile, abandoned by people and by other projects.** (213–14)

Through Norbert, Latour offers a trenchant passage of heterogeneous constructivism. The only purely technological objects are the defunct ones, the refuse left behind after commerce with humans inventing, engaging with, and maintaining them has ceased. Until then, prior to the possibility of a quasi-autonomous self-organization along Simondon's lines, the technical object assumes existence as a hybrid entity produced by a continuous cocreation. Such a genesis must also involve in some fashion the laborious negotiations of a project phase, which only then may allow for the precipitation of an "instituted object" into the sociotechnical world. Nonetheless, the ongoing existence of this being as a working object will depend on the holding together of a network binding the cohort of allies needed to keep things going.

But conversely, how can an actor-network bind *itself* together, other than by producing its own boundaries, however provisional, that is, by becoming a *systemic* network binding the continuous work of all the actors in its series? The discourse of second-order systems theory radically extends the implications of Latour's descriptions by providing an *operational* supplement, a more robust account of the forms and conditions of the cognitive—that is, autopoietic—processes assumed there. Aramis was a project to construct a hybrid system incorporating psychic, technological, and social subsystems within its boundaries. Within that larger complex, the cognitive productions of its human operators and the computations of its mobile units are on the same plane. Each possesses relative degrees of autonomy to be defined and adjusted in the total operation of the system. It is never a matter of Aramis *versus* its human observers, but of whether the project for the Aramis *system* can constitute and distribute cognition and computation viably among its systemic components. In Latour's text, "a continuous passage, a commerce, an *interchange*" posit but do not yet account for the technical system as the continuous production—in the rigorous terminology of social systems theory—of a composite sociotechnical autopoiesis. Even as projects, technical systems are objects of a particular type—specifically, machine systems coupled to a larger metabiotic ecology. As compounded of actors with the observing capacities of psychic and social systems, they will or will not be able to distribute heterogeneous cognitive functions so as to hold together a range of elements that exist *as such* only in relation to the interrelations of the systems that produce them.

With regard to this meditation on systematicity, Simondon's discourse of the late fifties is nearly as far along as Latour's of the early nineties. They both press to but do not cross the threshold of systemic self-reference as an operational demand and outcome of a system capable of self-observation. Simondon writes: "The principle of progress is none other than the way in which the object causes and conditions itself in its operation and in the feed-back effect of its operation upon utilization. . . . These relationships make it possible for the object to discover obstacles within its own operation on the basis of certain limits in the conditions of its use" (25). This passage describes a proper quasi-cognitive process instituted in technical objects. As Latour implicitly insists, it is the coupling of technical objects to social systems that must complete the operational circuit.

Similarly, Latour's constructivism wants the second-order epistemological component that would give teeth to Norbert's observations about **"a variable-ontology world"** resulting from **"the interdefinition of the actors"** (173).[17] Norbert declares that **"VAL, because it exists, unifies points of view. It transforms people's opinions of it into 'simple' points of view about an object that remains independent of them. With Aramis there is nothing of the sort. Since it does not exist, it cannot unify points of view"** (77). In this applied observation, Latour reinvents one of the wheels of second-order cybernetic constructivism:

> Under what conditions, then, do objects assume "objectivity"? Apparently, only when a subject, S_1, stipulates the existence of another subject, S_2, not unlike himself, who, in turn, stipulates the existence of still another subject, not unlike himself, who may well be S_1.
>
> In this atomical social context each subject's (observer's) experience of his own sensori-motor coordination can now be referred to by a token of the experience, the "object," which, at the same time, may be taken as a token for the externality of communal space.
>
> With this I have returned to the topology of closure . . . where cognition computes its own cognitions through those of the other: here is the origin of ethics.[18]

Aramis's minimal ontology or lack of achieved being as an autonomous object, as an operational transportation system, is better stated in terms of its inability to sustain such cognitive recognitions in its many observers. It cannot yet be the token for an eigenbehavior that would stabilize and prolong a provisional recursive consensus, the autopoiesis of communications for which it would be the enduring theme. At most, through the "white magic" (73–74) of ANT's pursuit of an adequate account of a failed fabrication, Aramis gains a *textual* substance persisting for a while as the complex social-systemic element called *Aramis*.

Norbert comments that **"the actors also provide themselves with the means to pass from one point of view to another, and they unify, from their own point of view, and each for himself, the multiplicity of points of view thus deployed. Each constructs his own instrument in order to elaborate a synoptic view. All the actors thus repair, for themselves,**

the disorder they create by multiplying perspectives" (170). Latour's methodological rule for ANT here again complements a more rigorously theorized systems-theoretical description of "variable ontology" in the mode of increasing complexification. "By theoretically reducing social complexity in the form of a coherent social theory, social reality inevitably increases in complexity since another social construct has been achieved. . . . Reality, by being observed, described, and analyzed, becomes further complicated than it had been before it was observed."[19] Or, again, observing systems reduce their own complexity relative to their environment by increasing *its* complexity.[20] And while every observing system constantly generates one blind spot or another for itself, this in no way has prevented the technological ethics of Simondon, the hybrid socioliterary work of Latour, and the epistemological constructivism of second-order systems theory, especially when shaken together in a critical cocktail, from unveiling much of what the "technical object" has been hiding in plain sight.

5 MEDIATIONS OF GAIA

Ecology and Epistemology from Gregory Bateson and Félix Guattari to Avatar

THE THEORIES OF COGNITION we have been exploring are rooted in the cellular sentience posited by biological systems theory and validated by contemporary molecular biology and microbial ecology. Let us now fit this picture into a corresponding conception of the biosphere. Prior to and beyond any specific consciousness, without mind, it is nonetheless perfused with cognitions from which higher-order cognitive consortia arise. A self-maintaining system of ecosystems, the biosphere is truly an "autopoietic planet," Margulis and Sagan's telling phrase in *What Is Life?* (19). But as Victoria Alexander writes in *The Biologist's Mistress*, "Nature, which does not have a brain, must wait upon the coincidence of analogous things coming near enough to each other, like ligands and receptors, to have an effect. Nevertheless, we may say that any selection that makes use of analogous structures is mind-like" (111). And out of such resonant and, so to speak, meaningful couplings of sunlight, Earth, and life, the biosphere also becomes mind-like, self-observing, nonconscious yet cognitive in its own right. This final chapter reads the theory of metabiotic autopoietic systems back to biotic autopoiesis and its subsequent developments, not only in the direction of linguistically mediated meaning systems but also in the direction of Gaia altogether. Delusions of spiritual or rational dominion and humanist grandeur aside, our corner of the cosmos resides within an ecology of worldly systems, in the midst of microbial and terrestrial affinities, running the gamut from thermodynamical and geobiological systems to the technological networks that mediate minds and their societies wherever and in whatever form they emerge from and fall back into the Gaian matrix.

Cycle and Flow

The word *ecology* was invented by German naturalist Ernst Haeckel and first published in his *General Morphology* of 1866. British biologist E. R. Lankester transmitted it to English in translations of Haeckel. His natural-scientific neologism named a "branch of biology that deals with the relationships between living organisms and their environment," and came to refer also to "the relationships themselves, esp. those of a specified organism" *(Oxford English Dictionary, or OED)*. Within a few decades, with the specification of the human organism, this lively disciplinary concept leaped from the natural to the social sciences. Anthropological and sociological usages developed by the early twentieth century. The abstract form of this semantic dynamic came to be codified as "the interrelationship between any system and its environment; the product of this" *(OED)*. Gregory Bateson's 1972 career-spanning compendium of his professional papers, *Steps to an Ecology of Mind,* makes a seminal extension of the natural concept toward what he calls "an ecology of ideas."

For what began shortly after Darwin's publication of the theory of evolution as one among many newly specialized biological subdisciplines, then, ecology stands out from the pack for the persistence, range, and prominence of its cultural overdeterminations. In particular, it has been asked to answer a conceptual call for a natural science of virtual relationality to come forward alongside and thus repair the epistemological deficiencies built into other positive scientific disciplines devoted but delimited to disciplinary objects out of context. Ecology is and always has been extendible. The relational principle that drives the extendibility of the concept of ecology also exposes another matter that has always been latent in its notion: ecology is systems theory. And just as some, present company included, may get a bit messianic about systems theory, so too has ecology inspired an unusual amount of philosophical as well as political fervor, due in large part to its open-ended potential for holistic or systemic application.

One can read about this inspirational tenor of the topic in Sharon E. Kingsland's national history of the discipline, *The Evolution of American Ecology, 1890–2000.* Consider the career of American botanist Frederic Clements. At the turn of the twentieth century, "Clements was one of the few people who had a clear vision of ecology as a distinct subject. . . .

Plant associations were 'complex organisms,' which interacted with their environments and had developmental histories like individual organisms" (144). Already the holistic drift of Clements's organismic ecology was manifest. Moreover, "by 1935 his arguments for the importance of ecology were taking on an almost religious tone. . . . Far from being a specialized field like physiology or morphology, ecology was 'a point of view and a plan of attack'" (151). In Clements's development of its theory, twentieth-century ecology is doing something like biosociology along residually nineteenth-century lines of organicist analogy. The extension of its constructions of botanical community toward political ecology is irresistible. Clements made ecology speak patriotic socialism to a mid-1930s American heartland gripped by both depression and drought: "Society was also a complex organism evolving in harmony with its environment: it was imperative therefore that the environment 'be so fashioned as to call forth progress and not retrogression [with] organs working in unison within a great organism'" (162–63).

However, during the same period when Clements was propounding sociopolitical morals based on his ecological vision of the communal succession of complex botanical organisms, also in 1935, eminent British ecologist Arthur Tansley launched a critique of Clements's organismal approach, for which critique he coined the term *ecosystem*.[1] Clements's complex organism minimized animal symbionts and excluded humans altogether. In contrast, according to Kingsland, Tansley thought "the ecosystem concept . . . made it easier to see how humans were part of the system, not standing outside it. Tansley had a holistic perspective not unlike that of Clements, but he wanted to envision the whole in a way that included humans as intrinsic parts of the system" (185). Tansley's redescription of ecology explicitly as a science of diverse environmentally situated systems, adding in but also going beyond the human element, makes the holistic possibilities of the discipline even more all-encompassing. In Kingsland's depiction, Tansley's rationale for substituting ecosystem in place of complex organism reads like a dress rehearsal for the neocybernetics of the 1970s, that is, for the programmatic inclusion of the observer within the system to be observed.

Standing behind Tansley's ecosystem concept is Alfred Lotka's 1925 text, *Elements of Physical Biology*. A figure there titled "The Mill-Wheel of Life," in illustration of his heuristic idea of a "World Engine" driven by the sun, diagrams the interrelation between energy and life. Sunlight

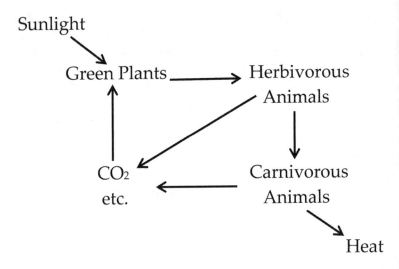

Figure 7. "The Mill-Wheel of Life," after Alfred Lotka, *Elements of Physical Biology* (1925).

flows through a cascade of geobiological cycles, driving the circular operation of a global ecosystem embedded within its physical and thermodynamic environments.[2]

Additionally, three years before Tansley named and codified the ecosystem concept for ecology, Walter B. Cannon introduced the concept of homeostasis—the circular mechanism of negative feedback by which organic systems maintain their bodily operations at a steady state—into the theoretical repertoire of physiology. Both are seminal systems concepts for the cyclical operations of self-regulating processes; both are precursor formations bound up into the emergence of the first cybernetics. Ecosystem ecology, in particular, hitches itself to the cybernetic wagon. The infusion of mathematical physics into ecology allows it to roam more freely beyond its biological origins and connect itself more firmly to the material and energetic conditions of the physical environments to which it has always been nominally referred. In other words, the cybernetic development of the ecosystem concept brings ecology directly into the systems-theoretical treatment of system-environment relations. The ecological thinker most responsible for the early cultivation of this ecocybernetic trend was expatriate British ecologist G. Evelyn Hutchinson, a family friend and Cambridge University chum of Gregory Bateson's older brothers, before they died in the Great War.

In his Foreword to *Steps to an Ecology of Mind,* Bateson recalls the circumstances by which, despite being an anthropologist by training, he falls in with the discourse of cybernetics:

> In 1942, at a Macy Foundation conference, I met Warren McCulloch and Julian Bigelow, who were then talking excitedly about "feedback." The writing of *Naven* had brought me to the very edge of what later became cybernetics, but I lacked the concept of negative feedback. When I returned from overseas after the war . . . I was privileged to be a member of the famous Macy Conferences on Cybernetics. My debt to Warren McCulloch, Norbert Wiener, John von Neumann, Evelyn Hutchinson, and other members of these conferences is evident in everything that I have written since World War II. (ix–x)

Hutchinson is not often remembered as a participant in the Macy Conferences, nor is it often recalled that in the person of Hutchinson, ecology had a place at the first cybernetic table. Bateson's invitation to him to join that conversation appears to have impressed on Hutchinson the aptness of ecosystem ecology for cybernetic appreciation. He presented the paper "Circular Causal Systems in Ecology" at an early iteration of the Macy Conferences on Cybernetics gathering in 1946, under the title "Feedback Mechanisms and Circular Causal Systems in Biological and Social Systems." In it, he applies the concept of homeostasis to extant ecological methods and observations, noting as a "circular causality" that ecology concerns itself with "*groups* of organisms," which "may be acted upon by their environment, and they may react upon it" (221).

The ecological framework of the organism in developmental relation with its environment sets up a circular feedback scheme primed for cybernetic attention. Hutchinson continues: "Circular paths often exist which tend to be self-correcting within certain limits, but which break down, producing violent oscillations, when some variable in the system transgresses limiting values." Ecosystems are stable within operational limits, but vulnerable to fluctuations in variables coupled to their environments. Hutchinson's remarks underscore an ecological recognition that coalesces with the arrival of cybernetics: ecosystems are not just passive or mechanical mill wheels turned by the sun. They are self-constituting: they constitute themselves in the first place with the emergence of negative feedback loops for self-regulation. "It is, therefore, usual to find in natural circular systems various mechanisms acting to damp oscillations, and self-correcting mechanisms may be introduced at several points in the circular path" (221). Within this cybernetic framework, Hutchinson advances a biogeochemical approach to ecosystem ecology, with "an emphasis on the cycling of nutrients, such as carbon or nitrogen, through the biotic and abiotic components of the system in a roughly circular pathway"; by the 1950s, "analysis of the processes that defined ecosystems concentrated on these two ideas, the cycling of chemicals within the system and the flow of energy through the system."[3] Here is the cycle and flow of my section title, the fully Gaian complementarity of environmentally open physical and thermodynamical systems that flow through operationally closed ecological and geobiological systems that cycle—thanks in part, but not wholly, to those flows.

Two Ecologies: Bateson and Guattari

In 1989, Félix Guattari did radical cultural, political, and psychological theory under the sign of ecology, publishing a manifesto titled *The Three Ecologies*. It was originally to be an afterword for *Chaosmosis: An Ethico-Aesthetic Paradigm,* published posthumously in 1992. And while the details of *The Three Ecologies* are indeed explicitly ethico-aesthetic, their natural-ecological substance, apart from some introductory framing in the first few pages, is rather diffuse. This is not the case with Bateson's *Steps to an Ecology of Mind,* a work disseminating a seminal and explicit statement of a general ecological paradigm that remains conceptually bound to its natural-ecological and cybernetic occasions. Bateson's ecology of mind retains its strong purchase on our philosophical attention, I would argue, precisely because of its conceptual roots in and resonance with ecosystem ecology.

Guattari's discourse can be instructively juxtaposed to Bateson's. It is worth recalling that the "plateau" of Deleuze and Guattari's *Milles Plateaux* is a concept they adapt from Bateson's precybernetic anthropological work, *Naven.*[4] While, relative to Bateson, the ecological dimension of Guattari's late texts is indeed diffuse, it is not negligible, and we might tease it out in the following fashion. As I have already argued, ecology is a species of systems theory, perhaps even a keystone species. Bateson forcefully details how his ecology of mind is to be understood precisely as applied and, if you will, remediated cybernetics. Guattari's two works are also informed by systems discourses—specifically, Bateson's and Varela's—and as a result, it has a significant, not just nominal, ecological charge.

Nonetheless, it is ironic that Guattari's systems discourse labors under a general ban on the theoretical use of the word *system* in any positive sense. In this ban on speaking the name of systems except pejoratively, Guattari's text is symptomatic of the wider realm of Deleuzo-Guattarian discourse and, more generally, of that particular strain of continental but predominantly French theory that tends to lump cybernetics and systems theories together in a heap and keeps them all, perhaps as some sort of Anglo-Saxon intellectual vice, at arm's length.[5] This antisystemic syndrome and its ostensible rationale is beautifully encapsulated and issued as an edict in Foucault's preface to Deleuze and Guattari's *Anti-Oedipus*. Foucault remarks in that preface how "*Anti-Oedipus* (may its authors forgive me) is a book of ethics," which "carries with it a certain number of essential principles which I would summarize as follows if I were to make this great book into a manual or guide to everyday life" (xiii). By this seemingly ethical, indeed Mosaic gesture, Foucault confers on Deleuze and Guattari a sort of theoretical sanctification. And here, as Foucault extracts it from the discursive practice of *Anti-Oedipus,* is his most detailed commandment: "Withdraw allegiance from the old categories of the Negative (law, limit, castration, lack, lacuna), which Western thought has so long held sacred as a form of power and an access to reality. Prefer what is positive and multiple, difference over uniformity, flows over unities, mobile arrangements over systems. Believe that what is productive is not sedentary but nomadic" (xiii).

"Prefer . . . flows over unities, mobile arrangements over systems." It may be that we hear an echo of this credo in a remarkable passage early in *The Three Ecologies,* where Guattari affirms that an ethico-aesthetic realm of the subject needs to be reconfirmed against other theoretical agendas that minimize it:

> In the name of the primacy of infrastructures, of structures or systems, subjectivity still gets a bad press, and those who deal with it, in practice or theory, will generally only approach it at arm's length, with infinite precautions, taking care never to move too far away from pseudo-scientific paradigms, preferably borrowed from the hard sciences: thermodynamics, topology, information

theory, systems theory, linguistics, etc. It is as though a scientific superego demands that psychic entities are reified and insists that they are only understood by means of extrinsic coordinates. (25)

However, Foucault's fateful formulation of "flows over unities," as well as Guattari's opposition between processual subjects and rigid or static systems are too equivocal to withstand critical inspection.[6] You just cannot lump into the same polemical dismissal, on the one hand, the synchronic formations that structuralism from Saussure to Lacan calls semiotic systems, and on the other hand, the kinds of systems that are actually self-operating and self-regulating, that is, those cybernetic systems that are processual in their own right. And in this assumption that systemic unities can only be immobile or sedentary, in the manner of synchronic structures, this particular theoretical bias is insufficiently ecological. One must also factor into one's ontological picture those ecological cycles that arise as dynamical unities from the operational closure of their elements.

We have already observed the transversal relation of geobiological cycle and thermodynamic flow in Lotka's machinic assemblage of the "Mill-Wheel of Life." And Lotka, together with Tansley and Hutchinson, is in the direct line of ecological filiation that includes Bateson's appropriation of the ecosystem concept. Coming back to Bateson, let us move directly to the precise sense of his ecology of mind. In *Steps,* Bateson states that coming out of the Macy Conferences, he is led to "synthesize cybernetic ideas with anthropological data. . . . Broadly, I have been concerned with four sorts of subject matter: anthropology, psychiatry, biological evolution and genetics, and the new epistemology which comes out of systems theory and ecology" (x, xii). Taking the points bound up in that last clause, just as ecology is systems theory, the ecology of mind is a cybernetic epistemology for which observing systems and their environments are coconstructing. Nonetheless, the "mind" of Bateson's ecology of mind both transcends and encompasses the purposive or rational consciousness. In more recent parlance, it is distributed, ubiquitous, or indeed, "transversal." Guattari affirms in *The Three Ecologies:* "Bateson has clearly shown that what he calls the 'ecology of ideas' cannot be contained within the domain of the psychology of the individual, but organizes itself into systems or 'minds,' the boundaries of which no longer coincide with the participant individuals" (36).

However, Bateson's ecology of mind should not be depicted as a field, plateau, or territory, but rather, as a circuit coupling together systems and environments into larger wholes. Making an important aesthetic argument, Bateson's 1967 paper "Style, Grace, and Information in Primitive Art" states that "what the unaided consciousness (unaided by art, dreams, and the like) can never appreciate is the *systemic* nature of mind" (145). As with the processes of a natural ecosystem binding living beings and their environments into self-regulating circuits, the systemic nature or self-sustaining relationality of psychic phenomena is at once circular, social, and largely unconscious. "Life depends upon interlocking *circuits* of contingency, while consciousness can see only such short arcs of such circuits as human purpose may direct"; for this reason, "such phenomena as art, religion, dream" must come to the aid of "mere purposive rationality" (146).

In what is perhaps his most celebrated paper, written in 1970, "Form, Substance, and Difference," Bateson declares that "I now localize something which I am calling 'Mind' immanent in the large biological system— the ecosystem" (460). This paper also, uniquely in *Steps,* rehearses a definition of ecosystem ecology per se, the major forte of his colleague Hutchinson, in order to clarify the distinction as well as the correspondence between that discipline and his ecology of mind. As a direct adaptation of natural ecology, the ecology of mind retains the other ecology's cybernetic conceptuality and form, while refitting it, with due caution for operational differences, through information theory:

> Let us consider ecology. Ecology has currently two faces to it: the face which is called bioenergetics—the economics of energy and materials within a coral reef, a redwood forest, or a city—and, second, an economics of information, of entropy, negentropy, etc. These two do not fit together very well precisely because the units are differently bounded in the two sorts of ecology. In bioenergetics it is natural and appropriate to think of units bounded at the cell membrane, or at the skin; or of units composed of sets of conspecific individuals. These boundaries are then the frontiers at which measurements can be made to determine the additive-subtractive budget of energy for the given unit. In contrast, informational or entropic ecology deals with the budgeting of pathways and of probability. The resulting budgets are fractionating (not subtractive). The boundaries must enclose, not cut, the relevant pathways. (460–61)

In order to foreground physical and thermodynamic matters of energy budgets, Bateson mutes biogeochemical cycles in favor of bioenergetics. This move brings forward the face of ecosystem ecology more immediately juxtaposed to the statistical methods of information theory (by which methods that theory appropriates the thermodynamic term *entropy* for a measure of information), aligning while contrasting the physics of energy flows with the cybernetics of informatic transmission. However, the crucial matter of circular form returns in the profound remark that, for the observer of the ecology of mind, "the boundaries must enclose, not cut, the relevant pathways." Despite the self-organizing cycles that may arise within thermodynamic or dissipative systems with physical entropy, in the final instance, the "relevant pathways" for them are linear, they flow away from the system, thus any boundary posited for the sake of measurement will cut across them. However, in "informational or entropic ecology"—that is, in the information-theoretic approach to the circular operations and self-maintenance of an ecosystem, for which, as Maturana and Varela would say of an autopoietic system, there are neither inputs nor outputs—the "relevant pathways" are themselves circular. The ecology of mind refers us back once again to bounded operational form.

These considerations of circular form or "circuits of contingency" reach maximum profundity in their application to "units of survival," the unit here being very much the unity of the difference between a system and its environment. Bateson is pushing splendidly beyond neo-Darwinism to ecologize natural selection, or again, to meld the ecology of mind with the theory of evolution. This brings us to Bateson's 1969 paper, "Pathologies of Epistemology," that provides Guattari's epigraph to *The Three Ecologies*: "There is an ecology of bad ideas, just as there is an ecology of weeds." Bateson's joke here is, of course, that the concept of "weeds"—that is, useless or fungible organisms—is itself a "bad idea," one of the "epistemological fallacies of Occidental civilization" (483). Similarly,

> in accordance with the general climate of thinking in mid-nineteenth-century England, Darwin proposed a theory of natural selection and evolution in which the unit of survival was either the family line or the species or subspecies or something of the sort. But today it is quite obvious that this is not the unit of survival in the real biological world. The unit of survival is *organism*

plus *environment*. We are learning by bitter experience that the organism which destroys its environment destroys itself.

If, now, we correct the Darwinian unit of survival to include the environment and the interaction between organism and environment, a very strange and surprising identity emerges: *the unit of evolutionary survival turns out to be identical with the unit of mind.*

Formerly we thought of a hierarchy of taxa—individual, family line, subspecies species, etc.—as units of survival. We now see a different hierarchy of units—gene-in-organism, organism-in-environment, ecosystem, etc. Ecology, in the widest sense, turns out to be the study of the interaction and survival of ideas and programs (i.e., differences, complexes of differences, etc.) in circuits. (483)

The widest sense of Bateson's ecology of mind provides a general ecological paradigm, concerning "the interaction and survival of ideas and programs . . . in circuits." "Ideas and programs" don't just flow; precisely, they circulate within an ecology of systems. As "units of survival," such ideas or programs may be the coevolutionary Gaian complexes we have been used to as isolating, fallaciously, as "genomes," "individual organisms," or "separate species," but they may also be technical objects, machinic assemblages in the hybrid networks of the mechanosphere. Or they may be messages, like this one, seeking dissemination, response, and perhaps duration in social circulation. What Bateson has folded up into "Mind," I would want to unfold into the distinct systems of consciousness and communication. But that technicality does not diminish the epochal importance of his steps illuminating the relevant pathways to an ecology of ideas binding informatic processes and metabiotic systems—minds and societies—to the biosphere.[7]

The ecological dimension of Guattari's later work is ostensible in the term *ecosophy,* a name claiming a quantum of ecological wisdom, while leaving its ecological substance somewhat recondite. This discourse consistently centers instead on cultivating processes of subjectivation for its ethico-aesthetic paradigm, with its primary polemic remaining anti-Oedipal and counter-Lacanian. We hear that clearly in the following peroration from the last chapter of Guattari's *Chaosmosis,* "The Ecosophic Object," and perhaps we also detect in the midst of this passage one of these recondite allusions, this one to Bateson's own ecosophic thought:

> To speak of machines rather than drives, Fluxes rather than libido, existential Territories rather than the instances of the self and of transference, incorporeal Universes rather than unconscious complexes and sublimation, chaosmic entities rather than signifiers—fitting ontological dimensions together in a circular manner rather than dividing the world up into infrastructure and superstructure—may not simply be a matter of vocabulary! (126)

I read into "fitting ontological dimensions together in a circular manner" a Batesonian intertext evoking his circuits of ideas and programs in the ecology of mind. As we have noted, Guattari's *Three Ecologies* proceeds under an epigraph from Bateson and cites his ecology of mind explicitly. But it does so equivocally, and only in passing. Rather than draw that out further, however, I note instead one other singular and fleeting reference, at the end of this short work, in a documentary footnote Guattari places on the parenthetical remark: "(here I am opposing living autopoietic machines to mechanisms of empty repetition)" (40). The reference is to Francisco Varela's *Autonomie et Connaissance,* the 1989 French revision and translation of his 1979 work *Principles of Biological Autonomy.*

While the extant dialogue with Bateson in *The Three Ecologies* is curt at best, a dialogue with Varela's biological systems theory is writ large throughout *Chaosmosis.* The first reference to Varela comes early in the text: "We are not confronted with a subjectivity given as in-itself, but with processes of the realization of autonomy, or of autopoiesis (in a somewhat different sense from the one Francisco Varela gives this term)" (7). Guattari seizes the concept of autopoiesis, it would seem, to provide another mode of access to an ecology of mind for his ethico-aesthetic paradigm. While he rehearses its classical definition given by Maturana and Varela as an operational definition for living systems, he deploys autopoiesis synonymously with Varela's more general definition of systemic *autonomy,* of which autopoiesis is the biological instantiation. So for one, from *Autonomie et Connaissance,* Guattari gets a second-order or autopoietic ecology of mind without the detour through Bateson's earlier cybernetics. Guattari appropriates the concept of autopoiesis for its phenomenological as opposed to its biological register and as a semantic operator for rethinking subjectivity through a generalized sense of autonomy as nonpredetermined by drives and complexes. But also, in line with other thinkers of autopoiesis beyond the biological occasion, he extends the concept toward its general ecological possibilities, and he deploys the term *alterity* as a catchall denomination for the environments out of which systems arise by self-distinction and to which they must remain open for mediated transactions:

> Autopoiesis deserves to be rethought in terms of evolutionary, collective entities, which maintain diverse types of relations of alterity, rather than being implacably closed in on themselves. In such a case, institutions and technical machines appear to be allopoietic, but when one considers them in the context of the machinic assemblages they constitute with human beings, they become ipso facto autopoietic. Thus we will view autopoiesis from the perspective of the ontogenesis and phlyogenesis proper to a mechanosphere superposed on the biosphere. (39–40)

In his appropriation of the concept of autopoiesis for his vision of unpredetermined, chaosmotically unpredictable, singular yet collective potential subjectivities, Guattari anchors his ecosophic discourse to the ecological scaffoldings of second-order systems theory. In this text, despite its evocations of "Fluxes," the insistence on prioritizing flows over systems is largely absorbed now into a more complex concept of transversality. For instance, "The ecosystemic approach of Fluxes still represents an indispensable awareness of the cybernetic interaction and feedback involved with living organisms and social structures. But it is as much a matter of establishing a transversalist bridge between the ensemble of ontological strata which, each in their own way, are characterized by specific figures of chaosmosis" (124). In its counterinsistence on ontological autonomies, *Chaosmosis* enters on the discourse of self-referential systems and underwrites the operational cycles of systemic unities. It does so not without some semantic strain, but the systemic drift is unmistakable. And the concept of autopoiesis is particularly crucial here, because Maturana and Varela introduced this definition of living systems into cybernetic discussion under the name of "autopoietic machines." This hard cybernetic terminology in their earliest papers on autopoiesis licenses Guattari to do second-order systems theory under the name "machinic heterogenesis."

"Machinic Heterogenesis" is the title of chapter 2 of *Chaosmosis*. Throughout this text, "machine" is a way to say "system"—in the neutral sense of an integrated ensemble that effects a process—without saying "system." The concept of the machinic in Guattari is an antimechanistic affirmation of the primacy and necessity of systemic operationality or, again, of circular functions. But as a cultural revolutionary, he consistently presses his virtual ecology of abstract machines toward the possibility and potential emergence of the extraordinary, toward the actualization of febrile and fleeting existential singularities. This is the ecosophic beauty of Guattari's witness, and I would compare it directly to the aim of Bateson's thought as well. But whereas Guattari is an activist sermonizer, Bateson is more diffident, a natural philosopher who seeks to maintain a baseline of scientificity. Nonetheless, they share the good intentions of liberating the Western mind from its self-destructive linear fixations by opening it to extrahuman vistas and sweeping ecological contingencies. And returning in closing to the idiom of Varela, "machinic autopoiesis" also names something ecologically prior to aesthetics. In its ecological moment, autopoiesis is just the plain and simple basis of the mundane, moment-to-moment self-production of living beings altogether. It is the systemic basis of their mediated sentience and of their mediated sociality.

Ecological Resonance: *Darwin's Pharmacy*

Let us connect two other works that both discuss matters of ecological crisis but come from different planets in relation to an actual planetary discourse, Gaia theory. One is Luhmann's *Ecological Communication,* a sociological view of the systemic nature of the disconnection between modern social systems and the natural environment. The other is Richard Doyle's *Darwin's Pharmacy: Sex, Plants, and the Evolution of the Noōsphere,* a tour de force of personal memoir, rhetorical analysis, and discursive recovery addressing the literature, science, and practical application of psychedelic drugs in the context of that same disconnection between humanity and the biosphere. *Darwin's Pharmacy* is a contemporary example of the sort of ecological communication Luhmann discusses regarding German green politics in the 1980s. It is also a prescription aimed to cure the chronic syndrome of systemic detachment analyzed in Luhmann's social diagnosis. Doyle presses the case for an *ecodelic* therapy centered on immanent psychic constructions of worldly interconnectedness, experiences of Gaia sufficiently profound and persuasive to produce a paradigm shift in environmental policies. However, as the checkered career of Gaia discourse would indicate, to go from ecological consciousness to socially efficacious ecological communication is not as easy as throwing on a switch inside your brain. While Doyle suggests that his visionary experiences of global holism do not override or conjure away systemic differentiations and their operational contingencies, his important and hopeful message could be strengthened with some systems-theoretical exercise. At the same time, it could also show systems theory a way or two to loosen up.

For Luhmann, we recall, autopoietic, self-referential systems such as any given mind or society are the product of an operational closure by which they distinguish themselves from their environments and reproduce that distinction by an internal self-production. An autopoietic system is thus constitutionally prejudiced toward its own self-reference and is inclined to ignore its environment as long it gets from it what it needs to maintain its operations. Consider Western social systems writ large in relation to their environments: they have been happy to assume that their effects on their natural environments are prejustified by the system's own raison d'être, whatever that may be. As preordained or as part of God's plan, environmental consequences and displacements have been thought to be as natural as nature itself, and thus ethically neutralized. This would explain why it has taken our kinds of societies so long to arrive at the very concept of ecological consequences in their own right. We are now in the unhappy condition of having to consider that those time-honored, comforting, and very convenient assumptions about the perpetuity of our environmental impunity have been mistaken. And, as we know, some powerful social and corporate forces are trying with all their might to push our heads back into the sand.

Luhmann develops *Ecological Communication* from a 1985 address on the topic, "Can Modern Society Adjust Itself to the Exposure to Ecological Dangers?" This puts the issue well, for it has been a real question whether our kinds of societies can get over themselves long enough to realize that the abuse their environmental others can take has limits. His preface restates the "main argument of the address, namely that modern society creates too little as well as too much resonance because of its structural differentiation into different function systems" (xvii). Since autopoietic systems cannot receive transmissions but only construct external stimuli in terms of their own internal elements, *resonance* denotes that mode of relation between a social system in particular and its environment, in which the latter succeeds in setting the former "reverberating" (15). Resonance is the system-internal repercussion when its environment succeeds in irritating a social system sufficiently to get it to produce communication—which is what social systems do—taking that environment as its theme—to wit, ecological communication. "Too little" resonance denotes how difficult it typically is for a social system to construct for itself a message corresponding to its environment's condition. "Too much" means that once an ecological message manages to emerge somewhere in a society, there is no way to control or predict how it will travel among modern society's many semi-autonomous functional subsystems, how that theme will play out, or what it will lead to as it echoes and splinters among the political, legal, economic, academic, mass-mediated, and other function-systemic forms of its communication.

Luhmann's main argument is that the ecological question concerning modern society's difficulty in relation to environmental dangers has languished for want of a properly complex theoretical treatment, which he will now supply through his brand of second-order systems theory. The thesis regarding the proper "theoretical structure of the ecological question, above all of its fundamental paradox," arrives at the outset of his text. As usual, Luhmann's theory is that one must overcome traditional holism's monism, its drive toward an encompassing unity, by observing the paradoxical simultaneity of unity and difference. This familiar metathesis is particularly apt with regard to the current topic. An adequate theory of the ecological question

> has to treat all facts in terms of unity *and* difference, i.e., in terms of the unity of the ecological interconnection *and* the difference of system and environment that breaks the interconnection down. As far as the ecological question is concerned, the theme becomes the unity of the difference of system *and* environment, not the unity of an encompassing system. (5–6; my italics)

We can refer to the opening passage of Doyle's *Darwin's Pharmacy* to see what Luhmann is talking about. The introduction begins:

> Crawling with transactions, the contemporary Earth whirls and whorls, uncannily bereft of human agency. The global ecosystem, undeniably in crisis due to the presence and activities of humans and their fossil-fuel familiars, maintains itself far from equilibrium, surfing diverse gradients through raised ocean levels and proliferating vectors of disease. (5)

We note that the environmental terms Doyle appears to present as synonyms, that is, as a conceptual unity—"the Earth" and "the global ecosystem"—are immediately qualified toward a crucial distinction. The passage plays on, while not precisely observing, the paradox that, in order to be capable of observing it, a system must be operationally distinct from as well as immersed within its environment. On the one hand, the "contemporary Earth" and its totality of activities are elicited in sublime detachment from human beings; they are observed as "bereft of human agency." On the other hand, the "global ecosystem" is elicited insofar as it is beleaguered by humanity. It is not the Earth per se, it would seem, but the global ecosystem that is "undeniably in crisis due to the presence and activities of humans." Of course, it is for humans in particular to observe that the global ecosystem they specify by placing themselves as its keystone species is uncomfortably close to collapse due to their own modern industrial activities.

However, the ecosystem concept can be a booby trap for unwary ecological theory, in that it can all too readily override the difference between ecological system and ecological environment. For a closely related milieu of conceptual pitfalls around the problem of systemic differentiation, we can also consider the rhetorical as opposed to the scientific provenances of Gaia discourse. One frequently sees the notion of Gaia set forth in full organicist mode, in a manner that would render unobservable the very thing the speaker claims to see. Luhmann's systems theory is a deliberate conceptual prophylactic for just this sort of ecological theology. The rhetoric of *Darwin's Pharmacy* evokes Gaia in the service of a finer-grained ethical argument. In line with Lovelock's own rhetorical habits in works such as *The Revenge of Gaia,* Doyle constructs a Gaia girded like a Homeric warrior for anthropomorphic duty: "While trillions of dollars are spent in the pursuit of 'security,' a ubiquitous superpower—Gaia—launches global-defense operations against Homo sapiens of every demographic. Has yet another security briefing gone unheeded?" (5). Doyle's personification of Gaia is not so much organic as ironic. The image of Gaia in this instance is just a convenient projection, as it is not really Gaia that is to defend the globe against humanity's ecocidal attack; rather, *Homo sapiens* must use the idea of Gaia to make itself secure from the ecocidal effects of its own anthropocentrism.

The text continues in just this vein: the ethical as well as vital imperative is to get "humans to perceive the densely interconnected nature of their habitat," and especially to "make this perception available to those humans who so violently cling to visions of autonomy" (6, 8). Doyle's rhetorical stance is hyperbolic or, more precisely, psychedelic, to the extent that, ideological visions of cosmic autonomy aside, autopoietic systems such as minds and societies have no choice in the matter of their *operational* autonomy—a systemic autonomy always relative to the contingencies of their environmental milieu. Human minds and societies are both inextricably interconnected to their material and virtual environments and, at the same time, ineluctably self-enclosed and self-responsible as far as their own term of being is concerned. The overriding issue is how to get our particular autopoietic systematicities back into viable interrelation with Gaia's own autopoietic systematicities.[8] I see no real discrepancy between this vision of interconnection-in-distinction and Doyle's plea for a reworking of the self in the act of allowing oneself to take possession of a Gaian recognition that impels one into a web of worldly relations and the set of ecological responsibilities that come with them. Here, I am all with Doyle's visionary scheme for a repertoire of "rhetorical choices and means of persuasion . . . to make the perception of the Earth as a political plant planet palpable" (8).

The flowers of rhetoric to be picked for this critical ecological reformatting of the human sensorium are entirely organic—so to speak, cactus flowers. They are the sundry biochemical by-products that plants and their fungi companions have learned to produce in their natural evolutionary course. Doyle goes on to christen these psychotropic substances in Darwin's pharmacy "ecodelics." In this phase of his argument, he quotes a long passage from a mescaline trip report whose author, having eaten a large chunk of San Pedro cactus, experiences a heightened contentment with and beauty in nature, an indwelling that also evacuates a load of pent-up anger. Doyle interprets this report through his own lens of ecodelic monism. The crypto-theology of cosmic autonomy at the root of the pathology of the human disconnection from the rest of nature is to be overcome through the ecodelic experience of ecosystemic and environmental interconnectedness:

> At a moment when "egoic" consciousness—that form of human experience that insists on the radical distinction between self and cosmos, as the former insists on incessantly consuming and colonizing the latter—seems to have reached a pandemic, a humble cactus enables the news of our fundamentally nested nature. (12)

I have sketched an outline of Doyle's argumentative gambit at the point of its interfaces with systems-theoretical issues and Gaia theory. My main reservation with it is that, bound up in a rather undertheorized approach to his own forte of rhetoric, Doyle underplays the communicational and mediatic implications of his argument, which would put its feet more firmly on the ground—while playing up a hyperbolic psychic system. He conceives the Gaian mind as endowed with an ecodelic telepathy, a wireless connection to a communicating ecosphere—as if his heightened consciousness were not all the while autonomously and recursively constructing its gorgeous, sensorially distended but nonetheless singular awareness of its environment. Ecological consciousness and ecological communication here comprise a unified and collective human or transhuman self rather than a more realizable tableau of resonant multiplicities, a variable and contingent set of interpenetrated but operationally differentiated systems tuned to a higher key.

Once more: the operational closure of an autopoietic system is the condition of the possibility of its observing its environment at all—no closure, no life, no mind. Such closure interconnects while it separates, but it also brings about for that system the reduction of complexity without which it could not cope with the overwhelmingly greater complexity of its environment:

> The interconnection of system and environment is produced through the closing-off of the system's self-reproduction from the environment by means of internally circular structures. Only in exceptional cases (i.e., on different levels of reality, irritated by environmental factors), can it start reverberating, can it be set in motion. This is the case we designate as resonance.[9]

So far, this description is general enough to include the occasion of biological autonomy for which Maturana and Varela originally developed the concept of autopoiesis. When Luhmann transposes autopoiesis to the metabiotic realms of psychic and social systems, the milieu within which those systems dwell is also transposed, from the material milieu of living systems to that shared environment of virtual differences that enables the interpenetration of the separate autopoietic productions of minds and societies—the medium of meaning. This means that for any mind, despite experiential constructions to the contrary, there is no extrasensory hotline from it to the natural or supernatural world. All is already and necessarily mediated by the living systems—cells and organs—comprising the autonomous body from which that mind emerges.

As *Darwin's Pharmacy* amply documents, the mind under psyche-delics primarily needs to get or be given a handle on the tsunami of *meanings* that threatens to overwhelm its circuits. Hence, for the trip to go well, the psychonaut needs *sociality,* that is, mediated communications—guides and programming, for which Doyle's text is precisely an encyclopedic manual. In *Ecological Communication,* Luhmann continues:

> Meaning is a representation of world complexity that is actualizable at any moment. The discrepancy between the complexity of the actual world and consciousness's capacity for apprehension or communication can be bridged only when the scope of the actual intention is restricted and all else is rendered potential, i.e., reduced to the status of mere possibility. There is no such thing as a "stimulus inundation" since the neurophysiological apparatus already screens off consciousness drastically, and the operative medium of meaning has to work very hard to permit something that is well digested to become actual. (17)

But what is a trip if not "stimulus inundation"? Ecodelia would be the chemical dilating of the neurophysiological floodgates to allow for forms of radical resonance creating explosions of indeterminate but achingly meaningful meaning around the theme of Gaian embeddedness.

Avatar and Its Systems

Aeroflot

When the film *Avatar* debuted, I did not run out to see it. I managed to miss opportunities to experience it in a theater, let alone in 3-D. So this treatment of the cinematic text is extracted from its overlay of theatrical visual technologies. It is a small-screen treatment. How small, you ask? In June 2010, flying on Aeroflot from JFK Airport to a conference in Riga, Latvia, *Avatar* was an option on my entertainment center. So my maiden flight with *Avatar* was on a Russian airliner, on the seat-back screen, listening with headphones. The outlines of this discussion first took shape during that viewing. When I got home, I ordered the two-format set and watched the Blu-ray disk on my 42-inch LCD TV. Later that summer, when I had the notion to prepare an *Avatar* lecture for the International Research Institute for Cultural Technologies and Media Philosophy (IKKM), I put the DVD into my desktop drive and took notes and made drafts while it played on a 22-inch monitor. In more than one sense, the following treatment is a "close reading" of selected aspects of the narrative.

I examine the fictive technology that drives the story in relation to the other "networks" named in the text. The avatar system is a media system and also, of course, a dream-flight technology. It couples an informatic telecommunications apparatus with an organic, bioengineered humanoid effector to transport its paraplegic but virtually disembodied "driver" into an actual but alien body, with capable legs and access to wings. A brief review of Gaian science, aka Earth system science, in light of Bruno Latour's observations on both Gaia and *Avatar*, leads up to that central focus. The movie depicts Pandora's Gaia, Eywa, as "a global network," a telecommunications system in its own right. The avatar body is the cyberorgian microcosm of which Eywa is the superorganic macrocosm: both are embodied but metabiotic nodes in a mediatic network. And whereas direct connections to Eywa are possible through Pandoran biological organs, the avatar within its Earth-based system is both organic-cognitive and technological-informatic, both human(oid) and nonhuman—a doubly two-sided form. In the realm of the science-fiction film, it does not matter so much that *Avatar* and its systems have their conceptual wires crossed. One can still draw some wider cultural conclusions from a consideration of their schematics.

The Cybernetics of Gaia

In "An Attempt at a 'Compositionist Manifesto,'" Bruno Latour has jokingly accused director and screenwriter James Cameron of plagiarism, since his 2009 movie *Avatar*, set on the fictional planet of Pandora, "should really be called *Pandora's Hope!*"[10] *Pandora's Hope* affirms that at the bottom of modernity's technoscientific box of ills lies the hope of reassembling a new worldview in which human and nonhuman actors alike form alliances for the composition of an inclusive and networked collective. His "Compositionist Manifesto" reads the narrative outcome of Cameron's *Avatar* in this sanguine light: "I take this film to be the first Hollywood script about the modernist clash with nature that doesn't take ultimate catastrophe and destruction for granted—as so many have before—but opts for a much more interesting outcome: a new search for hope on condition that what it means to have a body, a mind, and a world is completely redefined" (471–72). Latour treats the story told by *Avatar*, then, as one that resonates with his own scholarly and philosophical call for the end of "nature" as constituted by modernity—that is, for the redistribution of worldly agency in a "nonmodernist" fashion.

However, with a relatively new polemical twist, Latour aligns his version of the movie's vision with a broad reading of Gaian science: "I am under the impression that this film is the first popular description of what happens when modernist humans meet Gaia" (471). And while this encounter is "not pretty," neither is it catastrophic, at least for the Pandorans. The peculiar and striking result is that Latour deflects the recent discourse of Gaia theory from the grim catastrophism of its progenitor, British atmospheric chemist James Lovelock, for instance, in *The Revenge of Gaia:*

> The period we are now in is close to a crisis point for Gaia. The sun is now too hot for comfort, but most of the time the system has managed to pump down carbon dioxide sufficiently and to produce enough white reflecting ice and clouds to keep the Earth cool and to maximize the occupancy of the Earth's niches. . . . But, like many regulating systems with a goal, it tends to overshoot and stray to the opposite side of its forcing. . . . This is why the usual state of the Earth at present is an ice age. The recent crop of glaciations the geologists call the Pleistocene is, I think, a last desperate effort by the Earth system to meet the needs of its present life forms. (43–45)

Lovelock's long-standing conviction is that Gaia has been in crisis throughout the Pleistocene era, such that he considers the current situation of global heating to be one of adding insult to injury. His cybernetic orientation goes back to his earliest versions of the Gaia hypothesis: the Gaian system is a natural homeostatic device, a planetary thermostat. Insofar as Lovelock's own thermostat, as it were, has been constantly set on crisis mode, however, he has obscured the vigorous systemic worldview otherwise there to be read in the wider discourse of Gaian science.[11] Witness Bruno Latour stepping in to restore Gaian science as a hopeful sign of cultural renovation. Lovelock's later career as a somewhat erratic cultural prophet of ecological dislocation seems to have freed Latour to coordinate the nonmodern aspect of Lovelock's maverick scientific contribution for his own agenda.

Latour's "Compositionist Manifesto" states, "There is no way to devise a successor to nature"—that is, to "nature" under the modern Constitution—

"if we do not tackle the tricky question of *animism* anew" (481). Now, the accusation of animism has plagued Gaian science from its inception. But for Latour, that is precisely its badge of honor, the mark of Gaia theory's nonmodernity, its groping toward a new formulation of the agencies of worldly assemblages. In a 2007 address to the British Sociological Association, Latour notes that "in spite of the goddess's name, Lovelock knows fully well that 'she' is not a person, not even an organism, but the emergent property of all the feedback mechanisms that, on the whole, have balanced themselves well enough over the last billion years to maintain life on Earth inside some fluctuating albeit restricted limits."[12] With this accurate synopsis of current Gaia theory, Latour affirms that, as Lovelock has argued for decades, the emergence of Gaian agency in the form of self-regulation at the level of the biosphere is not animistic—it is cybernetic. When Latour says, "Call it 'animism' if you wish," regarding "the odd resistance of reality: every consequence adds slightly to a cause," and more forcefully, "consequences overwhelm their causes," he parallels the neocybernetic dictum that, in the main, due to inner states that render them nontrivial, worldly processes are not deterministically linear but unpredictably recursive.[13] For instance, Gaia evolves precisely because it is the constantly emerging metabiotic consequence of feedback loops between biotic and abiotic processes. And yet, for the "modernist" sensibility, convinced that the world is essentially a scene of *inanimate* forces and effects, Gaia theory and other systems sciences still conjure the specter of animism—anthropomorphism, teleology, god knows what:

> It is this conceit that lies at the root of all the critiques of environmentalists as being too "anthropocentric" because they dare to "attribute" values, price, agency, purpose, to what cannot have and should not have any intrinsic value (lions, whales, viruses, CO_2, monkeys, the ecosystem, or, worst of all, Gaia). The accusation of anthropomorphism is so strong that it paralyzes all the efforts of many scientists in many fields—but especially biology—to go beyond the narrow constraints of what is believed to be "materialism" or "reductionism." It immediately gives a sort of New Age flavor to any such efforts, as if the default position were the idea of the inanimate and the bizarre innovation were the animate. Add agency? You must be either mad or definitely marginal. Consider Lovelock, for instance, with his "absurd idea" of the Earth as a quasi-organism—or the Navis with their "prescientific" connections to Eywa. ("Compositionist Manifesto," 481)

This is quite a superb moment of counterpolemic on Latour's part. Nonetheless, if we press the cybernetic subtext here, Latour's distinction between the modernist and the nonmodern mind-sets maps fairly well onto a distinction previously developed in the discourse of systems theory, between "control" and "autonomy":

> In system theory, the autonomy/control distinction appears more specifically as a recursion/behavior distinction. The behavioral view reduces a system to its input-output performance or behavior, and reduces the environment to inputs to the system.... The recursive view of a system, as expressed in the closure thesis, emphasizes the mutual interconnectedness of its components.[14]

In other words, stated in a neocybernetic idiom, it is entirely possible for Gaia to be a self-referential cognitive system producing self-maintaining regulatory dynamics without having to assume the agency or anima of a *conscious* system. In a way reminiscent of the anthropomorphic automated subway system in Latour's *Aramis,* the narrative of *Avatar* is also the story of a remote control regime forced to take into account the emergent autonomies of its own effectors.

As Latour rightly insists, only in a network that couples together human and nonhuman actors can such autonomies be fully distributed. Such a network is properly observed as a system of discrete and differential subsystems. All technological systems "need allies, friends, long chains of translators. There's no *inertia,* no *irreversibility;* there's no *autonomy* to keep them alive.... No; for technologies, every day is a working day.... You can't manage if there's no one left working to maintain the technologies that are up and running."[15] That is, the extratechnological *maintenance* of a technological subsystem is part of the overall system: technologies are "self-maintaining" only when human actors are coupled to the nonhuman mechanisms. Within the terms of these conditions, however, the story of *Avatar* really does retell with the highest Hollywood production values a classic Latourian fable about the emergence of systemic autonomy within sociotechnical networks by the transformation of passive intermediaries into active mediators. At the same time, the movie's very derivativeness reminds us that for all his creative brilliance, Latour has repurposed a ready-made master plot from the annals of cybernetics.

The Avatar System

This neocybernetic itinerary from first-order control regimes to second-order autonomies recurs in the transition *to* the movie *Avatar* from Cameron's prior megahit, *Titanic*. In *The Language of New Media*, Lev Manovich recalls how the beginning of *Titanic* shows "an operator sitting at the controls . . . wearing a head-mounted display that shows an image transmitted from a remote location. This display allows him to remotely control a small vehicle, and with its help, explore the insides of the 'Titanic' lying on the bottom of the ocean. In short, the operator is 'telepresent'" (164). Manovich addresses informatic tele*presence* as a precondition for active remote control, tele*action*. A telepresence system draws signs from remote objects, allowing an operator to control the activity of the remote equipment producing the signs. The frame narrative of Cameron's *Titanic* places into the cinematic frame a representational technology for rendering an observer telepresent at an extreme location. Then teleaction adds interactivity to the control regime. According to Manovich, telepresence "can be thought of as one example of *representational technologies used to enable action, that is, to allow the viewer to manipulate reality through representations*":

> The ability to receive visual information about a remote place in real time allows us to manipulate physical reality in this place, also in real-time. If power, according to Latour, includes the ability to manipulate resources at a distance, then teleaction provides a new and unique kind of power—real-time remote control. . . . Coupled with a computer used for real-time control, electronic telecommunication leads to a new and unprecedented relationship between objects and their signs. It makes instantaneous not only the process by which objects are turned into signs but also the reverse process—the manipulation of objects through these signs. (165, 169–70)

Informatic teleaction turns worldly phenomena at one location into transmissible signals received elsewhere, within a total circuit of telecommunication through which cognitive responses to those signifiers can be sent back to remote effectors and consequently alter the things that they signify. In this circuit, the signifying process does not merely represent a remote world but also allows it to be worked over and in some degree refashioned. However, what would happen if the remote effectors of a teleaction system declared independence from their previous operators in favor of a new set of allegiances and obligations?

Let us now fast-forward to *Avatar*. The avatars in *Avatar* are designed to be remotely controlled teleactive informatic devices. But in addition to being remotely controlled effectors, the avatars in *Avatar* are also cognitive systems interacting with and within a living and social world. *Avatar* lifts the informatic interactivity of a virtual reality or cyberspace scenario and couples it to a realm of autopoietic cognition. For a tale of rebellious teleactivity within the "natural" alien storyworld of Pandora, this cinematic fiction imagines the anthropomorphic fulfillment of a biocybernetic system by submitting a media technology to a condition of humanoid embodiment. A narrative realization of embodied mediation, the avatar in *Avatar* is the organic metamorphosis of a media system.

At closer range, and as first focalized by the human characters, an unlinked avatar is an inert but living husk—a body awaiting animation. Bioengineered on Earth and grown in vitro en route, they appear as unborn adult fetuses floating in their amniotic vats. Dialogue informs us of their hybrid genome, mixed from human and Na'vi DNA, allowing the neural connections needed to hardwire the crossover from a human mind to a Na'vi body. Fresh avatar bodies are decanted fully ready to be operated, and as Jake Sully reports early on to his video log, he is there "to drive these remotely controlled bodies," once his mind is linked to his avatar's sensory and motor systems. In other words, an avatar is both the object of real-time remote control through its driver's teleaction—essentially and by design, a drone—and also the living effector by which its telepresent operator can interact with or manipulates other objects or persons at the avatar's location. An individual avatar, then, is just one node of a complex and regimented system, one component of a biotechnological consortium and technosocial network that reaches back to a genetic-engineering infrastructure on planet Earth.

Moreover, in a way that the filmic discourse never spells out, the avatar system must also be assumed to incorporate a transceiving apparatus, an interactive telecommunications link. By some means of mutual neural-psychic signaling, information about the perceptions and actions of a linked and functioning avatar is transmitted back to and received by the driver as he or she lies physically immobilized in a closed berth at a link station and experientially immersed in that prosthetic body. The intentions and decisions of the remote driver must also be instantaneously transmitted to and received, reconstructed, and enacted by the avatar. On the side of the human driver's instrumentation, there may be some exterior transceiver attached to the link station, but on the side of the avatar, there must be a transceiving device of some sort embedded within or genetically engineered into its body. In sum, one is to imagine a technologically instantiated, mutual and material informatic circuit between the cultured and vat-grown hybridized Na'vi avatar body and the human mind in seemingly detached command, a command-and-control circuit to both carry out the driver's intended behaviors and feed information back, registering the avatar's complex of bodily experiences. The cinematic discourse is content to have this material telecommunicational matter covered over as cybernetic telepathy.

The story will dismantle the corporate engineers' assumption of such operational detachment in favor of the inexorable if unintended attachments built into any technological system. Simondon remarks during the heyday of the first cybernetics that the progressive *concretization* of the technical object leads to a state analogous to a natural system, "as if an artificial object differed in no way from a physical system studied in all knowable aspects of energy exchange and of physical and chemical transformations"; as with unforeseen developments in the Avatar system. "In the concrete object each piece is not merely a thing designed by its maker to perform a determined function; rather, it is part of a system in which a multitude of forces are exercised and in which effects are produced that are independent of the design plan."[16]

The Link

This overdetermined media technology works insofar as it corresponds to its audience's more or less unconscious desire for such a hybrid or cyborg fusion to exist. The proxy and sign of such a desire is deposited in a magic little word: when the system works, there is a *link*. Jake Sully's first time linking up with his avatar is figured as a telematic leap. And quite helpfully for entertaining twists and turns of the story, the link between driver and avatar is inherently precarious. The link comes with contingencies of attachment: while the avatar is active, its driver must be alert but immobilized; in order for the driver to take care of his or her own bodily needs, their avatar must sleep. While linked, the driver is literally helpless, a kind of fetus umbilically connected to a technological womb and vulnerable to a forced abortion. These contingencies lead to any number of adventurous scheduling issues, vigorously exploited by the plot.

But more important than these manufactured complications are the formal implications of the avatar regime. Both as an observing system in its own right and as an element of the tale under the viewer's observation, this hybridic biocybernetic apparatus generates significant existential contradictions. Just as technics is constitutionally paradoxical, the cultural unconscious of this technological fabulation is meaningfully paradoxical. Stated in the idiom of form theory, the operational entity constituted by the avatar system is already a *two-sided form*. This particular formation already alerts us that the story at hand will climax with a posthuman metamorphosis that resolves the current overload.[17]

Concerning two-sided forms, consider the famous duck-rabbit image, for which it is easy to conceptualize but impossible to observe both images at once, that is, to observe the unity of its two possible constructions. To see one is to not see the other. At best, one oscillates ever so rapidly between the two options. As viewers of *Avatar*, we are afforded a second-order observation and understanding of the avatar system's functions. But for us, as well as for its sentient components as observers in their own right, while the system operates, only one side of its function can be indicated and observed at any given moment. The text of the film constantly cuts back and forth between two different bodies that are called by the same name. The question is: are they actually occupied by an identical mind? As I construct the story, the idea is that, due to its doubled bodily experiences, the person possessing this mind—"Jake Sully"—is gradually going to become someone else. Nevertheless, to speak about this process precisely, we have to pry apart its main components and keep them distinct. Otherwise, our own narrative desire to reify the metaphor will condense them back into a spuriously seamless unity, the supposed psychic unity of our two-sided protagonist.

Jake's two-sided nature has already been intimated by his having an identical twin, now dead, whose murder back on Earth has displaced Jake into his twin's place as avatar driver. The question now becomes, who is "Jake Sully" when he drives and therefore inhabits his Na'vi avatar? His apprehended avatar gives the Na'vi its driver's name. However, that avatar is also an embodied being, and when the being in question is the person of the avatar in action, it is precisely *not* Jake Sully—precisely not, let us say, *Jake S*. When Jake S and his avatar body are linked, we can call the embodied being that breathes the Pandoran air (which is unbreathable by humans) *Jake A*. While Jake A is active, Jake S is elsewhere.

When the nearly naked Neytiri first looks down from her tree limb and recognizes this "dreamwalker" as an avatar (its Levis give it away) lost and floundering in her home forest, she understands it for what it has come to mean to her people, an interloping predator, an invasive falsity that disguises an alien intent. This perception is directly articulated later by the warrior Tsu'tey when due to a broken link, Jake A collapses in their midst: "Look! It is a demon in a false body!" Neytiri's initial and immediate inclination is to slay the trespasser. However, she is stayed by the first of several animistic plot devices—the testimony of the "seeds of the sacred tree" that hover about him, detecting something genuine and worth preserving in this dubious being, and that she understands to be "a sign from Eywa."

From then on, Neytiri takes the person of this avatar at face value. But we must decline the invitation to identify with her empathy and stay instead at our proper level of narrative observation. The problem is that the text equivocates with regard to how entirely immersed the mind of Jake S is in the body of Jake A. Can the mind of Jake S, while it is linked to Jake A, really detach itself from the thoughts and utterances that are proper to the psychic and social systems that are simultaneously coupled by that avatar body? Or, again, can the mind of Jake S be at once both a first-order hetero-observer and a second-order self-observer? After their night of lovemaking, Neytiri whispers to Jake A: "I am with you now, Jake. We are mated for life." Right then, Jake S opens his eyes in the link berth, breaking his link with the postcoital avatar. Even after a broken link, however, the consequences of newly forged attachments continue.

Displacements of the Link

The Bond

The cinematic discourse fills these logistical and existential gaps in the workings of the avatar system with other signs elsewhere in the story. We can call these particular folds in the narrative discourse *displacements of the link*. They are precisely metonymies of the narrative desire pressing toward the ultimate condensations or metaphorical epiphanies of the story's conclusion. I draw out two of these displacements: With regard to the first, many Pandoran life forms have an organ not possessed by terrestrial animals. On the first evening of Jake A's existence as a link-driven human-Na'vi hybrid, it bunks in the avatar camp, over-seen by the den mother of the avatar project, scientist Grace Augustine in her avatar incarnation. Jake A notices how his braided Na'vi ponytail ends in a cluster of waving filaments. Grace A remarks dismissively, "Don't play with that, you'll go blind." But her masturbation joke strikes home: its function is neural intercourse. The ease of its operation stands counter to the massive media-systemic technicalities, the complica-tions of the link needed to connect a human mind to its living avatar body. This Pandoran organ suggests that a relatively immediate organic coupling of one sensorium to another is as easy as twisting two wires together.

In the Na'vi language, the function of this organ is *tsaheylu*—a mak-ing of "the bond," direct neural contact between two beings, and also between the Na'vi altogether and Eywa, defined in the online Na'vi-English dictionary as "world spirit, Gaia."[18] As the story progresses, through acts of *tsaheylu,* Jake A bonds with and rides on a series of ani-mals, hears the Tree of Voices, and finally, connects with the Tree of Souls, the main line to Eywa. The Pandoran bond, then, is a naturalized displacement of and organic supplement to the biotechnological link between a human driver and its avatar. What then happens when Jake A, which being achieves personhood only through the link with Jake S, makes the bond with another Pandoran being? In a manner parallel to the delegation of narrative focalization from a narrator to one or more characters, this delegation of teleactive agency produces a mediation within a mediation. The mind attached to the avatar momentarily takes up a further attachment to *another* creature, adding it to the network under composition. In the process, the human link is remediated by the Na'vi bond, yielding a second-order displacement of the sentience that frames and is framed by these embedded levels.

We come once more to metempsychosis, narrative signs of the leap of the soul from one body to another. The avatar system is designed to produce telecommunicational leaps for discrete periods of time. Befitting the informatic structure of these species-specific phatic or connective operations—the link and the bond—the narrative discourse provides both with distinct signs. The cinematic sign of the link is a pulsing energy vortex that suggests the mind or spirit's speed-of-light leap across space to make contact between its sender and receiver. This visual signature also marks Ellie Arroway's ride across the galaxy in *Contact.* In *Avatar,* it marks

Jake's phatic links, and also, tellingly, the moment when the soul of the mortally wounded Grace Augustine makes *tsaheylu* with Eywa, but does not as hoped return to life in the body of her avatar.

Otherwise, when established between Pandoran vertebrates, the cinematic sign of the bond is an opening or dilating eye. In the film's informatic semiotics, the link is presented as a transmission, the bond as a reception. Short of death, they both convey the establishing of a two-way circuit, but the link is focalized from the position of the sender, the bond by another's observation of the receiver. The failure of Grace's soul to pass through the "eye of Eywa" and back into a mortal body is at the same time its successful transmission *to* Eywa. The scientist's dying words would affirm the suggested metaphysics: "I'm with her, Jake. She's real." Her ascension to the world spirit is figured by a tubular conduit into a burst of white light. In contrast, in the movie's final scene, when the mind of Jake Sully succeeds in passing through the eye of Eywa permanently into his avatar body, the reception of his living metempsychosis is figured as Eywa's accomplishment and marked instantaneously by the sign of the bond: we watch his Na'vi eyes open wide. The informatic link is now bodily bonded to biotic and metabiotic cognition.

To sum up this phase of the discussion, *tsaheylu*—the bond—may be understood as a displacement and renaturalization, an organic interiorization of the exterior *connectivity* of the teleactive link. Autopoietic bodily organs are not just coupled to but also take the place of computerized telecommunicational prostheses. Playing out its imaginary cross of the informatic and the cognitive, the technological and autopoietic, *Avatar* fuses these two together by telling a tale of posthuman metamorphosis, a story of metempsychosis by embodied mediation. I will come back to this.

Eywa

In a second, more recondite displacement of the link, what is displaced and renaturalized is whatever it is that *powers* it. At one level, this is a practical matter of storyworld logic, but it is never addressed in the given discourse of the film. This occulting of power sources is entirely typical and endemic, especially to science-fiction cinema. For instance, no one asks the text of *Star Wars* to give an accounting of how a star cruiser repeatedly hits transgalactic warp drive. The genre banks on a limitless energy account. Viewing *Avatar*, if one is worried about verisimilitude, one just assumes that back at headquarters, the primary link station taps into whatever generators run the base. When Grace and her avatar team repair to the "mobile link at site 26," and then later, when they haul that module all the way to the outskirts of the Tree of Souls, we assume the availability of mobile generators and their fuel sources. Similarly but more mysteriously, we must assume that avatar bodies can tap their organic metabolisms to run the recondite circuitry of their embedded or bioengineered transceivers.

However, in this second or further displacement of the implications of the link, we go from occulted energy sources to *occult* energy sources. In *Avatar*, all explicit discourse about energy, electrical or otherwise, in the service of communication is offered in reference to Eywa, the biosphere and/or biospirit of Pandora itself. Or, in short, energy becomes anima. This element of the fabula emerges from bits and pieces of dialogue. Out in the Pandoran forest, inserting an electrical probe into a tree, avatars driven by Grace and her colleague Norm make scientific conversation: "That is signal transduction from this root to the root of the tree next to it." "So it's probably electrical, based on the speed of the reaction." Before his conversion experiences, Jake S reports to his ongoing video log about Neytiri: "She's always going on about the flow of energy, the spirits of animals. I really hope this tree-hugger crap is not on the final." Grace gives him an ethnographic tip: "Try to see the forest through her eyes." A bit later, he is more receptive: "I'm trying to understand this deep connection the people have to the forest. She talks about a network of energy that flows through all living things. She says, all energy is only borrowed." The importance of Grace's ongoing witness of Jake S's cultural transformation is that through her mediation, native Na'vi beliefs about natural energies are granted human scientific validation through empirical measurement. Grace observes satellite images of the Tree of Souls: "It's their most sacred place. See the Flux Vortex in these false-color images? . . . There is something really interesting going on in there biologically."

This verbal and visual imagery conveys the perennial Western muddle between science and spirituality, physics and metaphysics, energy and anima—Bruno Latour country indeed, and the air that science fiction breathes. We get a stereotypical polarization between the callous and mercenary insensitivity and convenient racism of the corporate exploiters and the incommunicable intuitions of the indigenous exploited race. Nonetheless, the scripted vocabulary of the film approaches the profundity of actual Gaian science, the vigorous systemic worldview I alluded to earlier—the interconnectedness and systemic coevolution of life and its environment, the autopoietic biosphere that our culture is genuinely and desperately trying to bring to working cognition. In this mass-mediated entertainment, however, that vista must come into view through neural metaphors for geobiological processes, leading off into New Age equivocations between energy, mind, and spirit. Latour would seem to contend that, such as it is, this vision of an interconnected biosphere is at least one step beyond the dead atomistic reductionism of the modernist sensibility.

Couched in this popular vehicle, the properly sundry material and conceptual couplings of electronic, computational, and organic systems are reified and distributed in a Pandoran approximation of Gaia. From this complex of information and cognition, however, the narrative solicits animism rather than cybernetics—spiritual forces rather than emergent systemic functions. But when Grace pleads with her corporate masters for a moratorium on the assault on Home Tree, she does so both to honor the validity of Na'vi spiritual beliefs and in order to preserve its scientific usefulness as a field site. There is no necessary contradiction between these intentions:

> "Those trees were sacred to the Omaticaya in a way that you can't imagine. . . . I'm not talking about some kind of pagan voodoo here, I'm talking about something real, something measurable in the biology of the forest. . . . What we think we know is that there is some kind of electrochemical communication between the roots of the trees. Like the synapses between neurons. And each tree has 10^4 connections to the trees around it. And there are 10^{12} trees on Pandora. . . . It's more connections than the human brain—get it? It's a network. It's a global network and the Na'vi can access it, they can upload and download data, memories—at sites like the one you destroyed."

These heterogeneous informatic and cognitive systemic elements flow into the validated reality of Eywa, and like Gaia for real, Eywa is priceless, beyond all corporate accounting. Eywa is also the measurable reservoir and emergent personhood of the "network of energy that flows through all living things" on the planet, for which reason, as Jake S has now realized, the Na'vi have no need for the beads and trinkets with which the Earthling exploiters want to buy their planet.

Eywa presides at extreme moments, such as the scene of the ritual effort to save Grace from her deadly wounds. Here at the threshold of death or transcendence, the filmic discourse gives us direct second-order observations of the two-sided form of the avatar system. We see it when Jake S undergoes his metempsychosis into Jake A. Grace's dying human body also lies directly next to her avatar, which itself cannot live without a mind to drive it, but which is also the potentially permanent receptacle of her telecommunicated personhood. As the scene proceeds, the imagery of Eywa is driven to a spectacle of pagan delirium. With native drums pounding and the people gathered together, each in Lotus position around the many-rooted Tree of Souls, the Na'vi bond directly to Eywa through their glowing *tsaheylu* connectors, tap into, access, and augment Eywa's global network. But what is more telling and less clichéd is this scene's amplification of embodied mediation. Up from Pandora, more filaments like root hairs above ground proliferate around Grace and her avatar, called forth to wire together Eywa's mediation of the organic transmission of this person from one body to another, trying for enough bond-width, so to speak, to transmit an entire soul. But Grace makes it only halfway. Both of her bodies die, as "all that she is" ascends to Eywa.

Embodied Mediation

"In the place the eye does not see," in the avatar body of Jake A and in the name of Grace, Jake S takes his righteous revenge against his forsaken corporate nation. The human system-designers of the Na'vi avatars do not appear to have taken into consideration the potentially corrupting or emancipating influence on their human drivers of the *tsaheylu* filaments that come along with the Na'vi genome. Jake S goes off the reservation at least in part because through his immersion in Jake A he gets close enough to the Na'vi to access *their* network and measure the difference between his own, relatively clunky virtual technological link and Jake A's elegant and consummate organic bond. Jake S ultimately transforms into Jake A due to the formal pull of his avatar body's enhanced ability to mediate its world, the gratifying access his Pandoran frame has to Eywa's organic Internet.

The desire to return from technological exteriorizations to bodily reconnections is a significant trend in technoscience fictions of metamorphic displacements. Such stories seek to remediate disembodied mediations, to turn signs back into concrete things, to transform the word back into flesh, while at the same time overcoming the discreteness and separation of bodies and minds in some more encompassing holistic ensemble. If a human technology is not available for these purposes, an alien body or metaphysics can be made to do. For instance, in another striking narrative of human/alien encounter leading to a posthuman metamorphosis—Octavia Butler's brilliant *Xenogenesis* trilogy (republished in the omnibus edition titled *Lilith's Brood*)—the alien Oankali seduce their human partners with organic capacities entirely reminiscent of the digital networks arising in the author's world in the eighties. Kittler might read the Oankali's advanced memory and communication functions as "alien-ated" media devices personifying the posthuman destination of the digital convergence of previously separate data streams. Even in the long slumber of the chrysalis phase of their developmental metamorphoses, like sleeping monitors or voice-activated recorders, the Oankali are always *on*. These alien designers of construct bodies resemble self-reproducing organic computers with nervous systems that naturally undergo metamorphic upgrades, passing on accumulated genetic memories that are downloaded by lateral cellular transfer from one generation to the next.

Moreover, Butler's aliens also come organically equipped with sensory tentacles for direct neural connections among discrete bodies. Here is a telling prior telling of embodied mediation—the fictional return of technological and telecommunicational functions to organic conditions and capacities. As with the *tsaheylu* connectors on Pandora, the attraction of such organs is that through them, communication no longer has to suffer real-world delays, need not go through the "bottleneck of the signifier" or the detour of social systems operationally distinct from the psychic systems that they mediate.[19] In the first book of the *Xenogenesis* trilogy, the human heroine Lilith witnesses how, through neural interconnection, the Oankali can communicate without language. More so than Jake S in his link berth, more like the Na'vi around the Home Tree, the Oankali signify a social intimacy and solidarity that puts the fallibility of linguistic interaction in the shade: "Controlled multisensory stimulation. Lilith suspected it was the closest thing to telepathy she would ever see practiced."[20]

And while this first of presumably many *Avatar* movies to come does not exploit the suggestion of Grace's earlier wisecrack by presenting Neytiri and Jake A making the *tsaheylu* bond ponytail to ponytail—for their mating scene, these filaments are discretely put away from cinematic display—Butler goes the distance. The *Xenogenesis* trilogy develops the sexual exchanges of her human and alien characters through the inclusion of an *ooloi*, a bodily-specialized member of the Oankali trained to be a sexual and reproductive mediator, with supplemental limbs extruding sensory filaments for binding the intercourse of mating pairs or clusters into a directly neural affair. Making love to her human mate, Joseph, with her bonded ooloi, Nikanj, in their midst, Lilith

> never knew whether she was receiving Nikanj's approximation of Joseph, a true transmission of what Joseph was feeling, some combination of truth and approximation, or just a pleasant fiction. . . . Nikanj focused on the intensity of their attraction, their union. It left Lilith no other sensation. It seemed, itself, to vanish. (162)

In its telling of embodied mediation, *Avatar* begins with the temporary technological metempsychoses produced when the avatar system beams the minds of the drivers into the bodies of their vehicles. In yet another personified semiolepsis, with his avatar body already prepared by hybridization with his identical twin brother's genome, Jake Sully's incorporeal being undergoes metempsychotic interludes linked with his avatar. But on Pandora, because the mind of Eywa is at the same time the body of Eywa, the planet and its life forms are envisioned as an emergent networked sentience, a globally embodied media system with which its life forms may be bonded. If he is to become "one of the people," the human being Jake Sully must slough off the mortal coil of his human form and leap through the eye of Eywa into his proper quasi-Pandoran body. Just as, with her victory, Eywa throws off the temporary Earthborn irritant of the RDA mining company from her system, so too, in an equal and opposite reaction, Jake S performs a permanent metempsychosis through a final, one-way transmission *into* the body of Jake A, and therefore into Eywa. At that point, the Pandoran system reasserts its operational closure, its planetary autonomy.

Performance Capture

Another media technology vanishes from *Avatar*'s text, and yet is greatly in evidence among its promotional paratexts. It could be thought of as yet another displacement of the link, but one outside the text to begin with, and by which the movie's imagery of corporealized mediation is returned to exterior technological conditions. My earlier works *Allegories of Writing* and *Posthuman Metamorphosis* variously elaborate the thesis that, as constructed in a given narrative medium as an element of the fabula, the metamorphic body is itself an allegory of the transformativity of that medium. Thus, for instance, stated deconstructively, a literary character that undergoes a bodily metamorphosis is an allegory of writing—of erasure and translation, of the transposability and iterability of written signifiers, the deviations and corruptions of texts. *Posthuman Metamorphosis* states a related idea systems-theoretically:

> Posthuman metamorphs couple the media systems that enact them to the social systems communicating them. The medium—whether the words of a text, the code of a program, a narrative frame, or a bodily frame—transforms the forms it brings forth. . . . Narratives of metamorphosis are allegories of narrative communication. (177)

The transformativity of narrative mediums extends beyond literary semiosis to any regime of the trace and its erasure, to anything that fits under the headings of analog and digital media technologies founded on informatic and communicational coding and storage regimes. When cinema is the medium of the metamorphosis, it leaves its own particular traces on the cinematic text and its fabula. *Avatar* draws to a head just how many different media technologies are currently available for remediation within the cinematic medium. Thus, a significant amount of social chatter around this movie, when not obsessing its themes or complaining about its derivativeness, has been about the backstory of its innovations in CGI, computer-generated imagery. But I have not yet found discussed any notion that the story told by *Avatar* is an allegory of the media technology that went into its own production.

You will have noticed, however, that my initial focus on Cameron's telepresence system for filming the sunken Titanic suggested viewing that prior episode as an anticipation of *Avatar*'s cinematic fantasy of the avatar as a literally embodied teleaction system within which its operator is bodily immersed. In the same vein, an actual production technology—one that, unlike the 3-D rendering, remains outside any version of the text of the film—presents the most telling subtext for the avatar system inside the film. This technology is the "performance-capture" process perfected by Cameron's production team. It marks an advance on previous motion-capture processes because it bypasses the need to fill in the finer details of facial expressions with animation. Sometimes dubbed "e-motion capture," it yields the faces of main characters believably "human-like," even when their bodies are those of three-meter-tall blue humanoids with tails. Right here, the animism of the fable reverts back to the hyperanimation of its text's technological instance.

YouTube is full of *Avatar* clips showing this production technique.[21] A window with a finished scene is placed next to another showing a film of the performance-capture "filming" of the acted component of the scene. These clips render the two-sided form of the avatar system once again, through a display allowing a second-order observation of both sides of the production process. The actor's body is wrapped in the usual motion-capture garb, to which has been added the performance-capture enhancement of a head-mounted camera aimed back at the actor's face. The data from that real-time, high-definition facial scan is then transmitted to the CGI computers, out of which process comes the realized representation of the screen character. In a word, as in a video game, the metamorphosed cinematic representation is precisely the *digitized* avatar—as it were, the transmitted emotive soul in a new, virtual body—of the performance-captured actor. The CGI studio capture of the actor in cinematic performance is the actual transmission of which the temporarily or permanently transmitted mind of the human driver into its Na'vi avatar is the allegorical sign.

On this level at least, *Avatar* is an allegory of computer-generated cinema. Its discourse is the inverted sign of its own production process. I have remarked earlier that *Avatar* takes the digital interactivity of a virtual-reality or cyberspace scenario and sends it through a biocybernetic system that everts it into a tale of teleactivity within a natural storyworld. The fable told by *Avatar* envisions the renaturalization of the technological by way of the spiritual. But then, as Luhmann suggests, "What is 'Spirit' if not a metaphorical circumlocution for the mystery of communication?"[22] *Avatar* and other tales of embodied mediation dramatize a desire for which no amount of communication will ever suffice, and which thus keeps the mysterious wheels of social autopoiesis turning: the desire to return from signs back to things by way of souls. At every level, *Avatar* is self-contradictory and wrapped up in its own paradoxes. But that is not a fault, really; it is the most authentic thing about this fantasy. This is what can happen when, as Latour suggests, "a new search for hope" is enacted "on condition that what it means to have a body, a mind, and a world is completely redefined." However, the existence and the exhilaration of the text that tells this story rests on what is actually and always possible, taken out to an extreme—the transformation of objects into signs, or more precisely, the augmenting of objects by the supplements of their signs. Placed into its total package, further refining a process for the informatic duplication of physical bodies in digital bits, *Avatar* celebrates the power of media-technological links to manipulate reality through its representations.

Driven by such powerful media technologies in its making, in its telling, and in its tale, *Avatar* is a many-leveled parable about the always precarious status of individual and social autonomy. *Mind of My Mind, Eternal Sunshine of the Spotless Mind, Memento,* and *Aramis* are comparable parables. Systemic autonomy is never absolute; it arises, if at all, from an operational closure producing selective openness toward its environment. The possibility of cognition is won upon the construction of the operational autonomy of the cognitive system. One can proceed from there to couple cognitive systems to each other, to other kinds of systems, and to mediatic and other technological structures. But the operational outcomes in every case will depend from moment to moment on how viably the cognitive work is distributed through its systemic ecology. Three of the five narratives we have examined stage and mediate a fictional network centered on a technological system that, when it fails or even when it works all too well, fails to deliver the social goals for which it is designed. In the stories of the characters involved, this lapse is usually a desirable outcome, a fortunate failure. But in any event, as usual, the fault lies not with our designed systems, but with ourselves, their designers.

Gaia and Self-Reference

As a conclusion, let us return from these narrative mediations to the technoscientific and epistemological mediations that brought to mind the ecosystemic object James Lovelock comes to call Gaia. His initial intuition occurred in 1965, while he was working in Pasadena, California, at the Jet Propulsion Laboratory (JPL) on a contract to develop scientific instrumentation for Mars landers. His first recognizably Gaian papers derive from these specific efforts, which occurred just before a NASA weather satellite gave the Earth its first good and complete technological image of itself at the end of 1967, an image that appeared a year later on the front cover of the first *Whole Earth Catalog*. But British contractor Lovelock had been immersed in the American NASA milieu since 1961. His work there was directed to a mission driven both politically and scientifically by the quest to find, as well as send, life beyond the Earth: "At this time scientists still seemed to think that life flourished on Mars. I recall Carl Sagan enthusing over the wave of darkness that crosses Mars when winter ends. He and many others saw this phenomenon as indicative of the growth of vegetation. . . . This image of Mars sustained their belief in biological life-detection techniques."[23]

Lovelock refers here to the life-detection schemes put forward at JPL by his biologist colleagues, who assumed for Mars, Earth-style life in a watery medium, the detection of which demanded probes making contact with the surface of Mars. By 1964, he had devised a scheme for life detection based on a different principle, the search for an entropy reduction, that is, for a signature of some counterentropic ordering commensurate with the living organization of matter and energy relative to abiotic processes. Entropy is fundamentally a thermodynamic and thus a physical concept, and Lovelock's paper, "A Physical Basis for Life-Detection Experiments," declares an alternative to *biological* life-detection techniques. Where and how is such a signature to be found? The title of his next proto-Gaia paper, lead-authored by Dian Hitchcock, states this explicitly: "Life Detection by Atmospheric Analysis." The premise of his life-detection argument makes the crucial move out of normal science and into the Gaian cosmos. At that time, Earth's atmosphere was assumed to be almost entirely a geological and hence a fundamentally abiotic phenomenon.[24] Lovelock ventured the countervailing, now universally accepted idea that the atmosphere of a planet on which life exists will be to a significant extent the *product* of those living processes—enough so for that atmosphere to contain chemical by-products of life, in proportions improbable on an abiotic planet, to be detected and deciphered.

The brilliance of his scheme, now normal astrobiology, is its economy. One does not need to go to Mars or any other planet to apply it. For the exoplanets that have been detected in succeeding decades, as well as for those of our own solar system, atmospheres can be assessed here on Earth by spectrographic analysis.

The crucial turn toward Gaia proper came in September 1965, when Lovelock encountered—newly acquired from the 42-inch telescope NASA had installed at the Pic du Midi Observatory in the Pyrenees—infrared spectrographs of the atmospheres of Venus and Mars. They showed atmospheric entropies off the charts. Both planetary atmospheres were dominated by CO_2 and chemically inert, virtually at thermodynamic equilibrium. Whatever combustion or reduction of chemical potential had ever been possible there had long since burned out. According to Lovelock's scheme, the verdict on Mars was obvious: it harbored no life. When the Viking explorer landed on Mars a decade later, its probes found what Lovelock predicted—no life.

Gaia theory regarding a "living Earth" is born out of this prediction of Mars's lifelessness. Lovelock first conceived it by turning his interrogation of other planetary atmospheres back on the Earth. Now he notes with new eyes that our atmosphere is at a cosmically improbable chemical disequilibrium, and that evidence is abundant for the overall constancy of that imbalance over geological time. Earth's atmosphere has been a highly combustible mixture of reactive gases for hundreds of millions of years, but rather than burning out, it has maintained its lower entropy. The idea of Gaia as a self-regulating systemic unity is ignited in the vessel of this conceptual conundrum over atmospheric chemistry, a conundrum largely unrecognized as such before Lovelock did so in the mid-1960s: "If the air is burning, what sustains it at a constant composition? . . . It came to me suddenly, just like a flash of enlightenment, that to persist and keep stable, something must be regulating the atmosphere and so keeping it at its constant composition. Moreover, if most of the gases came from living organisms, then life at the surface must be doing the regulation."[25]

The idea of Gaia emerges when a cosmological gaze is returned upon the planetary conditions of its own possibility. The cultural resonance of Lovelock's Gaia is bound up with a self-referential turn in the cosmic gaze, an epistemological loop, an outward-inward re-turn beyond and back to the Earth. This can occur not just in creative or scientific imagination but for real only when a technology exists to make it possible. You have to be able to get a camera literally far enough away from the Earth that, when you look back at it, you can see it whole, and then, farther yet, in relation to other cosmic objects. And just as the Gaia hypothesis is taking its baby steps, a self-referential cosmology of the Earth as seen in the newly arriving space photographs is being mediated—articulated and celebrated—by the *Whole Earth Catalog*. Both Gaia and the *Catalog* partake of a space-oriented technoculture of systems thinking. Let us look at just one item published there, a review we touch on in chapter 3, von Foerster's write-up of Spencer-Brown's *Laws of Form*. I will draw out of that review only an impression of the importance of *Laws of Form* for an articulation of the logic of self-reference concurrent with the emergence of Gaia theory.

Von Foerster's review begins with a bang: "The laws of form have finally been written!"[26] He is playfully picking up the prophetic suggestion of Spencer-Brown's epigraph, from Blake's *America: A Prophecy*: "Tho' obscur'd, this is the form of the Angelic land," with an annunciation of this present revelation.[27] He begins his synopsis of the text by drawing a distinction between laws and descriptions: "Laws are not descriptions, they are commands; injunctions: 'Do!' Thus, the first constructive proposition in this book is the injunction: 'Draw a distinction!' an exhortation to perform the primordial creative act."[28] We see why *Laws of Form* is now a bible for constructivists. The world derives not from a timeless essence or classical Platonic form, but with a critical act that cuts a cosmos out of primal chaos. Or, again, in Spencer-Brown's terms for the application of the laws, to produce an indication, to point to something, one marks its distinction from the unmarked state. The laws describe the algorithms of such processes, of which descriptions are the product. Thus, any description, any specific indication—that is to say, the possibility of any cognition or observation whatsoever—in obeying the laws of form, must await the injunction that calls it forth. It depends on the particular distinction, or distinction of a distinction, by which it is marked out and constituted, and this cognitive contingency goes all the way down until one is back to chaos—or at least, until one is prior to autopoiesis.

Von Foerster rolls the cognitive processes of the laws of form forward from the primal distinction:

After this, practically everything else follows smoothly: a rigorous foundation of arithmetic, of algebra, of logic, of a calculus of indications, intentions and desires; a rigorous development of laws of form, may they be of logical relations, of descriptions of the universe by physicists and cosmologists, or of functions of the nervous system which generates descriptions of the universe of which it is itself a part.

His itinerary of the procession of *Laws of Form* is itself highly compressed, but as I read this passage, it concludes with a description of outer- or heteroreference ("descriptions of the universe") followed by one of self-reference ("descriptions . . . of functions of the nervous system which generates descriptions of the universe"), and so returns to its starting point, that is, to *its* conditions of possibility. In the terms I suggest with regard to the conception of Gaia theory, here once again is a looping, an outward-inward re-turn of the cosmic gaze. "Descriptions of the universe" could be anything at all, the world or any of its furnishings. But let us indicate, for instance, Mars as the object of an observer that has, so to speak, stepped out of the universe it observes in order to be "objective." This is the God's-eye view of normal science. However, to distinguish "functions of the nervous system which generates descriptions of the universe of which it is itself a part" is, in this instance, to return the cognition of Mars to the formation of its Earthly observer. In second-order cybernetics, the observer, along with whatever objects it as an observing system succeeds in constructing, reenters itself back into the universe of which its nervous system or cognitive apparatus "is itself a part." In short, the form of the observer is reentered into the form of the observed, and vice versa. Their distinction has been operationally affirmed but systemically sublated.

Gaia theory's development of the vision of the systemic integration of living things into their planetary and cosmic environments parallels the renovation of the observer's relation to its universe in second-order systems theory. Ontological propriety is surpassed by systemic construction over the void. The planetary self-reference of Gaia theory resonates with the cognitive self-reference of epistemological constructivism. In either case, dichotomies of subject and object, or life and environment, are sublated in favor of participation within higher-order systemic ensembles. Just as a living cell or an individual organism is both distinct from and an emergent element conditioned by the metabiotic system called Gaia, Gaia is both distinct from and an emergent element within the larger system of an evolving cosmos that mainstream astrobiologists are now content to call "the living universe." The universe and its constituents are as much elements of Gaia as it is of them.

ACKNOWLEDGMENTS

Neocybernetics and Narrative features work developed during a 2010–11 senior fellowship at the International Research Institute for Cultural Technologies and Media Philosophy (IKKM) at Bauhaus University, Weimar, Germany. The intellectual intensity of IKKM has stamped the primary arguments here concerning the heteroreception of the trace, noise and form, reentry and time, objects and projects, and the depiction of embodied mediation. In the years since, I have extended this work and fashioned it as a deliberate framework for gathering in other research investigating and interrelating systems theory, media theory, and narrative theory.

I want to thank the many people who made my sojourn at IKKM possible, productive, and pleasant. Priority of place goes to my stateside sponsor, longtime interdisciplinary collaborator, and the stately queen of the fourth dimension, Linda Henderson, and to my primary IKKM contact and benefactor, Bernhard Siegert. I owe special debts to my department chair at the time, Sam Dragga, for smoothing my extended absence from the home campus, and to Texas Tech University for conferring me a Horn professorship on my return. Thanks as well to IKKM's congenial codirector, Lorenz Engell, and to all the terrific people who graced my time at the institute: my assistant, Irma Klerings, and Kristina Hellmann on the staff; my colleagues, particularly Gertrud Koch, Irit Rogoff, Eric Alliez, and Erich Hörl; others at IKKM who became friends and musical partners, Michael Cuntz, Anne Ortner, and Martin Schlesinger; and finally, the crew at Bauhaus University, Weimar, who opened their homes and found me a place in the band, Markus and Joanna Schlaffke and Wolfram Hoehne.

Many other colleagues and friends extended their encouragement and critique toward the completion of this work. I am grateful for the hospitality and generosity of Yves Abrioux, Jan Alber, Tori Alexander, Sandy Baldwin, Jim Bono, Søren Brier, Linda Brigham, John Bruni, Oron Catts, Paul Cobley, Rich Doyle, Sabine Flach, Bernie Geoghegan, Phillip Guddemi, Mark Hansen, Kate Hayles, Jamie Hutchinson, John Johnston, Edgar Landgraf, Tim Lenoir, Ira Livingston, Bob Markley, Steven Meyer, Colin Milburn, Allen Miller, Tom Mitchell, Hans-Georg Moeller, Albert Müller, the late Sonja Neef, Maria O'Connell, Laura Otis, the late Jim Paxson, John Protevi, Hans-Jörg Rheinberger, Alexander Riegler, Judith Roof, Martin Rosenberg, Manuela Rossini, Dorion Sagan, Michael Schiltz, Henning Schmidgen, Philipp Schweighauser, Chris Shaw, Jan Söffner, Joy Stocke, Henry Sussman, Joe Tabbi, Bill Thompson, Evan Thompson, Dirk Vanderbeke, Tyler Volk, Peter Weingart, David Wellbery, Chris Witmore, and Cary Wolfe.

I am happy to acknowledge, in addition to IKKM, the following institutions and organizations for sponsoring invitations to present work that has found its finished form in this book: Writing Science Symposium, Stanford Humanities Center, Stanford University; Department of English, Rice University, Houston, Texas; Department of Philosophy, Brock University, St. Catharines, Canada; Comparative Literature Program, Department of Languages, Literatures, and Cultures, University of South Carolina; Society for Media Studies 2010 meeting, Bauhaus University, Weimar, Germany; Max Planck Institute for the History of Science, Berlin, Germany; Center for Research on Literature and Cognition, University of Paris 8, France; 2011 Heinz von Foerster Congress, Vienna, Austria; Morphomata Symposium on Cosmology and Cosmopolitanism in Media and Culture, University of Cologne, Germany; School of Sociology and Philosophy, University College Cork, Ireland; Southern Comparative Literature Association, 2012 conference, Las Vegas, Nevada; and the international symposium on the Ecological Paradigm: Issues and Perspectives of a General Ecology of Media and Technology, Ruhr University, Bochum, Germany.

NOTES

Introduction

1 Maturana, "Interview on von Foerster," 39.

2 von Foerster, "Thoughts and Notes on Cognition," 47. See Clarke, "From Information to Cognition." I discuss this passage in the section of chapter 2 on Serres's "The Origin of Language."

3 Margulis and Sagan, *What Is Life?* 78.

4 Varela with Johnson, "On Observing Natural Systems," 27. I discuss this Varela text in the "Origin of Language" section of chapter 2.

5 von Foerster, "On Constructing a Reality," 217. For insight into the gestation of this seminal statement, see Müller, "Computing a Reality."

6 I examine the concept of interpenetration in social systems theory in more detail in the "Telepathy" section of chapter 1.

7 For expert and extensively documented introductions to cognitive approaches to narrative, see Herman, "Cognitive Narratology"; and Tabbi, "Cognitive Science."

8 See Noë, *Out of Our Heads.*

9 See Thompson, "Life and Mind"; and Protevi, "Beyond Autopoiesis." In recent years, Tom Froese and his collaborators have achieved a considerable international profile at the intersection of enactive cognitive science and phenomenology. See Froese, "From Cybernetics to Second-Order Cybernetics," and "From Second-Order Cybernetics to Enactive Cognitive Science." See also Froese and Stewart, "Life after Ashby"; and Froese and Ziemke, "Enactive Artificial Intelligence."

10 For instance, Froese and Di Paolo's "Sociality" strikes me as taking systems theory back into the equivocal box of humanist "intersubjectivity." See the critique of intersubjectivity in the "Society and System" section of chapter 2. The epistemological Varela bears recovering beneath the phenomenological Varela. For Luhmann's treatment of phenomenology relative to systems theory, see Luhmann, "The Modern Sciences and Phenomenology," a 1995 lecture commemorating Husserl's 1935 Vienna lectures.

11 For greater detail on Luhmann's theory of communication, see Wolfe, "Meaning as Event-Machine"; on cognition, see Luhmann, "Cognitive Program of Constructivism"; and Thyssen, "Luhmann and Epistemology."

12 See Ben-Jacob, "Social Behavior of Bacteria." The abstract for this article concludes: "Bacteria must be able to sense the environment and perform internal information processing for thriving on latent information embedded in the complexity of their environment. I then propose that by acting together, bacteria can perform this most elementary cognitive function more efficiently as can be illustrated by their cooperative behavior" (315). Note the traditional informatic ontology, with "latent information embedded in . . . their environment"; however, what is important is the recognition of bacterial cognition. See also Ben-Jacob et al., "Bacterial Linguistic Communication and Social Intelligence"; and Lilly, *Mind of the Dolphin.*

13 For a detailed statement and ratification of this epistemological description from within object-oriented ontology, see Bryant, *Democracy of Objects,* 26, 135–62. His treatment of autopoietic systems theory suggests a positive alignment of systems theory's constructivist epistemology with the new realist ontologies. Compare Scholl, "Between Realism and Constructivism." Bryant cites the opening sentence of the first chapter of Luhmann's *Social Systems:* "The following considerations assume that there are systems. Thus they do not begin with epistemological doubt" (12; in Bryant, *Democracy of Objects,* 137). Luhmann poses this initial premise as a paradox for his theory of operational closure to unfold: "The concept of system refers to something that is in reality a system and thereby incurs the responsibility of testing its statements against reality" (*Social Systems,* 12).

14 Luhmann, "Self-Organization and Autopoiesis," 144.

15 See Geoghegan, "From Information Theory to French Theory."

1. Systems, Media, Narrative

1 Barthes, "Introduction to the Structural Study of Narratives," 79.

2 Maxwell, "On Governors."

3 Margaret Mead, quoted in Brand, "For God's Sake, Margaret," 33; Rosenblueth, Wiener, and Bigelow, "Behavior, Purpose, and Teleology," 19.

4 von Foerster, "Cybernetics."

5 Morowitz, *Energy Flow in Biology,* 2; italics in the original. The ensuing cultural hypertrophy of *flow* as all-purpose cosmic dynamism hitches a ride from physical, thermo- and hydro-dynamical usages to our current universalized "space of flows": "The information society . . . is constructed around flows: flows of capital, flows of information, flows of technology, flows of organizational interaction, flows of images, sounds, and symbols" (Castells, *Rise of the Network Society,* 1:411–12).

6 Luhmann, *Social Systems,* 8.

7 Bateson, cited in Brand, "For God's Sake, Margaret," 33. His reference is to Warren McCulloch, neurophysiologist and cyberneticist, Massachusetts Institute of Technology (MIT) colleague of Norbert Wiener, and coconvener of the Macy Conference on Cybernetics. McCulloch was also instrumental in establishing von Foerster's American career.

8 von Foerster, "Interview."

9 Their definitive statement is Maturana and Varela, *Autopoiesis and Cognition.* See also Maturana and Varela, *Tree of Knowledge.*

10 Biological autopoiesis has been studied in relation to computational self-organization, theories of the origin of living systems, neurophysiology and neurophenomenology, artificial life, artificial intelligence, and Gaia theory. See Winograd and Flores, *Understanding Computers and Cognition;* Luisi, "Autopoiesis"; Thompson, *Mind in Life;* Bourgine and Stewart, "Autopoiesis and Cognition"; and Froese and Ziemke, "Enactive Artificial Intelligence."

11 See Clarke, "Neocybernetics of Gaia," and "Autopoiesis and the Planet."

12 An excellent introduction is Moeller, *Luhmann Explained.* For literary applications, see Wellbery, "Observation, Difference, Form"; McMurry, *Environmental Renaissance;* Clarke, *Posthuman Metamorphosis;* and Lippert, "Narrowing Circles."

13 Luhmann, *Social Systems,* 29.

14 Luhmann, "Cognitive Program of Constructivism," 147.

15 For an updated overview, see Winthrop-Young, *Kittler and the Media.*

16 Kittler, *Gramophone,* xxxix. See also Winthrop-Young and Gane, "Friedrich Kittler," in particular, discussing Sybille Krämer's contribution to the special number of which their text is the introduction (10–11).

17 Kittler, *Gramophone,* 1, 262.

18 von Neumann, "General and Logical Theory of Automata," 294.

19 Latour, *We Have Never Been Modern,* 46.

20 A complementary if alternative view is Winthrop-Young, "Silicon Sociology."

21 See Clarke, *Posthuman Metamorphosis,* chapter 1.

22 See Clam, "System's Sole Constituent, the Operation."

23 For an economical overview, see Luhmann, "What Is Communication?" I briefly expound this text in the "Society and System" section of chapter 2.

24 This ontological, hence atemporal aspect of the form of the trace has been well stated: "A mark or sign intended as an indicator is self-referential. The self is the whole space including the mark and the observer. But the mark points, in the first place, to its own location, and in this process becomes a locus of reference. The mark refers to itself. The whole refers to itself through the mark" (Kauffman, "Self-Reference and Recursive Forms," 53). However, I have constructed my origin scenarios to be indifferent to the matter of intention and to suggest that, for its observer, the trace will be construed as self-referential, whether it is intended as an indicator or not.

25 Ellie Arroway's cosmic ride can be viewed at http://www.youtube.com/watch?v=Z8axMaBL4uo.

26 See Aragno, "Mind's Farthest Reach," which documents the tenacity of the facticity approach to telepathy in the milieu of depth psychology.

27 Derrida, "Telepathy." See also Miller, *Medium Is the Maker.*

28 Nicholas Royle, a literary critic at the University of Sussex and the English translator of Derrida's "Telepathy," initiated the narrative approach, which he develops through a literary reading of Derrida's deconstructive critique of Freud's texts recording his psychoanalytical vacillations over telepathy. See Royle, *Telepathy and Literature,* and 'Telepathy Effect.'

29 Myers is cited in Peters, *Speaking into the Air,* 105. See also Luckhurst, *Invention of Telepathy.*

30 The *Wings of Desire* subway scene can be viewed at http://www.youtube.com/watch?v=2izlo8UX_PA&feature=bf_prev&list=PLE37F26B3E0A2C7F1.

31 Royle, *Telepathy and Literature,* 5.

32 Royle, "'Telepathy Effect,'" 256.

33 Ibid., 259. See also Culler, "Omniscience," 184, 196, which references Royle's work on telepathy.

2. Communication and Information

1 A well-considered information-centered treatment of Serres's cybernetics is Paulson, *Noise of Culture*; however, Paulson subsumes autopoiesis under information theory. See also Schweighauser, *Noises of American Literature.* The ongoing glamour and catchall usage of the informatic concept of noise is evident, for instance, in Lowe and Schaffer, *N01se.* A properly literal and hence massive and compendious approach to noise per se, weighing in at 912 pages all told, is Schwartz, *Making Noise.*

2 Weaver, "Recent Contributions," 4.

3 Luhmann, *Social Systems,* 83. Luhmann's note to this passage cites Edgar Morin, Henri Atlan, Michel Serres, and Jean-Pierre Dupuy. Thanks to Philipp Schweighauser for this reference.

4 The authority for this modern usage is typically attributed to Book III of John Locke's *An Essay Concerning Human Understanding* (1690): "To make Words serviceable to the end of Communication" *(Oxford English Dictionary).* The term derives from the Latin *communicare,* "to impart, share," literally, "to make common," from *communis,* "in common, public, general, shared by all or many."

5 Craig, "Communication."

6 Manovich, *Language of New Media,* 162.

7 Kittler, "History of Communication Media."

8 Chang, *Deconstructing Communication,* 39.

9 Habermas, *Theory of Communicative Action,* 1:386.

10 For another approach to this theoretical nexus, see Leydesdorff, "Luhmann, Habermas."

11 Luhmann, "What Is Communication?" 161.

12 Wiener, *Human Use of Human Beings,* 8.

13 Weaver, "Recent Contributions," 17–18.

14 See Kahn, "Concerning the Line."

15 Bateson, "Form, Substance, and Difference," 453.

16 Bateson, *Steps,* xxv.

17 See Terranova, "Communication beyond Meaning."

18 Luhmann, *Social Systems,* 39–40.

19 Serres, "Origin of Language," 76–77. Contributed to a special issue of *Critique* on *La Psychanalyse vue de dehors,* Serres's "Le point de vue de la bio-physique" is the source text for what comes into English translation, by way of its republication in *Hermès IV: La distribution,* as "The Origin of Language: Biology, Information The-

ory, and Thermodynamics." Thanks to Henning Schmidgen for assistance confirming this documentation.

20 The source text for "Platonic Dialogue" is Serres's 1966 article "Le troisième homme ou le tiers exclu." Thanks to Bernhard Siegert for this reference.

21 Weaver, "Recent Contributions," 7–8.

22 The Avon reprint of *Human Use* is based on its substantially revised 1954 second edition. Chapter 11, "Language, Confusion, and Jam," does not appear in the original 1950 edition.

23 However, according to the theological analogues Wiener purveys in the second edition of *Human Use,* Serres would seem to place us back into a Manichaean universe of "positive malicious evil" (11), in which nature itself is out to jam human communicative purposes.

24 Compare Sloterdijk, *World Interior,* on the classical reverence for the perfect sphere as both geometric and cosmological ideal, over against the noise of the empirical world: "The Greek prejudice in favour of rounded totality would survive until the days of German Idealism. . . . The rise of the world form over the world material was guided by an aesthetics of completion. . . . The beautiful in its pure form can safely be left to the idealists, while the half-beautiful and the ugly occupy empiricists" (15–16).

25 This observation marks the triumph of the informational perspective then abroad across Western science and discourse. Although it is mostly offstage in this discussion, molecular biology, which also fit itself directly to the informational paradigm, is in its heyday: genetic replication is transmission, the genome is the hereditary signal, and mutation is the noise. See Shapiro, *Evolution,* cited in the introduction, for a thorough update on molecular biology. In the terms I am rehearsing here, notions of mutational "noise" (and its more recent variant, "junk DNA") have receded in the face of better molecular understandings of cellular-systemic processes.

26 Nearly four decades later, a similar lack of specification inhabits Katherine Hayles's informatic reprise of this universalization of thermodynamic and physicochemical modeling. While it is true that "boundaries have not been rendered unimportant or nonexistent by the traffic across them," loose notions of "code" and "permeation" substitute here for Serres's earlier "information" and "flow." Hayles still blends cognitive systems into the transmission model along with technological and computational systems: "boundaries of all kinds have become permeable to the supposed other. Code permeates language and is permeated by it; electronic text permeates print; computational processes permeate biological organisms; intelligent machines permeate flesh. Rather than attempt to police these boundaries, we should strive to understand the materially specific ways in which flows across borders create complex dynamics of intermediation" (Hayles, *My Mother Was a Computer,* 242). For a related criticism of this passage, see Clarke and Hansen, "Neocybernetic Emergence," 93.

27 See Clarke, "From Information to Cognition."

28 For more on von Foerster's "On Self-Organizing Systems," see Clarke, "Heinz von Foerster's Demons."

29 von Foerster's "Thoughts and Notes on Cognition" was originally published directly following Maturana's "Neurophysiology of Cognition," the lead chapter of *Cognition: A Multiple View.*

30 For a thorough treatment of related issues, see Brier, "Construction of Information and Communication."

31 Kingsland, *Evolution of American Ecology*, 185. I come back to this in the "Cycle and Flow" section of chapter 5.

32 For another approach to this point of intersection between Serres, Atlan, and Luhmann relative to the role of noise in systems, with particular reference to affect, see Stenner, "Is Autopoietic Systems Theory Alexithymic?" 166–69.

33 See Atlan, *L'Organisation biologique*, 232–33, 243–53. A diagram of von Foerster's self-organizing demons from "On Self-Organizing Systems" appears on 244. See also Atlan, "Hierarchical Self-Organization." Milan Zeleny notes that he included this Atlan paper in his collection on autopoiesis to provide a conceptual counterpoint: "The theory of autopoiesis implies that notions of coding, programming, and transfer of information become misleading if used as explanatory notions at the cellular level. A good, up-to-date exposure to the theory of information appears to be useful for comparative purposes and as a reference" (183).

34 Serres, "Origin of Language," 82.

35 Luhmann, *Art as a Social System*, 6.

36 Kittler, *Gramophone*, 83.

37 Luhmann, *Art as a Social System,* 26–27.

38 Luhmann, *Social Systems,* 172.

39 Spencer-Brown, *Laws of Form*; Luhmann, "Medium of Art"; Baecker, *Problems of Form*; Luhmann, "Paradox of Observing Systems"; Clarke, *Posthuman Metamorphosis*; Schiltz, "Space Is the Place"; Landgraf, *Improvisation as Art*; Moeller, *Radical Luhmann.*

3. Feedback Loops

1 Kauffman, "Self-Reference and Recursive Forms," 53.

2 Franklin, "News under Fire."

3 Kuntz, "What We Said."

4 "Web Site Picks Year's Top Word," CNN.com, December 26, 2003. Article available at http://www.cnn.com/2003/TECH/internet/12/26/top.word.reut/index.html.

5 Savidge, "Embedded for Life."

6 Roberts, "Self-Reference in Literature," 40.

7 Bolter and Grusin, *Remediation,* 5.

8 Kuntz, "What We Said."

9 On the virtualization of the body, see Lévy, *Becoming Virtual.*

10 For a literary application of this text, see Knoop, "Fictional Communication."

11 See http://en.wikiquote.org/wiki/Gertrude_Stein.

12 Latour, *We Have Never Been Modern*, 117.

13 Brand, "For God's Sake, Margaret," 37.

14 Spencer-Brown, *Laws of Form*. *Laws of Form* and its reception in the work of von Foerster and Varela is the subtext of Kauffman's treatment of self-reference sampled at the beginning of this chapter.

15 von Foerster, "On Constructing a Reality," 211.

16 von Foerster, *"Laws of Form."* I return to this text in chapter 5, apropos its affordance of a perspective on the epistemology of the Gaia hypothesis.

17 As Varela remarks at the beginning of his earliest treatment of *Laws of Form:* "Whether in dealing with the organization of systems or with the structure of languages, hardships with self-referential situations have the same root: the distinction between actor or operand, and that which is acted or operated upon, collapses" (Varela, "Calculus for Self-Reference," 5).

18 Luhmann, "Control of Intransparency," 363–64. Emphasis in the original. See also Gonzalez-Diaz, "Paradox, Time, and De-Paradoxication in Luhmann."

19 Woolf, *Mrs. Dalloway*, 3. For more on the relation of narrative forms, systems theory, and Spencer-Brown's calculus of distinctions, see Clarke, *Posthuman Metamorphosis*, chapters 3 and 4.

20 For a dense linguistic analysis and short history of free indirect discourse treated under the phrase "represented speech and thought," see Banfield, *Unspeakable Sentences.* Banfield treats the opening passages of Woolf's *Mrs. Dalloway* on 65–67.

21 Moretti, *Graphs, Maps, Trees*, 82.

22 Bordwell, *Narration in the Fiction Film*, 25, 62.

23 For diagrams of the figural narrative situation in form notation, see Clarke, *Posthuman Metamorphosis*, 85–87.

24 Luhmann, *Social Systems:* "Systems with temporalized complexity *depend on constant disintegration.* Continuous disintegration creates, as it were, a place and a need for successive elements . . . . Temporalized systems must be fast ("hot"). . . . True system performance resides in *conditioning the interdependence of disintegration and reproduction.* A structure is then what can unfold, that is, extend yet constrain, this interdependence" (48).

25 Genette, *Narrative Discourse*, 34.

26 Richardson, "Beyond Story and Discourse," 53.

27 See Royle, "'Telepathy Effect.'"

28 Luhmann, *Art as a Social System*, 7.

29 Luhmann, *Social Systems*, 42.

30 See Chatman, "Backwards."

31 Hansen, "Backmasked Messages," 181.

4. Observing *Aramis, or the Love of Technology*

1 See Deleuze, "Review"; Toscano, "Gilbert Simondon"; and Stiegler, *Technics and Time.*

2 Simondon, *On the Mode of Existence of Technical Objects*, 11.

3 Ellul, *Technological Society*, xxv, 138.

4 See Latour, *We Have Never Been Modern*, 51.

5 Simondon, *On the Mode of Existence of Technical Objects*, 35.

6 Latour with Herzberg, *Aramis: Analyse Socio-Technique d'un Echec.*

7 References to Simondon reappear in Latour's recent work as well. See Latour, "Reflections"; "Can We Get Our Materialism Back, Please?"; and "Prendre le pli des techniques."

8 In terms that Simondon goes on to develop elsewhere, Latour's concern could be said to be with the preindividual phase of the individuation of the technical object, but that later dialect of Simondon's work does not appear in *Aramis.* See Simondon, "Genesis of the Individual."

9 Ellul, *Technological Society,* 133–34, 138.

10 Ibid., ix. See Moskowitz, "How Science Fiction Got Its Name." On the idea of scientifiction, see also Bould and Vint, "Learning from the Little Engines That Couldn't."

11 See Latour and Powers, "Two Writers Face One Turing Test"; and Latour, "Powers of the Facsimile."

12 In *Labyrinths,* Borges observes how the virtual embeddedness of literary texts within the wider world invites exploitation by authors intent on playing with ontological distinctions: "Every novel is an ideal plane inserted into the realm of reality; Cervantes takes pleasure in confusing the objective and the subjective, the world of the reader and the world of the book" (194).

13 MacKenzie had already been acknowledged in a footnote to the preface of *Aramis:* "D. MacKenzie, *Inventing Accuracy: A Historical Sociology of Nuclear Missile Guidance*" (17).

14 Bernward Joerges is a professor of the philosophy and sociology of science and technology at the Technical University of Berlin. See, for instance, Joerges, "Technology in Everyday Life."

15 Bould and Vint, "Learning from the Little Engines That Couldn't," 144. See Laurier and Philo, "X-Morphizing," 1060.

16 Simondon, *On the Mode of Existence of Technical Objects,* 53.

17 See Nowotny, "Actor-Networks vs. Science," for a cogent accounting of Latourian versus systems-theoretical constructivisms.

18 von Foerster, "Objects," 266–67.

19 Moeller, *Radical Luhmann,* 84–85.

20 Luhmann, *Social Systems:* "Only complexity can reduce complexity" (26).

5. Mediations of Gaia

1 See Tansley, "The Use and Abuse of Vegetational Concepts and Terms."

2 Lotka, *Elements of Physical Biology,* 334.

3 Kingsland, *Evolution of American Ecology,* 185.

4 Deleuze and Guattari, *Thousand Plateaus,* 21–22.

5 Serres is perhaps the most notable exception here. While less well-known in Anglophone circles, sociologist turned complexity theorist Edgar Morin is another, although problematic, French systems thinker. Sojourning at the Salk Institute and encountering von Foerster at the end of the 1960s, Morin's six-volume magnum opus, *La Méthode,* purveys subtitles with self-reflexive or second-order phrasings, such as *La Nature de la*

Nature, La Vie de la Vie, and *La Connaissance de la Connaissance.* A later Salk Institute sojourner, Bruno Latour, makes a joke at Morin's expense in the pages of *Aramis,* when the young engineer complains to Norbert H.: "But I thought we had to take *everything* into account. I even read some philosopher, I think, or a sociologist, Edgar Morin, who said that every techno-bio-political problem was also a political-techno-biological problem . . . and that the politics of chips were also the chips of politics or something like that" (152). Unfair or not, it is a cautionary passage: unless recursive formations are immunized against regress through operational and temporal distinctions—basically, the sort of methods of deparadoxication that *Laws of Form* provides to Luhmann's difference-theoretical systems theory—cybernetic holism can revert to an untenable monism, or end up in a cosmic mishmash. Whether this is a valid reading of Morin, I cannot say, but the stereotype of cybernetic philosophy as prone to New Age self-indulgence is not entirely without warrant. That is all the more reason to distinguish and affirm rigorous self-referential systems theory against less stringent versions.

6 Compare Guattari, *Three Ecologies:* "Process, which I oppose here to system or to structure, strives to capture existence in the very act of its constitution, definition and deterritorialization" (30).

7 For a recent collection reviving Bateson for contemporary application to biological systems, see Hoffmeyer, *Legacy for Living Systems.*

8 On autopoietic Gaia, see Clarke, "Autopoiesis and the Planet."

9 Luhmann, *Ecological Communication,* 15.

10 Latour, "Attempt at a 'Compositionist Manifesto,'" 471.

11 For more on Gaia and glaciations, see Lovelock, *Ages of Gaia,* chapter 6; on Gaia as a thermostat, see Lovelock, *Gaia,* chapter 4. On Gaia and systems theory, see Clarke, "Neocybernetics of Gaia."

12 Latour, "Plea for Earthly Sciences," 72.

13 Latour, "Attempt at a 'Compositionist Manifesto,'" 482, 484. On nontrivial machines, see, for instance, von Foerster, "For Niklas Luhmann."

14 Varela, *Principles of Biological Autonomy,* 86.

15 Latour, *Aramis,* 86.

16 Simondon, *On the Mode of Existence of Technical Objects,* 31.

17 "A difference-theoretical theory of form . . . treats forms as pure self-reference, made possible by the marking of the form as a boundary that separates two sides—made possible, in other words, by the fact that form is essentially a boundary." Luhmann, *Art as a Social System,* 28. See "Two-Sided Form" in Clarke, *Posthuman Metamorphosis,* 87–89.

18 *Na'vi-English Dictionary,* v.13.05, compiled by Mark Miller. http://eanaeltu.learnnavi .org/dicts/NaviDictionary.pdf.

19 "Texts and scores—Europe had no other means of storing time. . . . All data flows . . . had to pass through the bottleneck of the signifier." Kittler, *Gramophone, Film, Typewriter,* 4.

20 Butler, *Lilith's Brood,* 107.

21 A good short example, "Zoe Saldana vs. Neytiri," is available at http://www.youtube .com/watch?v=fOHPCI_9-eQ&feature=related.

22 Luhmann, *Art as a Social System*, 10.

23 Lovelock, *Homage to Gaia*, 248.

24 An overview of these doctrinal commitments is given in Lovelock and Lodge, "Oxygen in the Contemporary Atmosphere."

25 Lovelock, *Homage to Gaia*, 253.

26 von Foerster, "*Laws of Form*."

27 Spencer-Brown, *Laws of Form*, iv.

28 von Foerster, "*Laws of Form*."

BIBLIOGRAPHY

Alexander, Victoria N. *The Biologist's Mistress: Rethinking Self-Organization in Art, Literature, and Nature.* Litchfield Park, Ariz.: Emergent, 2011.

Aragno, Anna. "The Mind's Farthest Reach: Dream-Telepathy in Psychoanalytic Situations: Inquiry and Hypothesis." *Signs—International Journal of Semiotics* 5 (2011): 29–70.

Atlan, Henri. "Hierarchical Self-Organization in Living Systems: Noise and Meaning." In *Autopoiesis: A Theory of Living Organization,* edited by Milan Zeleny, 185–208. New York: Elsevier North Holland, 1981.

———. *L'Organisation biologique et la théorie de l'information.* Paris: Hermann, 1972.

Baecker, Dirk, ed. *Problems of Form.* Stanford, Calif.: Stanford University Press, 1999.

Bal, Mieke. *Narratology: Introduction to the Theory of Narrative.* 3rd ed. Toronto: University of Toronto Press, 2009.

Banfield, Ann. *Unspeakable Sentences: Narration and Representation in the Language of Fiction.* Boston: Routledge and Kegan Paul, 1982.

Barthes, Roland. "Introduction to the Structural Study of Narratives." In *Image, Music, Text,* translated by Stephen Heath, 79–124. New York: Hill and Wang, 1978.

Bateson, Gregory. "Cybernetic Explanation," in Bateson, *Steps,* 399–410.

———. "Form, Substance, and Difference," in Bateson, *Steps,* 448–66.

———. "Pathologies of Epistemology," in Bateson, *Steps,* 478–87.

———. *Steps to an Ecology of Mind.* New York: Ballantine, 1972.

———. "Style, Grace, and Information in Primitive Art," in Bateson, *Steps,* 128–52.

———. "A Theory of Play and Fantasy," in Bateson, *Steps,* 177–93.

Ben-Jacob, Eshel. "Social Behavior of Bacteria: From Physics to Complex Organization." *European Physical Journal B* 65 (2008): 315–22.

Ben-Jacob, Eshel, et al. "Bacterial Linguistic Communication and Social Intelligence." *Trends in Microbiology* 12 (2004): 366–72.

Bolter, Jay, and Richard Grusin. *Remediation: Understanding New Media.* Cambridge, Mass.: MIT Press, 1999.

Bordwell, David. *Narration in the Fiction Film.* Madison: University of Wisconsin Press, 1985.

Borges, Jorge Luis. *Labyrinths: Selected Stories and Other Writings.* Edited by Donald A. Yates and James E. Irby. New York: New Directions, 1964.

Bould, Mark, and Sherryl Vint. "Learning from the Little Engines That Couldn't: Transported by Gernsback, Wells, and Latour." *Science-Fiction Studies* 33 (2006): 129–48.

Bourgine, Paul, and John Stewart. "Autopoiesis and Cognition." *Artificial Life* 10 (2004): 327–45.

Brand, Stewart. "For God's Sake, Margaret: Conversation with Gregory Bateson and Margaret Mead." *CoEvolution Quarterly* 10 (Summer 1976): 32–44.

———, ed. *Whole Earth Catalog.* Menlo Park, Calif.: Portola Institute, 1968–71.

Brier, Søren. "The Construction of Information and Communication: A Cybersemiotic Reentry into Heinz von Foerster's Metaphysical Construction of Second-Order Cybernetics." *Semiotica* 154 (2005): 355–99.

Bryant, Levi R. *The Democracy of Objects.* Ann Arbor, Mich.: Open Humanities Press, 2011.

Burnett, Judith, Syd Jeffers, and Graham Thomas, eds. *New Social Connections: Sociology's Subjects and Objects.* Houndmills, Basingstoke: Palgrave Macmillan, 2010.

Butler, Octavia. *Lilith's Brood.* New York: Warner, 2000.

———. *Mind of My Mind* (1976). In Butler, *Seed to Harvest,* 255–451. New York: Warner Books, 2007.

Calvino, Italo. *Cosmicomics.* Translated by William Weaver. New York: Harvest, 1968.

Cameron, James, dir. *Avatar.* Twentieth-Century Fox, 2009.

Castells, Manuel. *The Rise of the Network Society—The Information Age: Economy, Society and Culture.* Oxford: Blackwell, 1996.

Chang, Briankle G. *Deconstructing Communication: Representation, Subject, and Economies of Exchange.* Minneapolis: University of Minnesota Press, 1996.

Chatman, Seymour. "Backwards." *Narrative* 17, no. 1 (2009): 31–55.

Clam, Jean. "System's Sole Constituent, the Operation: Clarifying a Central Concept of Luhmannian Theory." *Acta Sociologica* 43, no. 1 (January 2000): 63–79.

Clarke, Bruce. *Allegories of Writing: The Subject of Metamorphosis.* Albany: State University of New York Press, 1995.

———. "Autopoiesis and the Planet." In *Impasses of the Post-Global: Theory in the Era of Climate Change,* vol. 2, edited by Henry Sussman. Ann Arbor, Mich.: Open Humanities Press, 2012. http://www.openhumanitiespress.org.

———. "From Information to Cognition: The Systems Counterculture, Heinz von Foerster's Pedagogy, and Second-Order Cybernetics." *Constructivist Foundations* 7, no. 3 (2012): 196–207.

———. "Heinz von Foerster's Demons: The Emergence of Second-Order Systems Theory." In Clarke and Hansen, *Emergence and Embodiment,* 34–61.

———. "Neocybernetics of Gaia: The Emergence of Second-Order Gaia Theory." In *Gaia in Turmoil: Climate Change, Biodepletion, and Earth Ethics in an Age of Crisis,* edited by Eileen Crist and H. Bruce Rinker, 293–314. Cambridge, Mass.: MIT Press.

———. *Posthuman Metamorphosis: Narrative and Systems.* New York: Fordham University Press, 2008.

Clarke, Bruce, and Mark B. N. Hansen, eds. *Emergence and Embodiment: New Essays on Second-Order Systems Theory.* Durham, N.C.: Duke University Press, 2009.

———. "Neocybernetic Emergence: Retuning the Posthuman." *Cybernetics and Human Knowing* 16, nos. 1–2 (2009): 83–99.

Clarke, Bruce, and Linda D. Henderson, eds. *From Energy to Information: Representation in Science and Technology, Art, and Literature.* Stanford, Calif.: Stanford University Press, 2002.

Clarke, Bruce, with Manuela Rossini, eds. *The Routledge Companion to Literature and Science.* New York: Routledge, 2010.

Craig, Robert. "Communication." In *Encyclopedia of Rhetoric,* edited by Thomas O. Sloane. New York: Oxford University Press, 2001.

Culler, Jonathan. "Omniscience." In *The Literary in Theory,* 183–201. Stanford, Calif.: Stanford University Press, 2007.

Deleuze, Gilles. "Review of Gilbert Simondon's *L'individu et sa genèse physico-biologique* (1966)." Translated by Ivan Ramirez. *Pli* 12 (2001): 43–49.

Deleuze, Gilles, and Félix Guattari. *Anti-Oedipus: Capitalism and Schizophrenia.* Translated by Robert Hurley, Mark Seem, and Helen R. Lane. New York: Viking, 1977.

———. *A Thousand Plateaus: Capitalism and Schizophrenia.* Translated by Brian Massumi. Minneapolis: University of Minnesota Press, 1987.

Derrida, Jacques. "Differance." In *Speech and Phenomena and Other Essays on Husserl's Theory of Signs,* translated by David B. Allison. Evanston, Ill.: Northwestern University Press, 1973.

———. "Telepathy." Translated by Nicholas Royle. In *Psyche: Inventions of the Other,* vol. 1, edited by Peggy Kamuf and Elizabeth Rottenberg, 226–61. Stanford, Calif.: Stanford University Press, 2007.

Doyle, Richard. *Darwin's Pharmacy: Sex, Plants, and the Evolution of the Noösphere.* Seattle: University of Washington Press, 2011.

Ellul, Jacques. *The Technological Society.* Translated by John Wilkinson. Introduction by Robert K. Merton. New York: Knopf, 1965.

Franklin, Nancy. "News under Fire: Real-Time Reporting in the Fog of War." *New Yorker,* April 7, 2003. http://www.newyorker.com/archive/2003/04/07/030407crte_television.

Froese, Tom. "From Cybernetics to Second-Order Cybernetics: A Comparative Analysis of Their Central Ideas." *Constructivist Foundations* 5, no. 2 (2010): 75–84.

———. "From Second-Order Cybernetics to Enactive Cognitive Science: Varela's Turn from Epistemology to Phenomenology." *Systems Research and Behavioral Science* (2011): 631–45.

Froese, Tom, and Ezequiel A. Di Paolo. "Sociality and the Life-Mind Continuity Thesis." *Phenomenology and the Cognitive Sciences* 8 (2009): 439–63.

Froese, Tom, and John Stewart. "Life after Ashby: Ultrastability and the Autopoietic Foundations of Biological Autonomy." *Cybernetics and Human Knowing* 17, no. 4 (2010): 7–50.

Froese, Tom, and Tom Ziemke. "Enactive Artificial Intelligence: Investigating the Systemic Organization of Life and Mind." *Artificial Intelligence* 173, nos. 3–4 (2009): 466–500.

Genette, Gérard. *Narrative Discourse: An Essay on Method.* Translated by Jane E. Lewin. Ithaca, N.Y.: Cornell University Press, 1980.

Geoghegan, Bernard. "From Information Theory to French Theory: Jakobson, Lévi-Strauss, and the Cybernetic Apparatus." *Critical Inquiry* 38, no. 1 (Autumn 2011): 96–126.

Gibson, William. *Neuromancer.* New York: Ace, 1984.

Gondry, Michel, dir. *Eternal Sunshine of the Spotless Mind.* Focus Features, 2004.

Gonzalez-Diaz, Emilio. "Paradox, Time, and De-Paradoxication in Luhmann: No Easy Way Out." *World Futures* 60 (2004): 15–27.

Guattari, Félix. *Chaosmosis: An Ethico-Aesthetic Paradigm.* Translated by Paul Bains and Julian Pefanis. Bloomington: Indiana University Press, 1995.

———. *The Three Ecologies.* Translated by Ian Pindar and Paul Sutton. New York: Continuum, 2008.

Habermas, Jürgen. *The Theory of Communicative Action.* Translated by Thomas McCarthy. 2 vols. London: Polity Press, 1986.

Hansen, Per Krogh. "Backmasked Messages: On the Fabula Construction in Episodically Reversed Narratives." In *Unnatural Narratives—Unnatural Narratology,* edited by Jan Alber and Rüdiger Heinze, 162–85. Berlin: De Gruyter, 2011.

Hayles, Katherine. *My Mother Was a Computer: Digital Subjects and Literary Texts.* Chicago: University of Chicago Press, 2005.

Herman, David. "Cognitive Narratology." In *The Living Handbook of Narratology.* Hamburg, Germany: Hamburg University Press, 2013. http://wikis.sub.uni-hamburg.de/lhn/index.php/Cognitive_Narratology.

Hitchcock, Dian R., and James E. Lovelock. "Life Detection by Atmospheric Analysis." *Icarus* 7 (1967): 149–59.

Hoffmeyer, Jesper, ed. *A Legacy for Living Systems: Gregory Bateson as Precursor to Biosemiotics.* New York: Springer, 2008.

Hutchinson, G. Evelyn. "Circular Causal Systems in Ecology." *Annals of the New York Academy of Sciences* 50 (October 1948): 221–46.

Jakobson, Roman. "Linguistics and Poetics." In *Style in Language,* edited by Thomas Sebeok, 350–77. New York: John Wiley and Sons, 1960.

Joerges, Bernward. "Technology in Everyday Life: Conceptual Queries." *Journal for the Theory of Social Behaviour* 18, no. 2 (1988): 219–37.

Joyce, James. *Ulysses.* New York: Vintage International, 1990.

Kahn, Doug. "Concerning the Line: Music, Noise, and Phonography." In Clarke and Henderson, *From Energy to Information,* 178–94.

Kauffman, Louis H. "Self-Reference and Recursive Forms." *Journal of Social and Biological Structures* 10 (1987): 53–72.

Kingsland, Sharon E. *The Evolution of American Ecology, 1890–2000.* Baltimore, Md.: John Hopkins University Press, 2005.

Kittler, Friedrich. *Gramophone, Film, Typewriter.* Translated by Geoffrey Winthrop-Young and Michael Wutz. Stanford, Calif.: Stanford University Press, 1999.

———. "The History of Communication Media." *CTheory.net,* 1996. http://www.ctheory.net/articles.aspx?id=45.

Knoop, Christine Angela. "Fictional Communication: Developing Gregory Bateson's 'Theory of Play and Fantasy.'" *Kybernetes* 36, no. 7 (2007): 1113–21.

Kuntz, Tom. "What We Said and What We Meant, A to Z." *New York Times,* December 28, 2003, sec. 4, 2.

Landgraf, Edgar. *Improvisation as Art: Conceptual Challenges, Historical Perspectives.* New York: Continuum, 2011.

Latour, Bruno. *Aramis, or the Love of Technology.* Translated by Catherine Porter. Cambridge, Mass.: Harvard University Press, 1996.

———. "An Attempt at a 'Compositionist Manifesto.'" *New Literary History* 41 (Summer 2010): 471–90.

———. "Can We Get Our Materialism Back, Please?" *Isis* 98 (2007): 138–42.

———. *Pandora's Hope: Essays on the Reality of Science Studies.* Cambridge, Mass.: Harvard University Press, 1999.

———. "A Plea for Earthly Sciences." In Burnett, Jeffers, and Thomas, *New Social Connections,* 72–84.

———. "Powers of the Facsimile: A Turing Test on Science and Literature." In *Intersections: Essays on Richard Powers,* edited by Stephen J. Burn and Peter Demsey, 263–92. Champaign, Ill.: Dalkey Archive Press, 2008.

———. "Prendre le pli des techniques." *Réseaux* 28, no. 163 (2010): 13–32.

———. "Reflections on Etienne Souriau's *Les Modes d'existence.*" In *The Speculative Turn: Continental Materialism and Realism,* edited by Graham Harman, Levi Bryant, and Nick Srnicek, 304–33. Melbourne, Australia: re.press, 2011.

———. *We Have Never Been Modern.* Translated by Catherine Porter. Cambridge, Mass.: Harvard University Press, 1993.

Latour, Bruno, with Nathaniel Herzberg. *Aramis: Analyse Socio-Technique d'un Echec.* Rapport de fin de contrat, RATP-INRETS, Réseau 2000. 1988.

Latour, Bruno, and Richard Powers. "Two Writers Face One Turing Test: A Dialogue in Honor of Hal." *Common Knowledge* 7, no. 1 (1998): 177–91.

Laurier, Eric, and Chris Philo. "X-Morphizing: Review Essay of Bruno Latour's *Aramis, or the Love of Technology.*" *Environment and Planning A* 31 (1999): 1047–71.

LeClair, Tom. *In the Loop: Don DeLillo and the Systems Novel.* Urbana: University of Illinois Press, 1987.

Lévy, Pierre. *Becoming Virtual: Reality in the Digital Age.* Translated by Robert Bononno. New York: Plenum Trade, 1998.

Leydesdorff, Loet. "Luhmann, Habermas, and the Theory of Communication." *Systems Research and Behavioral Science* 17, no. 3 (2000): 273–88.

Lilly, John Cunningham, M.D. *The Mind of the Dolphin: A Nonhuman Intelligence.* Garden City, N.Y.: Doubleday, 1967.

Lippert, Florian. "Narrowing Circles: Questions on Autopoiesis and Literary Interpretation after Dietrich Schwanitz." *Cybernetics and Human Knowing* 16, nos. 1–2 (2009): 125–41.

Lotka, Alfred J. *Elements of Physical Biology.* Baltimore, Md.: Williams and Wilkins, 1925.

Lovelock, James. *The Ages of Gaia: A Biography of Our Living Earth.* New York: Norton, 1988.

———. *Gaia: A New Look at Life on Earth.* New York: Oxford University Press, 1979.

———. *Homage to Gaia: The Life of an Independent Scientist.* Oxford: Oxford University Press, 2000.

———. "A Physical Basis for Life-Detection Experiments." *Nature* 207 (1965): 568–70.

———. *The Revenge of Gaia: Earth's Climate in Crisis and the Fate of Humanity.* New York: Basic Books, 2006.

Lovelock, James, and James P. Lodge Jr. "Oxygen in the Contemporary Atmosphere." *Atmospheric Environment* 6 (1972): 575–78.

Lowe, Adam, and Simon Schaffer. *N01se: Universal Language, Pattern Recognition, Data Synaesthetics.* Cambridge: Kettle's Yard, 2000.

Luckhurst, Roger. *The Invention of Telepathy: 1870–1901.* Oxford: Oxford University Press, 2002.

Luhmann, Niklas. *Art as a Social System.* Translated by Eva Knodt. Stanford, Calif.: Stanford University Press, 2000.

———. "The Cognitive Program of Constructivism and a Reality That Remains Unknown." In Luhmann, *Theories of Distinction,* 128–52.

———. "The Control of Intransparency." *Systems Research in the Behavioral Sciences* 14 (1997): 359–71.

———. *Ecological Communication.* Translated by John Bednarz Jr. Chicago: University of Chicago Press, 1989.

———. "The Medium of Art." In *Essays on Self-Reference,* 215–26. New York: Columbia University Press, 1990.

———. "The Modern Sciences and Phenomenology." In Luhmann, *Theories of Distinction,* 33–60.

———. "The Paradox of Observing Systems." In Luhmann, *Theories of Distinction,* 79–93.

———. "Self-Organization and Autopoiesis." In Clarke and Hansen, *Emergence and Embodiment,* 143–56.

———. *Social Systems.* Translated by John Bednarz Jr. with Dirk Baecker. Stanford, Calif.: Stanford University Press, 1995.

———. *Theories of Distinction: Redescribing the Descriptions of Modernity.* Edited by William Rasch. Stanford, Calif.: Stanford University Press, 2002.

———. "What Is Communication?" In Luhmann, *Theories of Distinction,* 155–68.

Luisi, Pier Luigi. "Autopoiesis: The Logic of Cellular Life." In *The Emergence of Life: From Chemical Origins to Synthetic Biology,* 155–81. Cambridge: Cambridge University Press, 2006.

Manovich, Lev. *The Language of New Media.* Cambridge, Mass.: MIT Press, 2001.

Margulis, Lynn, and Dorion Sagan. *What Is Life?* Berkeley: University of California Press, 2000.

Maturana, Humberto. "Interview on von Foerster, Autopoiesis, the BCL and Augusto Pinochet." In Müller and Müller, *An Unfinished Revolution?* 37–51.

———. "Neurophysiology of Cognition." In *Cognition: A Multiple View,* edited by Paul L. Garvin, 3–23. New York: Spartan Books, 1970.

Maturana, Humberto, and Francisco Varela. *Autopoiesis and Cognition: The Realization of the Living.* Boston: D. Reidel, 1980.

———. *The Tree of Knowledge: The Biological Roots of Human Understanding.* Rev. ed. Boston: Shambhala, 1998.

Maxwell, James Clerk. "On Governors." *Proceedings of the Royal Society of London* 16 (1868): 270–83.

McMurry, Andrew. *Environmental Renaissance: Emerson, Thoreau, and the American System of Nature.* Athens: University of Georgia Press, 2003.

Miller, J. Hillis. *The Medium Is the Maker: Browning, Freud, Derrida and the New Telepathic Ecotechnologies.* Brighton: Sussex Academic Press, 2009.

Moeller, Hans-Georg. *Luhmann Explained: From Souls to Systems.* Chicago: Open Court, 2006.

———. *The Radical Luhmann.* New York: Columbia University Press, 2012.

Moretti, Franco. *Graphs, Maps, Trees: Abstract Models for a Literary Theory.* New York: Verso, 2005.

Morin, Edgar. *La Méthode, 1: La Nature de la Nature.* Paris: Éditions du Seuil, 1977.

Morowitz, Harold J. *Energy Flow in Biology: Biological Organization as a Problem in Thermal Physics.* New York: Academic Press, 1968.

Moskowitz, Sam. "How Science Fiction Got Its Name." In *The Prentice Hall Anthology of Science Fiction and Fantasy,* edited by Garyn G. Roberts, 1127–35. Upper Saddle River, N.J.: Prentice-Hall, 2001.

Müller, Albert. "Computing a Reality: Heinz von Foerster's Lecture at the A.U.M. Conference in 1973." *Constructivist Foundations* 4, no. 1 (2008): 62–69.

Müller, Albert, and Karl H. Müller, eds. *An Unfinished Revolution? Heinz von Foerster and the Biological Computer Laboratory/BCL 1958–1976.* Vienna: Echoraum, 2007.

Noë, Alva. *Out of Our Heads: Why You Are Not Your Brain, and Other Lessons from the Biology of Consciousness.* New York: Hill and Wang, 2009.

Nolan, Christopher, dir. *Memento.* Newmarket, 2000.

Nowotny, Helga. "Actor-Networks vs. Science as a Self-Organizing System: A Comparative View of Two Constructivist Approaches." In *Self-Organization: Portrait of a Scientific Revolution,* edited by Wolfgang Krohn, Günter Küpper, and Helga Nowotny, 223–39. Dordrecht, Netherlands: Kluwer Academic, 1990.

Ovid. *Metamorphoses.* Translated by Horace Gregory. New York: Mentor, 1960.

Paulson, William R. *The Noise of Culture: Literary Texts in a World of Information.* Ithaca, N.Y.: Cornell University Press, 1988.

Peters, John Durham. *Speaking into the Air: A History of the Idea of Communication.* Chicago: University of Chicago Press, 2000.

Protevi, John. "Beyond Autopoiesis: Inflections of Emergence and Politics in Francisco Varela." In Clarke and Hansen, *Emergence and Embodiment,* 94–112.

Pynchon, Thomas. *The Crying of Lot 49.* New York: Harper and Row, 1990.

Richardson, Brian. "Beyond Story and Discourse: Narrative Time in Postmodern and Nonmimetic Fiction." In *Narrative Dynamics: Essays on Time, Plot, Closure, and Frames,* edited by Brian Richardson, 47–63. Columbus: Ohio State University Press, 2002.

Roberts, David. "Self-Reference in Literature." In Baecker, *Problems of Form,* 27–45.

Rosenblueth, Arthur, Norbert Wiener, and Julian Bigelow, "Behavior, Purpose, and Teleology." *Philosophy of Science* 10 (1943): 18–24.

Royle, Nicholas. "The 'Telepathy Effect': Notes toward a Reconsideration of Narrative Fiction." In *The Uncanny,* 256–76. New York: Routledge, 2003.

———. *Telepathy and Literature: Essays on the Reading Mind.* Oxford: Basil Blackwell, 1991.

Sagan, Carl. *Contact.* New York: Pocket Books, 1986.

Saussure, Ferdinand de. *Course in General Linguistics.* Translated by Wade Baskin. New York: McGraw-Hill, 1966.

Savidge, Martin. "Embedded for Life." CNN.com, July 4, 2003. http://www.cnn.com/2003/US/07/04/wbr.embedded.life/index.html.

Schiltz, Michael. "Space Is the Place: The Laws of Form and Social Systems." In Clarke and Hansen, *Emergence and Embodiment,* 157–78.

Scholl, Armin. "Between Realism and Constructivism: Luhmann's Ambivalent Epistemological Standpoint." *Constructivist Foundations* 8, no. 1 (2012): 5–12.

Schreber, Daniel Paul. *Memoirs of My Nervous Illness.* Translated and edited by Ida MacAlpine and Richard A. Hunter. Cambridge, Mass.: Harvard University Press, 1988.

Schwartz, Hillel. *Making Noise: From Babel to the Big Bang and Beyond.* New York: Zone Books, 2011.

Schweighauser, Philipp. *The Noises of American Literature, 1890–1985: Toward a History of Literary Acoustics.* Gainesville: University Press of Florida, 2006.

Serres, Michel. *Genesis.* Translated by Geneviève James and James Nielson. Ann Arbor: University of Michigan Press, 1995.

———. *Hermes: Literature, Science, Philosophy.* Edited by Josué V. Harari and David F. Bell. Baltimore, Md.: Johns Hopkins University Press, 1982.

———. "The Origin of Language: Biology, Information Theory, and Thermodynamics." In Serres, *Hermes,* 71–83.

———. *The Parasite.* Translated by Lawrence R. Schehr. Introduction by Cary Wolfe. Minneapolis: University of Minnesota Press, 2007.

———. "Platonic Dialogue." In Serres, *Hermes,* 65–70.

———. "Le point de vue de la bio-physique." *Critique* 32 (1976): 265–77.

———. "Le troisième homme ou le tiers exclu." *Les Études Philosophiques,* new series, 21, no. 4 (1966): 463–69.

Shapiro, James A. *Evolution: A View from the 21st Century.* Upper Saddle River, N.J.: FT Press, 2011.

Shelley, Mary Wollstonecraft. *Frankenstein; or, the Modern Prometheus. The 1818 version.* 2d ed. Edited by D. L. Macdonald and Kathleen Scherf. Peterborough, Ontario: Broadview Press, 2004.

Simondon, Gilbert. "The Genesis of the Individual." Translated by Mark Cohen and Sanford Kwinter. In *Incorporations,* 297–319. New York: Zone, 1992.

———. *On the Mode of Existence of Technical Objects.* Paris: Aubier, 1958. Translated by Ninian Mellamphy. Ontario: University of Western Ontario, 1980.

Sloterdijk, Peter. *In the World Interior of Capital: For a Philosophical Theory of Globalization.* Translated by Wieland Hoban. Malden, Mass.: Polity, 2013.

Spencer-Brown, George. *Laws of Form.* New York: E. Dutton, 1979.

Stanzel, F. K. *A Theory of Narrative*. Translated by Charlotte Goedsche. New York: Cambridge University Press, 1984.

Stenner, Paul. "Is Autopoietic Systems Theory Alexithymic? Luhmann and the Socio-Psychology of Emotions." *Soziale Systeme* 10, no. 1 (2004): 159–85.

Stiegler, Bernard. *Technics and Time, 1: The Fault of Epimetheus*. Translated by Richard Beardsworth and George Collins. Stanford, Calif.: Stanford University Press, 1998.

Tabbi, Joseph. *Cognitive Fictions*. Minnesota: University of Minneapolis Press, 2002.

———. "Cognitive Science." In Clarke with Rossini, *Routledge Companion*, 77–88.

Tansley, Arthur G. "The Use and Abuse of Vegetational Concepts and Terms." *Ecology* 16 (1935): 284–307.

Terranova, Tiziana. "Communication beyond Meaning: On the Cultural Politics of Information." *Social Text* 80 (Fall 2004): 51–73.

Thompson, Evan. "Life and Mind: From Autopoiesis to Neurophenomenology." In Clarke and Hansen, *Emergence and Embodiment*, 77–93.

———. *Mind in Life: Biology, Phenomenology, and the Sciences of Mind*. Cambridge, Mass.: Harvard University Press, 2007.

Thyssen, Ole. "Luhmann and Epistemology." *Cybernetics and Human Knowing* 11, no. 1 (2004): 7–22.

Toscano, Alberto. "Gilbert Simondon." In *Deleuze's Philosophical Lineage*, edited by Graham Jones and Jon Roffe, 380–98. Edinburgh: Edinburgh University Press, 2009.

Varela, Francisco J. "A Calculus for Self-Reference." *International Journal of General Systems* 2 (1975): 5–24.

———. *Principles of Biological Autonomy*. New York: North Holland, 1979.

Varela, Francisco J., with Donna Johnson. "On Observing Natural Systems." *CoEvolution Quarterly* 10 (Summer 1976): 26–31.

von Foerster, Heinz. "On Constructing a Reality." In von Foerster, *Understanding Understanding*, 211–27.

———. "Cybernetics." *Encyclopedia of Artificial Intelligence*. Vol. 1. New York: John Wiley and Sons, 1990.

———. "For Niklas Luhmann: 'How Recursive Is Communication?'" In von Foerster, *Understanding Understanding*, 305–23.

———. "Interview." *Stanford Electronic Humanities Review* 4, no. 2 (1994). http://www.stanford.edu/group/SHR/4-2/text/interviewvonf.html.

———. "*Laws of Form*." In Brand, *Whole Earth Catalog* (Spring 1970): 14.

———. "Objects: Tokens for (Eigen-)Behaviors." In von Foerster, *Understanding Understanding*, 261–71.

———. "On Self-Organizing Systems and Their Environments." In von Foerster, *Understanding Understanding*, 1–19.

———. "Thoughts and Notes on Cognition." In von Foerster, *Understanding Understanding*, 169–89.

———. *Understanding Understanding: Essays on Cybernetics and Cognition*. New York: Springer, 2003.

———. "What Is Memory that It May Have Hindsight and Foresight as Well?" In von Foerster, *Understanding Understanding,* 101–31.

von Neumann, John. "The General and Logical Theory of Automata." In *Collected Works,* vol. 5, edited by A. H. Taub, 288–318. New York: Pergamon Press, 1961–63.

Weaver, Warren. "Recent Contributions to the Mathematical Theory of Communication." In Claude E. Shannon and Warren Weaver, *The Mathematical Theory of Communication,* 3–28. Urbana: University of Illinois Press, 1949.

Wellbery, David E., ed. "Observation, Difference, Form: Literary Studies and Second-Order Cybernetics." *MLN* 111, no. 3 (1996).

Wenders, Wim, dir. *Wings of Desire [Der Himmel über Berlin].* Road Movies Filmproduktion, 1987.

Wiener, Norbert. *The Human Use of Human Beings: Cybernetics and Society.* Boston: Houghton Mifflin, 1950; 2d ed., New York, Avon, 1967.

Winograd, Terry and Francisco Flores. *Understanding Computers and Cognition: A New Foundation for Design.* Reading, Mass.: Addison-Wesley, 1987.

Winthrop-Young, Geoffrey. *Kittler and the Media.* Malden, Mass.: Polity, 2011.

———. "Silicon Sociology, or, Two Kings on Hegel's Throne? Kittler, Luhmann, and the Posthuman Merger of German Media Theory." *Yale Journal of Criticism* 13, no. 2 (2000): 391–420.

Winthrop-Young, Geoffrey, and Nicholas Gane. "Friedrich Kittler: An Introduction." In *Theory, Culture and Society* 23, no. 7 (2006): 5–16.

Wolfe, Cary. "Meaning as Event-Machine, or Systems Theory and 'The Reconstruction of Deconstruction.'" In Clarke and Hansen, *Emergence and Embodiment,* 220–45.

———. *What Is Posthumanism?* Minneapolis: University of Minnesota Press, 2011.

Woolf, Virginia. *Mrs. Dalloway.* New York: Harcourt, 2005.

Zemeckis, Robert, dir. *Contact.* Warner Brothers, 1997.

INDEX

abiotic, the, 11, 50, 144, 161, 178
actor-network theory (ANT), xix, 58, 112, 131, 136
Alexander, Victoria, 139
allegory, xvii, 20, 24, 35, 104; of media, 175–76; of narrative, 22, 29, 107, 109
animism, 161, 167, 170–71, 176
Anti-Oedipus (Gilles Deleuze and Félix Guattari), 145
Aristotle, 4, 93
artworks, 50, 70
autonomy, xiii, 4, 7, 17, 35, 48, 71, 82, 177; in *Aramis,* 116, 123–26, 129–36, 162; in *Avatar,* 162, 174; contingent, 13; in Richard Doyle, 156; in Félix Guattari, 151; idealized, 87; operational, xii, 13, 34, 177; phantom, 15; psychic, 34; systemic, xxi, 76, 157, 162, 177; in Francisco Varela, 150, 162
autopoiesis, xv–xvi, 6, 39, 41, 47, 50, 153, 180; and autonomy, 130, 150, 156–57; biotic, xi, xii, 12, 72, 130, 139; and cognition, xvii–xviii, 15, 20, 70, 136, 164; of communication, 17, 40–41, 137; of consciousness, 17, 72; and form, 73–76; and Gaia, xx, 6, 139, 156, 171; in Félix Guattari, 150–52; information theory and, 66–67, 71, 73; in Niklas Luhmann, xiv–xv, 6, 12–13, 71–72, 130, 153; and

machines, 14–15, 169; in Maturana and Varela, 5, 12–13, 130, 148; metabiotic, xiv, xx–xxi, 12–13, 35, 139; and noise, 75; operational closure of, 35, 37, 70, 130, 157; psychic, 35, 47, 71; scientificity of, 6; social, 7, 18, 40, 48–49, 177; and time, 105, 108; and Heinz von Foerster, 64
Avatar (dir. James Cameron), xx, 158–77; the avatar system, xx, 159, 163–72; and Bruno Latour, 159–62

Barthes, Roland, 1
Bateson, Gregory, ix, xx; and cybernetics, 4–5, 55, 86–89; and "ecology of mind," 140, 144–52; and ecosystem ecology, 147–49; and information, 53, 56, 147–48; *Steps to an Ecology of Mind,* xix, 86, 140, 143–49. *See also* ecology
Biological Computer Lab (BCL), x, 64–65
biology, x, xii, 12, 139, 161, 171. *See also* ecology
biosphere, 6, 139, 149, 151, 152, 161, 170–71. *See also* Gaia
Bloom, David, 82, 84
bodies, 40
Bordwell, David, 99
boundary: in Gregory Bateson, 86, 147–48; biotic (organic), 6, 130; disciplinary, 117; in Félix Guattari, 146; mediatic, 82,

boundary (cont.)
85; metabiotic (virtual), 6, 35–36, 47; narrative: 98–104; systemic (operational), xv, 6, 12, 31, 34–36, 48, 73–74, 94, 136

Butler, Octavia, xviii; *Mind of My Mind,* 32–35, 103; *Xenogenesis,* 8, 173–74

Cameron, James, 159, 163, 175–76
Cannon, Walter B., 142
Chang, Briankle, 46–47
chaos, 4, 9, 39, 80, 180; in Michel Serres, 58, 61, 68
Chatman, Seymour, 109–10
circularity, 4, 47, 86–87, 142, 152; in Gregory Bateson, 148, 150; and feedback, 89, 142–43; logical, 47; and the observer, x, 148; operational, 47; as recursion, 4; in self-referential systems, 65–67, 90, 144, 147, 157
Clements, Frederic, 140–41
closure, xviii, 137; autopoietic, 130, 153, 157, 186n13; of cognition, xv, 35, 41, 76, 177; and narrative, 96–99, 107; operational, xiii, 5–6, 14, 35–37, 47, 55, 131, 146, 162, 174; and reentry, 90, 96, 130; in relation to Michel Serres, 57, 62, 66–67, 70, 72
CNN (Cable News Network), 77, 83
code, xvii, 20, 41, 44, 48, 50, 54, 95, 134; linguistic, xvi, 46–47; in Michel Serres, 56, 60, 64, 68; symbolic, 55–56
CoEvolution Quarterly, 4, 79, 88
coevolution, 149; systemic, 6, 13, 48, 171
cognition, ix–xx, 6, 21, 39, 75–76, 94–95, 136, 171, 177; closure of, xv, 137; as consciousness, xi; biotic, ix–xiii, 66–67, 75, 139, 169; and mediation, 21, 87; metabiotic, xiv, 96, 169; and narration, 96–99, 103–4; noninformatic, 2, 65; and the observer, 68, 180–81; systemic, xi, 7, 12, 20, 47, 57, 89, 90, 162, 164; social, xiv, 48–49; in Heinz von Foerster, 64–65
cognitive science, xiv; enactive, xiv–xv

communication, xviii, 7, 20, 39–75, 89; and autopoiesis, 41, 137; in Gregory Bateson, 53, 55; emergence of, 40, 47; in Friedrich Kittler, 7–10, 54; and language, 43–44; literary, 1; in Niklas Luhmann, 45–49, 70–72, 75–76, 152–54, 158, 176; and narrative, 17, 108–9, 175; and media, 41–45, 54, 82; operationality of, xv, 7, 14, 24; in Michel Serres, 58–64; systemic autonomy of, xiv, 13, 14, 34, 149; technologies, 14, 45, 51; and telepathy, 25–27, 34–37; understanding/misunderstanding in, 48–49. *See also* telecommunication
complexity, 4, 35, 94, 104, 138, 158, 186n12; reduction of, 157, 192n20; in Michel Serres, 58, 70, 75; temporalization of, xix, 91, 94, 105, 191n24
Contact (Carl Sagan), 24, 168
control, 2, 4, 5, 79, 87, 89, 95, 103; in the avatar system, 163–65; limits to, xv; theory, x, 3, 51, 60, 87, 162
Cosmicomics (Italo Calvino), 18
coupling, structural, xx, 6, 37, 48
Craig, Robert, 42
Crying of Lot 49, The (Thomas Pynchon), 41–42, 49–50
cyberculture, ix, xv
cybernetics, 2, 5, 81, 86, 143, 145; in Gregory Bateson, 4, 53, 55–56, 87–88, 145, 150; first-order, xviii, xx, 3, 4, 12, 51–52, 68, 74, 79, 88, 142, 161; and Gaia, 159–61, 171; and informatics, x, xv, 7, 71, 148; second-order, xi, xvii, 2, 4, 5, 64–65, 88, 130, 181; in Michel Serres, 58, 62, 72; in Norbert Wiener, 51, 60–61, 88
cyborg, 43, 73, 165

Darwin's Pharmacy (Richard Doyle), xx, 152–58; "ecodelia," 156–58
Derrida, Jacques, 25, 47, 187n28; "Differance," 44; *The Post Card,* 30; "Telepathy," 30–34

hermeneutics, xvii, 7, 21

Hermes, 22, 23–24

holism, holistic, xxi, 55, 65, 89, 153, 173, 193n5; and ecology, 140, 141, 154

homeostasis, 2, 3, 129–30; cognitive, xiii; and feedback, 79–80, 143; physiological, 130, 143

Hutchinson, G. Evelyn, 142–44

imaginary numbers, 93

immediacy, 32, 72, 74, 85, 90; and embedded media, 82

informatics, 2, 12, 45, 64, 81; and first-order cybernetics, 7; narrative, 17; and noise, 51

information: and autopoiesis, 57, 71, 76, 108, 190n33; and communication, 17, 42–45, 48–50, 54; and cybernetics, x–xi, xv, 5, 51, 64–66, 74, 79, 171, 188n1; and ecology, 147–48, 186n12; and entropy, 10, 55–57; and matter, 52–53; and noise, 55; positivist approach to, xi, 186n5, 189n25; in Michel Serres, 58–64, 66–70, 188n1; and technology, 3, 9, 52, 132–33, 163–65; theory of, xvi–xvii, 2, 21, 39–41, 49–53, 69, 74, 81; and value, 50

interpenetration, xiv, 6, 14, 17, 35–36, 157

intersubjectivity, xviii, 45–47, 185n10

Iraq, War in, 82–85

Jakobson, Roman, 43–44, 46, 61

Kingsland, Sharon, 140–41, 144

Kittler, Friedrich, xvi, 21, 64, 71, 73, 173; *Gramophone, Film, Typewriter,* 7–12, 39–40, 53; "History of Communications Media," 45, 188n7

Lacan, Jacques, 8, 10, 30, 40

language, 43, 46, 53, 83, 168, 173; as a media technology, 15, 60; as a structure, xvi, 44, 48

lap game, xviii, 78–79

Latour, Bruno, xvi, 10, 15, 87, 163, 171, 177; *Aramis or the Love of Technology,* xix, 112–38, 162, 192n5; "Compositionist Manifesto," 159–61; and Gaia, xx, 159–62; and modernism, 87, 159–62, 171; and postmodernism, 10; and Gilbert Simondon, 111–12, 114–16, 131, 134–38; *We Have Never Been Modern,* 10, 87, 112. *See also* actor-network theory

Laws of Form (George Spencer-Brown), xviii–xix, 81, 90–96, 180–81

life: and cognition, xii, xv, 15, 139; in ecology, 141–42; and Gaia, 160–61, 171, 178–79; and mind, xv; and systems, 63, 67, 147, 157; and technics, 112, 125, 135

literature: and media theory, 9–10, 54; and narration, 29; and technics, 117, 134

logic, 4, 87; humanist, 5; posthumanist, 5; of recursion, 87, 180; of remediation, 84; telepathic, 28

Lotka, Alfred, 141–42, 146

Lovelock, James, 155, 160–61, 178–79

Luhmann, Niklas, 4; *Art as a Social System,* 70–75, 107, 193n17; and communication, 17, 47–49, 185n11; *Ecological Communication,* xx, 152–58; and *Laws of Form,* 90–91, 94–96, 193n5; *Social Systems,* 35–36, 56–57, 186n13, 191n24; systems theory of, xiv–xv, 5–6, 12–13, 40, 105, 108–9

machines, 3, 14–15, 189n26; and cybernetics, 15, 43, 51, 60; in Félix Guattari, 150–52; in Friedrich Kittler, 8–9; in Bruno Latour, 87, 114, 126, 136; as nonautopoietic, 14–15, 50; nontrivial, 92

Macy Conferences, 83, 143, 146

Manovich, Lev, 44–45, 163

Margulis, Lynn, 6, 139

Maturana, Humberto, 5; on cognition, x–xiii; "Neurophysiology of Cognition," xiii, 65; and Francisco Varela, 5–6, 12–13, 64, 130, 148, 151, 157

living, ix–x, xvii, 3–6, 12–13, 62–67, 73, 130, 150–51, 157; meaning, xiv, xvi, 14, 15, 36, 94, 139; media, xx, 20, 40–41, 47, 50, 82, 84, 159, 164, 174, 175; metabiotic, xiv, 6, 12–17, 149, 182; natural, xiii, xx–xxi, 4, 65–66, 79, 87, 165; nonautopoietic, xvi, 12, 14–15, 50; nondesigned, 65; observing, xiv, xvi, 1, 7, 15–20, 50, 76, 85–87, 90, 94–97, 103–7, 138, 146, 166, 181; open, 4, 63, 66; psychic, 1, 7, 17, 26, 34–36, 41, 47–48, 57, 71–73, 102–9, 129, 157, 173; self-referential, x, xv–xx, 4–5, 12, 35, 65, 74, 76, 95, 153; social, 1, 6–7, 12, 18–26 , 35–37, 47–49, 71, 87, 90–91, 105–9, 128, 130, 137, 152–54, 173; structural coupling of, xx, 6, 37, 48; technological, xix, 14–15, 24, 105, 132, 162, 165, 177; thermodynamic, 2, 51, 63. *See also* autopoiesis; boundary; closure; cognition; environment; interpenetration; observation; recursion; resonance

Tansley, Arthur, 141–42
technology, 8–14, 24, 51, 103, 117, 173, 180; communications, 8, 27; fictive, 159; media, xx, 44, 73, 164–65, 175–76; philosophy of, xiv, 111–14, 132; print, 54. *See also* machines
technoscience, 10, 71, 89; fictions of, 100, 128, 173
teleaction, 163–64, 175
telecommunication, 21; in *Avatar,* 159, 163–65, 168–71, 173
telepathy, xvii–xviii, 25–37, 47, 157, 174; cybernetic, 165; facticity of, 25, 30, 72; Derrida on, 30–34; and narrative, 27–29, 96; as viewed by systems theory, 34–37

telepresence, 45, 163, 175
Thompson, Evan, xv
Thousand Plateaus, A (Gilles Deleuze and Félix Guattari), 144
timbre, 52
time, 19, 21, 51; geological, 179; narrative, xix, 98–101, 105–10; "real," 44–45, 163–64, 176; systems, xix, 5, 73, 90–96; virtual, 44
time-axis manipulation (TAM), 52
Titanic (dir. James Cameron), 163, 175
trace, the, xvii, 14, 18–25
transmission, xvi– xvii, 27, 82, 153, 169, 172, 176; genetic, 189n25; informatic model of, 40–42, 46–48, 65, 68–76, 148, 189n26; and media, 10–11, 21, 39; neural, 174; and noise, 50–64; in telepathy, 31, 33; and the trace, 20
typewriter: Malling-Hansen writing ball, 9

Ulysses (James Joyce), 23

Varela, Francisco, xiii, xv, 5–6, 12–13; in Félix Guattari, 150–52; "On Observing Natural Systems," 65–66; *Principles of Biological Autonomy,* 130, 150, 162
von Foerster, Heinz, x–xiii, 5, 7, 57, 64–65, 69, 88, 91, 189–81
von Neumann, John, 9

What Is Life? (Lynn Margulis and Dorion Sagan), 139
Whole Earth Catalog, 4, 91, 178, 180
Wiener, Norbert, 51, 60–61, 88, 143
Wings of Desire (Wim Wenders), 27–29
writing, 7, 9, 15, 21, 42–45, 53, 113, 175; in *Aramis,* 121; in Michel Serres, 58–59, 64

zorbing, 85–86

(continued from p. ii)

BRUCE CLARKE is the Paul Whitfield Horn Professor of Literature and Science and chair of the Department of English at Texas Tech University. He is the author of *Allegories of Writing: The Subject of Metamorphosis*; *Dora Marsden and Early Modernism: Gender, Individualism, Science*; *Energy Forms: Allegory and Science in the Era of Classical Thermodynamics*; and *Posthuman Metamorphosis: Narrative and Systems,* and the coeditor of *From Energy to Information: Representation in Science and Technology, Art, and Literature*; *Emergence and Embodiment: New Essays in Second-Order Systems Theory*; and the *Routledge Companion to Literature and Science.*